I0540402

The Marks of A Leader

Defining Leadership Excellence in Crisis, Continuity, Disaster, and Emergency Management

Robert C. Chandler, Ph.D.

THE MARKS OF A LEADER
Defining Leadership Excellence in Crisis, Continuity, Disaster, and Emergency Management

Published by Emperiria Press
CrisisMasters Series
Jackson, Tennessee

ISBN: 978-1-971104-01-0
Library of Congress Control Number: 2026900006

Foreword by Robert S. Nakao, Executive Publisher, Contingency Planning & Management and Continuity Insights
Foreword by Jeff Robertson, Retired U.S. Coast Guard Officer and Former Assistant Commissioner, U.S. Customs and Border Protection

Book design by Norman Read
Cover design by Anna Baker
First Edition, January 2026

Printed in the United States of America

Dedication

*To all my teachers, mentors, coaches, and supportive colleagues—
across every level and stage of life—who sparked in me a love of
learning, instilled the value of evidence-based thinking, and
inspired a lifelong commitment to reflection, growth, and
continuous improvement.*

*Your guidance has shaped not only my work, but the person I have
become and the contributions I strive to make.*

*I also owe deep thanks to friends, including former students,
whose encouragement has carried me farther than they know.*

*Special thanks to Doug Albritton—I remain profoundly grateful for
everything you have done (and still do) for an old debate coach.*

I dedicate this book to you all.

Foreword: *The Marks of A Leader*
The Map

The tragedy of the Alfred P. Murrah Federal Building bombing in Oklahoma City on April 19, 1995, was an event that none of us will ever forget. At that time, as an experienced business-to-business publisher, I appreciated that there would be many other stories to share beyond the tragic loss of life, the political implications, and the physical destruction of the building. Shortly after, I founded *Contingency Planning & Management*, a magazine focused on disruptive events. The key to a successful media launch is developing a varied group of subject matter experts to provide guidance and direction on content. My search (pre-Google) for expert advice on crisis management eventually connected me with Dr. Robert Chandler.

Bob was widely recognized for his expertise in crisis management. Successful business resilience relies on strong leadership to address diverse disruptions, from man-made to natural disasters to technological failures. Effective crisis managers need clear vision, steady character, and decisive action. As our challenges grow more complex, adaptable, and ethical leadership is increasingly vital. This book examines the essential traits, habits, and mindsets that set genuine leaders apart from managers. Rather than offering quick solutions, it focuses on foundational leadership principles, such as self-awareness, trust, empathy, accountability, and vision. Drawing on real-world experience and research, Bob offers practical guidance for anyone seeking to enhance their leadership skills.

Over time, as discussions around business continuity reached executive leadership and boardrooms, my emphasis shifted from tactical responses to strategic planning. With crisis management emerging as a central topic of importance within organizations, this evolution led to the subsequent launch of Continuity Insights, a publication focused on business continuity for mid-to-senior-level management professionals. The demand for effective business continuity leaders rose significantly over time, and Bob became an increasingly important resource. I've organized various conferences and have frequently invited him to deliver keynote addresses and presentations on crisis leadership.

Leadership is fundamentally about taking responsibility for those under your guidance. It entails listening attentively before speaking, demonstrating integrity regardless of external observation, and making decisions consistent with purpose and ethical standards. Leadership does not stem from titles or organizational hierarchy; rather, it represents a manner of conduct. This book conveys more than theoretical concepts and instead draws upon practical insights, personal experiences, and enduring principles that have informed leaders across various industries and professions.

Within these pages, you, the readers, will not encounter

overused phrases or superficial solutions. Ultimately, the defining character of a leader is rooted in their identity, not merely their actions. This work is a thoughtful organization of crisis leadership. Each section examines core attributes, from discussing the foundations of crisis leadership, the marks of an effective leader, and how to apply the leadership model, serving both as a tool for self-evaluation and as a resource for further development.

Whether you're leading a team, a company, or a community, the principles in this book will challenge you. Let this book be your guide and steady voice, reminding you that while crises are inevitable, chaos is not. Leadership at these moments is not about heroics. It's about responsibility, the tools, and the courage to make effective decisions when it matters most. I am confident that readers will find this book both intellectually stimulating and practically applicable.

— Robert S. Nakao

Executive Publisher

Contingency Planning & Management; Continuity Insights

Foreword: The Marks of A Leader
The Compass

In a world marked by volatility and disruption, authentic leadership is not optional—it is essential. When disaster strikes or a crisis unfolds, leaders must rise above chaos to offer clarity, stability, and hope. The Marks of a Leader arrives at a pivotal moment, offering a framework not just for managing complexity, but for thriving within it.

Dr. Robert Chandler—known to many of us simply as Bob—has been a trusted colleague, advisor, and coach for years. I've had the privilege of working alongside him in real-world situations during my service with the U.S. Coast Guard and U.S. Customs and Border Protection. His ability to connect theory and practice is rare, and it's precisely what makes this book so impactful. George Bernard Shaw once quipped, "He who can, does. He who cannot, teaches." Clearly, Shaw never met Bob.

This book is both practical and scholarly, providing executives, administrators, crisis managers, and anyone in leadership under pressure with actionable insights they can implement immediately. It isn't a collection of abstract theories likely to gather dust; it's a hands-on guide rooted in experience, thorough research, and decades of coaching and fieldwork. What makes this volume unique is its emphasis on practicality without losing depth. It doesn't just describe what effective leadership looks like; it demonstrates how to practice it daily, especially when it's most critical. Readers will often return to its framework, using it both as a mirror for self-assessment and as a guide for growth.

Built on over 30 years of research, fieldwork, and scholarly inquiry, including Bob's foundational studies at Fort Leavenworth's CATTS Center and his longitudinal survey of practitioners, the insights here are lived, tested, and distilled into a legacy work. Its most significant contribution is the distinction between routine and crisis leadership. Bob's research shows that technical competence and credentials, while important, do not guarantee effectiveness in high-stakes environments. Leadership is situational, contextual, and closely tied to the moment—an insight with profound implications for how we train, evaluate, and support leaders across sectors.

Equally important is recognizing that crisis leadership can be developed. Someone effective in routine situations may not be crisis-ready—and vice versa—but with intentional preparation, leaders can learn to adapt, respond, and succeed when it matters most. This book helps organizations avoid costly mistakes by identifying and cultivating the unique skills needed for different environments.

The implications are revolutionary. The Marks of a Leader challenges linear models and fixed skills, proposing a flexible framework for human performance under pressure. It redefines leadership as a complex, adaptable craft—requiring rhetorical agility, emotional intelligence, and a thorough understanding of context.

The chapter lineup itself serves as a masterclass in leadership architecture. Each "mark" represents not just a trait, but a dynamic capability—something to be developed, tested, and refined. A few highlights include:

- "Communication and Listening" — Leadership is not only about output but dialogue. Listening is what makes communication relational and responsive.
- "Facilitating Followership" — A counter-narrative to charisma-driven models, it emphasizes creating the conditions where others choose to follow.
- "Closing the Continuous Preparedness Loop" — The culmination of Bob's career-long research, reframing preparedness not as a checklist but as a rhythm, a mindset, a loop without end.

Whether you're shaping strategy in the boardroom, guiding a department through change, or making quick decisions in the field, this book will enhance your ability to focus on what matters most during chaos and to lead with calmness and purpose.

Perhaps most importantly, The Marks of a Leader is not a resource to keep to yourself. Its lessons are meant to be shared so that leadership excellence becomes a collective standard rather than an individual exception. A team that shares a common vocabulary and framework can respond with greater unity, clarity, and resilience when unexpected events occur.

The value of this book lies in its ability to go beyond sectors and titles. By combining proven principles with practical examples, it empowers readers at all levels to see leadership not just as a role of a position, but as a duty to act decisively, ethically, and with foresight. It is rigorous enough for scholars, practical enough for field leaders, and visionary enough to reshape how we think about leadership development.

Ultimately, leadership isn't about titles, credentials, or authority; it's about stepping up with clarity, courage, and compassion when others look to you for guidance. This book provides both a compass and a call: a compass to navigate uncertainty with stability and wisdom, and a call to see leadership as a responsibility that goes beyond personal success to the resilience and well-being of others. If its lessons are absorbed and applied, they will shape stronger individual leaders and also build cultures of trust, adaptability, and collective strength. That is the true mark of leadership—and the lasting gift of this work. May the Marks of a Leader inspire and prepare you to lead well, especially when it matters most.

— Jeff Robertson

Retired U.S. Coast Guard Officer; Former Assistant Commissioner, U.S. Customs and Border Protection

Table of Contents

THE PATH TO
THE MARKS OF A LEADER

I n moments of calm, leadership is often celebrated for charisma, vision, or polished metrics—but in the raw chaos of crisis, when buildings shake, systems collapse, or violence erupts without warning, true leadership is measured in seconds, decisions, and lives saved. In those crucible moments, it's not the title on a badge or years in a role that defines a leader; it's the raw ability to stay focused, guide others through fear, and function with clarity amid unrelenting uncertainty.

Effective leaders in crises are not just responders or managers. They are stabilizers, decision-makers, and communicators. They inspire confidence when others freeze, adapt when plans collapse, take responsibility instead of hiding behind bureaucracy, and above all, act with integrity—even when the stakes are highest. Ineffective leaders, by contrast, can make a bad situation worse. Indecision, ego, poor communication, or denial can paralyze a response. Some delay action while seeking consensus or comfort. Others communicate poorly, causing panic or confusion. Some deflect blame rather than solve problems. In doing so, they jeopardize safety, trust, and the future of those they serve.

My interest in how leaders respond under pressure began in the mid-1980s, when I was a doctoral candidate at the University of Kansas. I was conducting field research at the Command and Tactical Training Simulation (CATTS) center, part of the U.S. Army's Battle Command Training Program at Fort Leavenworth. Under the guidance of my professors, Ken Johnson, Ph.D., and Cal W. Downs, Ph.D., I had the rare opportunity to observe military leaders in high-stakes training simulations designed to replicate the fog, friction, and fluidity of real combat. Our goal was simple yet profound: to understand what separates effective command performance from ineffective leadership under extreme, rapidly changing conditions, through extensive analysis of After-Action Reviews. That experience shaped my thinking about leadership, training, and the value of experiential learning—and planted the seed for a decades-long exploration of leadership in non-routine environments.

As my academic journey advanced, so did the scope of my research. I became more interested in how leaders perform not only in simulated environments but also during actual crises—such as earthquakes, wildfires, terrorist attacks, pandemics, and system failures—where uncertainty dominates and the margin for error is very small. This interest wasn't just academic; it was personal.

While serving on the faculty at Illinois State University, I began researching emergency warnings—starting with how people respond to tornado sirens and gradually expanding into law enforcement and fire department leadership. Some of the most memorable insights came not from formal interviews but from informal Saturday morning conversations with SWAT team members over "Big Farm Breakfast" at Bob Evans. Their stories—raw, candid, and often laced with humor—offered a window into the realities of leadership under pressure.

I also developed a training program for managers at State Farm Insurance, focused on team management, mentorship, performance appraisal, and communication. In parallel, I worked on a project evaluating how technical professionals perform during extreme events. These efforts led to presentations at professional expos and academic conferences, and eventually to an opportunity to join the faculty at Pepperdine University in Southern California, where I continued to expand my research and teaching.

At Pepperdine, one particularly revealing project involved assessing behavioral responses to SMS emergency notifications during a wildfire. Despite clear instructions to shelter in place, a small percentage of students and staff went toward the oncoming fire to take photos. Even some trained Residential Life Assistants made perplexing choices. Working with Everbridge, I helped test and improve emergency message templates, leading to well-known guidelines like the 3-3-30 rule and the 60 & 6 principle. Everbridge provided encouragement and resources that allowed me to fully develop the many models for emergency notification that are so widely referenced. That effort eventually led to the eventual publication of my book *Emergency Notification (2010 PSI Security)*.

A few years earlier, beginning around 1999, while living in Malibu, I began collaborating with my Pepperdine colleague Dr. J.D. Wallace on a study that laid the groundwork for this book. We developed a field research survey to capture the real-life experiences of those who had led during emergencies, disasters, and disruptions. We weren't interested in hypotheticals. We wanted to know: What traits and behaviors distinguish leaders who step up from those who struggle? What makes a leader credible, capable, and effective when the stakes are high?

That survey marked a turning point in my journey—from observing battle simulations reviews at the CATTS Center to organizing insights from exploratory interviews and small group projects. It helped transform intuitive observations into patterns, data, and models. It laid the foundation for what became the *Marks of a Leader* framework: a set of traits, behaviors, and characteristics consistently tested in high-pressure, high-consequence environments across disciplines.

Based on this growing research focal area, Pepperdine's senior leadership team, especially Dr. Nancy Magnusson Durham, asked me to prepare several detailed after-action reports following several critical incidents that occurred at the university. These reports documented what happened, what worked, what didn't, and what needed improvement. I conducted interviews, led focus groups and organized complex performance data, laying the groundwork for my developing expertise in campus safety, security, and resilience. I also managed continuity planning for student study abroad programs, which led to a year living in Florence, Italy. That year—2002—was marked by rising anti-American sentiment across Europe, with the looming Iraq War stirring tensions. On November 9, over 500,000 people marched through Florence in one of the largest peace demonstrations in post-war Europe. My family and 64 college students were living in the city center during these upheavals. The European Social Forum soon followed, drawing even more protesters and pushing the city's population to its limits. When the U.S.-led invasion of Iraq began in March 2003, students were traveling for spring break, and contingency planning became a daily exercise in navigating unpredictability and ensuring safety.

By the time I returned from Florence, I had completed the first draft of my book "Surviving the Pandemic," eventually published in 2009. The book explored the challenges of maintaining business and campus operations during a pandemic, with a particular focus on communication. At that time, it was met with skepticism. The book did not sell well in the marketplace. Some reviewers dismissed it as "alarmist", suggesting I was stuck in a medieval mindset unaware of modern medicine. They dismissed the possibility that a pandemic would result in shutting down businesses, schools, universities, supply chains, and generally disrupt daily life. However, when COVID-19 arrived in 2020, I couldn't help but wear a slight "I tried to warn you" grimace. The pandemic didn't just validate the book's premise; it also highlighted the urgency of preparing for the unthinkable. Now that COVID is mainly in the rearview mirror, that book deserves an update. Maybe that will be the next project for me. At least I now know what I wish I would have known then as the book probably will be more specific in the second edition version.

Living in Southern California also taught me about life's unpredictability and risk surprises. Over the years, I faced my first (and second) shelter-in-place wildfire emergencies, several minor earthquakes, and one moderate quake that shook buildings and nerves. A landslide once blocked campus access and disrupted municipal water supplies. An eight-day campus-wide IT outage, caused by a failed master switch installation, became a detailed case study I was asked to research and document. And then there were personal reminders of vulnerability: rattlesnakes in the garage, scorpions in the kitchen. These weren't just inconveniences—they were vivid reminders to me that leadership under non-routine threats, situations, and pressure isn't limited to battlefields or boardrooms. It happens in homes, schools, and communities.

This book is the tangible outcome of this inquisitive journey. It blends decades of research and observation with the voices of those who have led—or been led—during pivotal moments. It is written for leaders in education, public safety, business, healthcare, and government—anyone tasked with leading through complexity, ambiguity, and disruption. The aim is not to present abstract theory but to provide a practical, evidence-based framework for preparation, selection, training, and performance evaluation.

If leadership were easy, the situation wouldn't feel real. The real challenge arises when control is lost, options are uncertain, and fear spreads faster than facts. This book explores what happens in those moments—and how we prepare leaders not just to survive but to lead others through them with clarity, courage, and credibility.

Leadership can mean the difference between a coordinated response and organizational failure, between recovery and reputational damage, and between saving lives and experiencing tragic loss. Although my background is rooted in the social sciences of rhetoric and communication, this work is not just for academics. It's for practitioners who must make decisions when there's no time to think and no room for error.

In a crisis, leadership goes beyond titles. It becomes a test of character, clarity, and competence. The next crisis won't wait for perfect preparation. It will come without warning or apology. When it does, it will judge you—not by your intentions or credentials, but by your readiness. How you lead under pressure—how you communicate, decide, adapt, and care—will shape not only the outcome but also the trust, resilience, and recovery of those you serve.

This book is for those who carry the responsibility of leadership in high-pressure settings. Whether you work in education, public safety, government, healthcare, law enforcement, military, or business, the principles here will help you lead more effectively when it matters most. You'll find insights rooted in research and real-world experience—and, more importantly, actionable strategies. This is a practical guide, not just an academic one.

I have three goals for this book:

> ➤ To help readers identify the traits and mindsets that distinguish effective crisis leaders—those who earn trust, inspire action, and remain composed when others falter.
> ➤ To help readers avoid common leadership mistakes, such as blind spots, breakdowns, and habits that weaken mission success and team confidence.
> ➤ To help readers develop a leadership model based on core human factor dimensions and define the essential knowledge, skills, and attitudes for an effective Leader KSA Framework focused on resilience, readiness, and ethical responsibility.

Because when everything starts to fall apart, people won't follow a job title. They'll follow the leader who guides—someone who brings order to chaos, calms fears, and provides hope during uncertain times. That kind of leadership can be learned, practiced, and developed before a crisis happens. That's why this book exists.

History doesn't just remember leaders during peace and prosperity. It defines them—often permanently—by how they respond when everything falls apart. Moments of crisis reveal fault lines beneath our systems, communities, and assumptions. They test not only infrastructure and protocols but also the character, clarity, and courage of those in charge.

Since I started this inquiry over twenty-five years ago, the number of important case studies in crisis leadership has increased. From pandemics and terrorist attacks to school shootings and natural disasters, recent history has changed public expectations, trust in institutions, and the very concept of leadership.

At this stage in my journey during the trip from my starting point in the mid-1980s when I was first collecting data at the CATTS center until now, I occasionally reflect on the lasting impact of significant events that have occurred along the way that have been relevant to the Marks of a Leader framework. These would include the Columbine High School shooting in 1999, which forced educators and law enforcement alike to take on roles they weren't anticipated and, in some cases, not prepared for. It demonstrated the urgent need for threat assessment, proactive planning, and emotionally intelligent leadership in schools.

Just two years later, the September 11th attacks changed how emergency management, homeland security, crisis management, and crisis communication operate. Leaders at all levels faced impossible choices with lives at risk, showing both remarkable courage and major gaps in preparedness.

Hurricane Katrina in 2005 exposed systemic failures in emergency response, coordination, and fairness. The images from New Orleans remain a stark reminder of what happens when leadership struggles under pressure. The 2007 Virginia Tech massacre prompted higher education to reassess campus safety, mental health strategies, and interdisciplinary communication. Once again, it demonstrated the importance of leaders who can handle complex situations with compassion and clarity.

Then came a major crisis for which I had advocated preparedness in my (2009) book *Surviving the Pandemic*, the COVID-19 pandemic. From 2020 to 2023, institutions worldwide faced a stress test of historic proportions. It was not just a public health emergency; it challenged continuity, adaptability, and moral leadership. Schools, hospitals, businesses, and governments had to adapt quickly, often with incomplete information and conflicting demands. The pandemic revealed the fragility of many systems but also highlighted leaders capable of systemic thinking, transparent communication, and leading with both determination and empathy.

In each of these crises, the world changed—and so did people's expectations of leadership. They began demanding more than authority; they sought authenticity. Beyond competence, they wanted compassion. They desired guidance, not just orders. The era of command-and-control leadership is shifting toward a more human-centered, flexible approach—one that values emotional intelligence as much as operational expertise. We now live in a world shaped—and continuously reshaped—by crisis. The challenges ahead may differ from those we've faced, but the need for strong leadership remains constant. What we learn from history and how we prepare for the future will determine whether our institutions bend or break under pressure. This book is not just about understanding crisis leadership but about preparing for the world we already inhabit. A world where leadership isn't optional, and readiness isn't a luxury. It has become clear to me that the quality of leadership during emergencies directly influences outcomes—physical, emotional, operational, and political. These events weren't merely emergencies; they reflected deep organizational, social, and cultural fault lines. In nearly every case, public scrutiny didn't just assess the crisis—it evaluated the leaders. Today's leaders face a rapidly evolving risk landscape. Climate-related disasters are increasing in frequency and severity. Cyberattacks and infrastructure failures threaten continuity across many sectors. Mass shootings and targeted violence challenge schools, businesses, and public spaces. Misinformation and communication breakdowns hinder public responses and erode trust. Social unrest and political divisions heighten volatility in decision-making. The traditional, static, hierarchical "command and control" model no longer suffices. Crisis leadership must be adaptable, inclusive, and emotionally aware. It should focus on human behavior rather than only organizational structures. It needs to combine decisiveness with empathy, planning with flexibility. Continuity of operations should be a core leadership skill—not an afterthought. Despite the increasing frequency and severity of crises, many organizations still lack trained and tested leadership structures to manage them. Leadership development often emphasizes credentials and technical skills in ideal conditions rather than performance under pressure. This book shares insights from this journey, specifically reflecting on a long-term field research project aimed at identifying the human traits, characteristics, and abilities associated with leadership effectiveness in real-world emergencies.

CHAPTER 1

LEADERSHIP IN CRISIS, DISASTER, AND EMERGENCY MANAGEMENT

C rises, emergencies, disasters, and critical incidents are among the most intense, complex, and demanding situations that individuals, teams, and organizations face. Whether caused by natural forces, technological failures, public health emergencies, or deliberate acts of disruption, these events place extraordinary demands on human cognition, emotion, behavior, and coordination systems. The stakes—life, reputation, economy, and operations—are set in environments characterized by uncertainty, ambiguity, and time Pressure.

These events test not only technical systems and formal procedures but also the limits of human performance. The psychological, operational, and systemic demands of crises require more than checklists and contingency plans. They call for adaptive thinking, clear-headed leadership, cohesive team dynamics, and emotionally resilient individuals.

Understanding the complexity of these challenges is essential for preparing leaders and teams to perform effectively under pressure. Crises disrupt routines, test assumptions, overwhelm capacities, and often eliminate the luxury of time or complete information. They demand rapid interpretation, decisive action, and moral clarity—often amid fatigue, stress, and personal vulnerability. This chapter explores the layers of strain individuals and groups face, as well as the burdens carried by those in leadership roles.

The Importance of Effective Leadership

Crises—whether natural disasters, technological failures, pandemics, acts of violence, or organizational breakdowns—are inherently unpredictable, fast-moving, and high-stakes. In these moments, leadership becomes the decisive factor. It determines whether a situation spirals into chaos or is brought under control. Effective leadership isn't a luxury; it's essential. It shapes how information is interpreted, how decisions are made, how people respond, and ultimately, how successfully a crisis is managed and resolved. One respondent, a city emergency coordinator, put it plainly: "The plan mattered—but the person leading it mattered more."

Strong leadership directly influences the speed and quality of decision-making. Ambiguity, fragmented data, and compressed timelines characterize crises. Leaders must quickly evaluate changing conditions, synthesize input from multiple sources, and make critical decisions—often with incomplete information and no time for consensus. Hesitation, indecision, or poor judgment can worsen damage and delay response efforts. A hospital administrator recalled, "We had minutes to decide whether to evacuate. The leader didn't flinch—and those saved lives." In crisis, clarity and speed are inseparable.

Effective crisis leaders demonstrate a mix of decisiveness, critical thinking, and adaptive reasoning. They assess risks, anticipate cascading consequences, and stay flexible as new information becomes available. Their ability to act swiftly and wisely not only reduces harm—it builds confidence among responders and the public. One school superintendent shared, "She didn't have all the answers, but she had a calm voice and a clear plan. That's what kept us together." In high-stakes environments, leadership isn't just about control—it's about coherence.

Beyond tactical execution, effective leadership also shapes emotional tone. Leaders influence morale, trust, and psychological safety. Their presence can stabilize teams, reduce panic, and foster unity. A logistics officer noted, "He walked the floor, made eye contact, and asked how we were doing. That wasn't in the protocol—but it made all the difference." In moments of disruption, people don't just follow plans; they follow people. And the leaders who earn that trust are the ones who lead with clarity, courage, and compassion.

Ultimately, the significance of effective leadership during a crisis cannot be overstated. It is the force that transforms strategy into action, uncertainty into direction, and fear into focus. The next chapter will examine the behavioral traits that define such leadership—not as abstract ideals, but as observable, teachable, and repeatable practices. Because when the stakes are highest, leadership is not about position; it's about performance.

The Dual Burdens of Crisis Response

Every crisis presents two simultaneous battles: the external threat and the internal toll it takes on those who respond. While the public often sees the outward struggle, rescue operations, containment efforts, press briefings, the invisible burden is carried by crisis managers, first responders, medical professionals, and military personnel working at the brink of human endurance. Their focus remains outward: solving problems, saving lives, restoring order. But the inward costs—physiological strain, emotional exhaustion, and moral injury—are deep and often unspoken. One emergency coordinator reflected, "We were trained to handle the chaos. No one trained us for the grief."

Physiological stress responses spike during crises. Elevated heart rates, adrenaline rushes, sleep deprivation, and chronic fatigue become routine. Decision-making occurs under extreme pressure, where seconds can determine outcomes and mistakes have moral and human consequences. Responders stay in a heightened state of alertness—a volatile mix of focus and fear—that the human body isn't meant to sustain forever. Yet for many crisis workers, this "temporary" condition becomes normal. Without proper recovery, chronic activation of stress responses leads to exhaustion, weakened immunity, and long-term health problems. A paramedic shared, "I didn't realize how sick I'd become until the crisis ended—and I collapsed."

The psychological toll is equally profound. Repeated exposure to trauma, loss, and danger chips away at emotional resilience. Emergency workers witness suffering and death on a scale most people never encounter. Paramedics face raw vulnerability daily; soldiers make life-or-death decisions in morally complex situations; crisis managers must lead with confidence while hiding their own fears and grief. Over time, this emotional suppression can numb empathy, create emotional detachment, and lead to anxiety, guilt, or post-traumatic stress. One hospital administrator noted, "I kept it together for my team. But at home, I couldn't sleep. I couldn't stop seeing their faces."

Unlike most jobs, crisis responders can't simply clock out and leave the weight behind. The psychological residue—the memories, the moral burden of decisions, the faces of those lost—often follow them home. In cultures that prize toughness and stoicism, admitting distress may be seen as a sign of weakness. But unresolved trauma doesn't go away—it reemerges as burnout, depression, substance abuse, strained relationships, or decreased performance. A fire chief shared, "We lost a great leader not to the fire—but to the silence that followed." The cost of untreated emotional stress is not just personal—it affects the entire organization.

This accumulated stress impacts not only on individuals but also on the systems and communities they serve. When responders suffer in silence, staff turnover increases, cohesion weakens, and the quality of care or decision-making declines. A tired responder is more likely to make errors; a burned-out leader struggles to make balanced decisions. The mission itself becomes vulnerable when those carrying it are unsupported. Effective crisis leadership must recognize this dual burden—by fostering cultures of care, incorporating recovery into operations, and understanding that resilience isn't just about endurance but also about healing.

Leadership as a Moral and Ethical Duty

Effective leadership during a crisis is judged not only by operational results but also by how much care leaders show to those they lead. The ability to protect, support, and maintain a team under stress is not optional; it is fundamental to leadership. Psychological resilience, peer support, rest, and recovery are not luxuries or afterthoughts, they are essential parts of preparedness. One hospital administrator said, "We had protocols for everything—except how to help our people breathe again after the worst was over." Leaders must create systems that support both performance and recovery: access to mental health services, scheduled decompression time, counseling resources, and cultures that encourage honest conversations about stress and hardship. Resilience is often viewed as an individual trait, but in reality, it is a shared responsibility. Leaders who prioritize team well-being protect not only the people but also the mission. In high-stress situations, leadership must evolve beyond command-and-control to include care and continuity. A fire chief described his role during a prolonged wildfire response: "I wasn't just directing crews—I was checking in, making sure they ate, slept, and talked. That's what kept us going." Leadership that recognizes the human cost of crisis fosters trust, cohesion, and sustained effectiveness. The moral responsibility of leadership becomes even more significant during a crisis. Decisions made under pressure have ethical implications, and the emotional toll on responders can be deep. Those who carry the heaviest burdens—frontline workers, decision-makers, coordinators—deserve more than gratitude. They need leadership that actively supports their strength, safeguards their recovery, and respects their humanity. A paramedic stated, "We were praised in public, but behind the scenes, we were falling apart. What we needed wasn't applause—it was help." Ethical leadership means understanding that care is not a sign of weakness; it's a foundation of resilience. This responsibility extends beyond the immediate crisis. Leaders must ensure that recovery efforts are built into organizational routines, not improvised reactions. This involves embedding support systems into organizational culture, training leaders to recognize signs of distress, and establishing feedback mechanisms so teams can voice their needs. One emergency manager remarked, "After the hurricane, we had a debrief—but no follow-up. People drifted. We lost good people because we didn't close the loop." Leadership that embraces the full cycle from response to recovery builds organizations that are both operationally prepared and emotionally resilient. Ultimately, leading in a crisis is a moral and ethical act. It involves stewardship—of people, purpose, and potential. Leaders who meet this challenge are not just tacticians—they are guardians of human dignity. They understand that resilience is built not by pushing harder but by caring more deeply. In doing so, they foster cultures where strength is shared, recovery is valued, and leadership becomes a force for healing and action.

Emotional Intelligence and Team Stability Leadership

Crises often trigger waves of emotional chaos, confusion, grief, and uncertainty that ripple through teams, stakeholders, and communities. In these moments, people instinctively turn to leaders not just for guidance but for emotional grounding. Strategy might steer the plan, but emotional intelligence steers the people. Leaders who stay calm, empathetic, and transparent help stabilize the emotional atmosphere, reduce panic, and foster a shared sense of purpose—even amid chaos. One emergency manager described a leader this way: "She didn't just give orders—she gave us confidence. That's what kept us moving."

Emotional intelligence in crisis leadership involves more than just staying composed—it requires attunement. Leaders must read their team's emotional pulse, openly acknowledge stress, and respond with compassion. By encouraging open communication and validating emotional experiences, they build psychological safety, a space where people feel secure enough to speak up, seek help, and stay engaged. A hospital administrator recalled, "He started every shift with a check-in. Not about tasks—but about how we were doing. That changed everything." These small gestures lay a foundation of trust that sustains morale through prolonged or overwhelming challenges.

Resilient leaders' model emotional regulation. They don't suppress emotions—they manage them openly and constructively. This example helps others tune their responses. When leaders show vulnerability without losing clarity, they humanize the crisis and strengthen cohesion. One school superintendent shared, "I told my team I was scared too—but that we'd face it together. That honesty didn't weaken us—it united us." Emotional intelligence becomes a stabilizing force, allowing teams to navigate uncertainty with confidence and connection.

Significantly, emotional intelligence also improves decision-making. Leaders who understand their teams' emotional dynamics can anticipate conflicts, diffuse tension, and align efforts more effectively. They recognize when fatigue is affecting performance, when fear clouds judgment, and when empathy is more needed than efficiency. A logistics officer noted, "She paused a meeting to let someone cry. That wasn't weakness—it was leadership. After that, we worked better together." Emotional intelligence isn't just a soft skill—it's a strategic asset. In a crisis, emotional intelligence acts as the glue that keeps teams united. It shifts leadership from command to connection, from authority to authenticity. Leaders who develop this skill don't just manage events; they shape experiences. In doing so, they foster cultures where people feel seen, supported, and capable—even when the world feels unstable.

The Critical Function of Coordination and Collaboration

No single person can handle a crisis alone. An effective response requires a collective effort—one that crosses disciplines, departments, jurisdictions, and sometimes entire sectors. Leadership during these times isn't about giving orders from the top; it's about bringing together different skills into a clear, flexible response. One emergency manager compared it to "conducting an orchestra where half the musicians have never met and the music keeps changing." Coordination isn't just logistics; it's a leadership necessity.

Strong leaders act as integrators. They clarify roles, delegate wisely, and keep lines of communication open. They understand each team member's unique strengths and foster cooperation rather than competition. A hospital administrator recalled, "We had doctors, logistics, and volunteers all working together. The leader didn't micromanage—she aligned us." Such leadership builds unity and shared purpose, allowing teams to act quickly and precisely even under pressure.

Without strong coordination, a crisis response can quickly fall apart. Redundant efforts, missed handoffs, and conflicting priorities lead to delays and confusion. One respondent described a multi-agency drill where "everyone had a plan, but no one had a shared language." The result was friction, wasted time, and lost trust. In real emergencies, these failures can cost lives. Leaders need to anticipate these risks and build connections—shared protocols, cross-team liaisons, and real-time feedback loops.

Collaboration also requires humility and flexibility. Leaders must be willing to listen, adapt, and share authority. In complex crises, no single perspective is enough. One logistics officer said, "The best decision we made came from someone outside the command structure. The leader didn't care about rank—he cared about results." Openness to input strengthens coordination and enables teams to innovate under pressure. It transforms hierarchy into a network, and networks are more resilient.

Ultimately, coordination and collaboration are more than just operational tasks; they are signs of leadership. They show a leader's ability to connect with people, align efforts, and build momentum. In crises, the best leaders aren't those who control everything, but those who empower everyone. By doing so, they transform disjointed responses into unified action.

Communication as a Leadership Imperative

In crisis leadership, communication is not a peripheral skill, it is a core function. Stakeholders at all levels, team members, partner agencies, affected communities, and the media depend on timely, honest, and actionable information. Leaders often serve as the main conduit for this flow, shaping not only what is said but how it is understood. Poor communication can increase confusion, spread misinformation, and damage trust. One emergency manager reflected, "The facts were hard enough. What made it worse was the silence. People filled the gaps with fear." In contrast, clear and transparent messaging builds credibility and enables coordinated responses.

Effective crisis leaders balance urgency with accuracy. They understand that speed matters, but so does precision. Delivering brutal truths with empathy is a key part of ethical communication. A hospital administrator recalled, "We had to tell families there were no more beds. The way we said it mattered—it wasn't just data, it was dignity." Leaders also must customize their messages for different audiences—what a tactical team needs differs from what the public or press requires. This tailoring ensures relevance and reduces misinterpretation, especially in emotionally charged environments.

Listening is just as essential as speaking. Leaders who practice active listening—who observe reactions, ask clarifying questions, and stay sensitive to emotional cues—are better able to adapt their communication in real time. One school superintendent shared, "I thought I was being clear, but the staff looked confused. I paused, asked what they needed, and rephrased. That moment changed everything." Communication is not a one-way broadcast; it's a dynamic exchange that requires humility, responsiveness, and emotional intelligence.

The way leaders manage information flow directly impacts how a crisis is perceived and handled. Strategic communication can calm panic, clarify priorities, and reinforce shared purpose. Conversely, vague or inconsistent messaging can fracture teams and erode public trust. A logistics officer noted, "We had three versions of the plan circulating. People didn't know which one to follow. That cost us time." Leaders need to establish communication protocols, designate spokespeople, and maintain message discipline across channels.

Ultimately, communication during a crisis is not just tactical; it's a moral obligation. It reflects a leader's commitment to truth, transparency, and trust. The best crisis communicators don't just inform, they connect. They help people make sense of uncertainty, find direction amid disruption, and feel acknowledged even in chaos. In doing so, they elevate leadership from simply a role to a relationship—one built on clarity, compassion, and credibility.

Adaptability and Continuous Learning

In crisis leadership, rigidity can be a weakness. No plan remains effective once faced with a real-world emergency. Situations change quickly, new factors appear, and threats often take unexpected turns. Successful leaders adopt adaptability—not as a backup, but as a vital skill. They know that flexibility, innovation, and rapid adjustments are crucial for managing uncertainty. One emergency manager summarized this well: "We had a great plan for the first hour. After that, we had to improvise." Adaptability isn't about abandoning structure; it's about knowing when to adjust it.

This flexibility is strategic, not reactive. Adaptive leaders keep a close eye on conditions in real time, tweak tactics as needed, and welcome input from various sources. They avoid the trap of sticking to outdated assumptions or strict protocols. A hospital administrator shared, "We changed our triage model mid-response. It wasn't in the manual, but it saved lives." These leaders build cultures where ongoing learning and change are normal, not feared. Their teams feel empowered to speak up, try new approaches, and improve—even under pressure.

A mindset of continuous learning is what keeps adaptability effective over time. Strong leaders review incidents afterward, seek honest feedback, and apply lessons learned to plans. They see every crisis as a learning opportunity—not just to fix what went wrong, but to find ways to do better. One logistics officer explained, "After the flood, we didn't just rebuild—we redesigned. We asked what the crisis taught us." This reflective approach makes organizations more resilient and prepares teams to face future challenges with greater agility and insight. Importantly, continuous learning isn't just about technical skills; it also involves personal growth. Leaders need to evaluate how they show up emotionally, ethically, and interpersonally. Did they listen well? Did they communicate clearly? Did they foster trust? A school superintendent shared, "I realized I was too focused on logistics and not enough on morale. That changed how I lead now." These insights help leaders grow not only as strategists but also as stewards of human experiences.

Adaptability and learning are essential, not optional; they are traits that ensure survival. In high-pressure environments, the ability to pivot, reflect, and develop is what distinguishes reactive management from resilient leadership. The leaders who succeed are those who view every challenge as an opportunity to improve—not just the plan, but also the people and principles behind it.

Earned Trust as the Currency of Leadership

Trust is not "a given" during a crisis; it is built moment by moment through actions, presence, and integrity. In high-stakes settings, trust becomes the key currency of leadership. When leaders are viewed as competent, transparent, and principled, their guidance is followed, teams stay motivated, and stakeholders feel reassured. Conversely, when trust diminishes, resistance grows, collaboration weakens, and reputational damage can intensify the crisis. One emergency manager simply stated: "People didn't follow the plan—they followed the person they trusted to lead it."

Trust is established through visibility and accessibility. Leaders who demonstrate presence—both physically and emotionally—signal commitment. They don't hide behind titles or shy away from difficult conversations. They take responsibility, admit when they don't know, and communicate honestly. A hospital administrator recalled, "She stood in the hallway every morning, answered questions, and admitted what she didn't know. That's why we trusted her." This type of leadership not only provides information but also fosters psychological safety, which is crucial for effective decision-making and team cohesion under pressure.

Acknowledging uncertainty is a powerful way to build trust. During a crisis, no one expects perfection, but everyone values honesty. Leaders who admit what they don't know, explain what they're doing to find out, and stay open to input show humility and credibility. A school superintendent shared, "I told parents we didn't have all the answers, but we were listening and adjusting. That honesty calmed the room." Trust comes not from knowing all the facts but from how leaders manage the unknown.

A commitment to others' well-being is a vital part of trust. Leaders who focus on the safety, morale, and dignity of their teams gain loyalty that goes beyond mere adherence to standard procedures. One logistics officer remarked, "He checked on us before checking the numbers. That's why we gave him everything we had." In a crisis, people don't just need guidance—they need genuine care. When leaders consistently show concern, trust becomes a steadying force that helps teams handle uncertainty. Ultimately, trust earned is the foundation on which all other leadership functions rely. It enables coordination, communication, adaptability, and resilience. It transforms authority into influence and strategy into action. In a crisis, trust isn't just a soft virtue; it's a tangible asset. Leaders who realize this don't merely manage events—they influence outcomes by earning the right to be followed.

Conclusion: Leadership as a Vital Force

Leadership in a crisis is not just a supportive role—it is the critical force that determines whether a response succeeds or fails. It impacts how quickly teams come together, how clearly information is shared, how fairly resources are allocated, and how effectively people are protected and reassured. Beyond logistics and strategy, leadership shapes the emotional environment: it influences morale, trust, and the collective ability to recover. During disruptions, people don't just need plans—they need someone to believe in.

Importantly, leadership in a crisis isn't defined by rank, title, or credentials. It is demonstrated through actions. Decisiveness, emotional intelligence, clarity under pressure, adaptability, and integrity are not optional—they are necessary. These qualities distinguish confusion from coordination, escalation from containment, and fragmentation from resilience. One experienced responder said, "The best leaders weren't the ones with the loudest voices—they were the ones who made us feel safe enough to act." Leadership isn't just about control; it's about coherence.

As the risk environment becomes more unpredictable—shaped by climate change, cyber threats, misinformation, and social unrest—the demands on crisis leaders increase. Technical expertise alone is no longer enough. Today's leaders must be able to think clearly amid chaos, communicate with compassion to diverse audiences, and act ethically under pressure. Investing in leadership development is no longer a strategic choice; it's a necessity for survival. Organizations that fail to develop these skills risk not only operational failures but also reputational damage.

This chapter has identified leadership as a vital element in crisis management. It has highlighted the behavioral qualities that matter most when stakes are high and mistakes are costly. We see that leadership isn't just about what gets done, it's about how it gets done, and who is protected in the process. But understanding the importance of leadership is only the first step. To truly prepare leaders for crises, we must understand what undermines their clarity, confidence, and cohesion.

In Chapter 2, we focus on the pressures that make crisis leadership so challenging. We will examine the mental strain of decision-making under uncertainty, the emotional toll of responsibility, and the organizational friction that hinders action. We will explore the blind spots, breakdowns, and biases that weaken judgment and erode trust. These challenges are not hypothetical—they are real experiences that influence every moment of leadership during a crisis.

Before we can develop better leaders, we must understand what causes their success or failure. Chapter 2 begins this exploration not with criticism but with an effort to understand the unique challenges leaders face in critical situations. It maps the landscape of adversity so we can create leadership that lasts, adapts, and inspires. The road ahead may be uncertain, but the need for courageous, emotionally intelligent, and ethically grounded leadership has *never* been more urgent.

CHAPTER 2

THE CHALLENGES OF LEADERSHIP

Crises are defined not only by their severity but by their unpredictability, complexity, and potential for wide-ranging impact. Unlike routine operational problems, which follow familiar procedures and known variables, crises erupt suddenly, escalate rapidly, and often evolve in nonlinear, chaotic ways. They rarely conform to expectations, timelines, or prior experience. Whether natural (earthquakes, hurricanes), technological (cyberattacks, industrial accidents), or human-made (terrorism, organizational failures), these events disrupt systems, threaten lives, destabilize institutions, and overwhelm resources.

A key feature of a crisis is its rapid pace. Decision-makers often have little time to gather or verify information. Initial reports may be delayed, incomplete, or contradictory. Facts change as events unfold, and clarity might only emerge in hindsight—if at all. Leaders must act amid uncertainty, without full understanding or thorough analysis. What was true five minutes ago may no longer be accurate, requiring constant reassessment of facts, priorities, and strategies.

This fast-paced environment requires quick sensemaking—the process where individuals and teams interpret unfolding events to understand what is happening and what actions are necessary. In high-stakes situations, sensemaking isn't optional; it's a crucial survival skill. It involves synthesizing information from multiple sources, recognizing patterns amidst chaos, predicting second- and third-order consequences, and making decisions without a clear plan.

Importantly, sensemaking isn't a one-time event; it must be ongoing and adaptable, responding swiftly to changing circumstances and new information. Leaders need to interpret events, communicate their understanding, and adjust strategies in real time. This requires cognitive agility, emotional control, and situational awareness—traits that rigid protocols or manuals cannot replace.

Mental flexibility is essential. Clinging to outdated beliefs or trying to force a crisis into a familiar pattern can cause delays, errors, or missed opportunities. Effective crisis management depends on a team's ability to learn, adapt, and innovate under pressure, often with little prior experience or certainty.

In summary, crises disrupt traditional patterns and challenge simple solutions. Their complexity pushes us and their unpredictability demands leadership based on humility, clarity, and adaptability. Recognizing these qualities is vital—not only for helping individuals and organizations respond effectively but also for developing leaders capable of weathering storms and guiding others toward recovery.

Ambiguity and Uncertainty

In crisis situations, information is rarely complete, consistent, or reliable. Reports may conflict, communication channels can be disrupted, and monitoring systems might provide vague or delayed readings. The chaos of rapidly changing events often obscures the situation, leaving decision-makers with limited visibility.

This uncertainty presents a serious challenge. Leaders need to evaluate the situation quickly, often without knowing its full scope, duration, or ripple effects. Lack of clarity can lead to hesitation, misjudgments, or paralysis. Teams may struggle to prioritize actions, allocate resources, or coordinate efforts effectively. Overreacting to perceived threats or underestimating risks can worsen the crisis or endanger lives.

In these moments, critical thinking and situational awareness become essential. Leaders must interpret incomplete data, update assessments in real time, and adjust strategies on the fly. Developing tolerance for uncertainty—and learning to make informed decisions with imperfect information—are vital skills for anyone operating in high-stakes environments.

Crisis leadership demands not only decisiveness but also the ability to act clearly amid uncertainty. It requires a mindset that accepts complexity, anticipates change, and remains open to new information—even under high pressure.

Time Pressure and Decision-Making

Crises often require immediate action, sometimes within seconds. The urgency is real; delays can result in loss of lives, escalating threats, or system failures. Leaders must make significant decisions under extreme pressure, often with limited or conflicting information and little time for consultation or deliberation.

This fast-paced decision-making environment challenges even experienced professionals. The luxury of gathering complete data or reaching consensus is rarely possible. Instead, leaders must depend on intuition, experience, and heuristic reasoning—mental shortcuts that can be both useful and risky. Under stress, cognitive functions such as memory, focus, and analytical thinking can decline, increasing the likelihood of mistakes.

Despite these limitations, leaders are expected to stay calm, communicate effectively, and act decisively. The ability to quickly evaluate situations, prioritize correctly, and act with confidence is a vital trait of crisis leadership.

Preparation is key. Leaders who have built trust within their teams, established clear protocols, and delegated authority properly are better equipped to make rapid, sound decisions. These foundations allow for quick action without sacrificing clarity or cohesion.

Mastering decision-making under pressure is more than a technical skill; it's an essential leadership capability. In unstable, high-stakes situations, the ability to act swiftly and wisely can be the difference between escalation and containment, chaos and control.

High Stakes and Human Impact

In crisis situations, decisions have immediate and significant consequences. For those on the front lines—such as rescuing victims, providing medical care, and containing threats, the results of leadership are often measured in lives saved or lost. But the impact extends beyond individuals. Effective leadership can determine whether organizations recover or fail, whether communities heal or fracture, and whether public trust is maintained or shattered.

Mistakes or delays can lead to cascading effects: extensive damage, environmental harm, reputational harm, or long-term societal disruption. The pressure to succeed is unrelenting, creating a heavy psychological burden on responders and leaders alike.

This burden grows with public scrutiny. Leaders are judged not only by the results they deliver but also by their communication, transparency, and support for recovery. In this environment, anxiety, stress, and fatigue can impair judgment, strain relationships, and weaken team cohesion.

That's why the human side of crisis leadership is just as crucial as technical expertise. Resilience, emotional intelligence, and clear communication are not soft skills; they are vital survival tools. Leaders who remain calm, empathetic, and grounded help stabilize their teams and lead them through uncertainty with purpose and clarity.

Media Scrutiny and Public Pressure

Media scrutiny adds another layer of complexity to crisis leadership. Emergency managers and public officials often operate under intense public observation, with every decision analyzed in real time. Mistakes—whether real or perceived—can provoke swift criticism, erode trust, and complicate response efforts. The demand for quick, accurate updates often exceeds operational capacity. Leaders must balance the urgency of communication with the risk of sharing incomplete or changing information. The nonstop pace of media cycles can cause fatigue, burnout, and increased anxiety, especially when misinformation or rumors begin spreading. Negative portrayals in the media can have a personal impact. Public criticism, even if unfair, can lower morale, weaken confidence, and lead to emotional exhaustion. Leaders might find themselves managing not just the crisis but also how their decisions are perceived, the tone of their messaging, and the expectations of various stakeholders. Media pressure also influences political leaders, regulatory agencies, and public sentiment—often creating conflicting demands. Crisis managers must juggle transparency, accountability, and operational focus, all while maintaining composure under scrutiny. To stay resilient, leaders need effective stress-management strategies and organizational support. Clear communication procedures, media training, and access to peer and psychological support can help leaders remain focused and credible under intense public pressure.

The Human Cost of Crisis Leadership

Crisis work pushes human limits—physically, psychologically, and emotionally. For those in high-stress roles like crisis managers, first responders, trauma doctors, and combat soldiers, the effects are not just theoretical. They are real, measurable, and often long-lasting.

Hans Selye first explained the physiological basis of stress in his General Adaptation Syndrome (1936, 1950, 1976), describing how the body responds to prolonged stress through alarm, resistance, and exhaustion. Robert Sapolsky (2004) expanded on this in Why Zebras Don't Get Ulcers, illustrating how chronic stress damages cardiovascular and immune systems and affects cognitive and emotional regulation. Bruce McEwen's concept of allostatic load (1998, 2007) further shows how repeated stress responses change the body's physiology over time.

The Yerkes–Dodson Law (1908) highlights a common paradox for crisis professionals: performance improves with stress up to a point—beyond which it sharply declines. Many operate past that threshold, where adrenaline maintains performance but damages well-being.

Lazarus and Folkman's transactional model of stress and coping (1984) emphasizes that stress results not just from external events but also how individuals perceive threats and their response abilities—an essential insight into resilience and failure.

In military contexts, Dave Grossman (1995) and Jonathan Shay (1994, 2011) studied the psychological and moral injuries of combat. Their work introduced the concept of moral injury—the emotional and spiritual wounds caused by morally complex decisions. These insights have influenced research in healthcare, law enforcement, and emergency response.

Empirical studies back these findings. Hoge et al. (2004) found higher rates of PTSD, depression, and substance use among deployed soldiers. Civilian responders—firefighters, police officers, and emergency medical workers—show similar patterns of burnout, cardiovascular issues, and post-traumatic stress (Violanti, 2007; National Fallen Firefighters Foundation, 2004). In healthcare, Charles Figley's research on compassion fatigue (1995) and the Maslach Burnout Inventory (1981, 1997) documented emotional exhaustion from repeated exposure to suffering.

Emergency physicians, trauma nurses, and paramedics often experience the full burnout trilogy: emotional exhaustion, depersonalization, and reduced sense of accomplishment. Neuroscience explains why judgment and calmness often decline under pressure.

Daniel Kahneman (2011) demonstrated how stress shifts thinking from deliberate, analytical "System 2" to instinctive, reactive "System 1." Gary Klein's research on naturalistic decision-making (1998) shows how experience allows quick, accurate decisions under stress—but also how untrained instinct can lead to errors. The overall conclusion is clear: high-stakes work has predictable, measurable human costs.

Prolonged stress depletes physical resources, impairs cognition, and increases the risk of trauma, burnout, and moral injury. For leaders, this research imposes a moral duty. Achieving tactical success and operational efficiency alone is not enough. Effective leadership also involves protecting the physical, psychological, and emotional well-being of those who serve.

George Everly and Jeffrey Mitchell (1997), founders of Critical Incident Stress Management (CISM), emphasized that structured peer and psychological support systems are not optional—they are essential. When leaders prioritize wellness, rest, peer support, and access to care, they protect not only individuals but also their organization's long-term capacity. As the World Health Organization (2013) and the National Academies of Sciences (2021) point out, sustainable crisis response depends on systemic, leader-driven commitment to mental health and psychosocial support. Resilience isn't just a personal trait. —it's a collective responsibility. Leadership's role is to ensure those carrying the heaviest burdens are never alone.

The Multiple Burdens of Crisis Leadership

Crisis leadership is not just about taking the lead—it's about staying grounded even as everything around you shakes. The true test of leadership in high-pressure situations isn't in one heroic moment but in the ongoing ability to think clearly, act decisively, and lead with compassion under mounting stress.

Leaders in these scenarios face three overlapping challenges: cognitive overload, emotional strain, and organizational friction. Each of these can distort judgment, undermine confidence, and slow down performance. Together, they create the crucible where leadership is truly tested.

Cognitive overload occurs when leaders are inundated with information, much of it incomplete, conflicting, or constantly changing. The mental effort required to process, prioritize, and respond can quickly become overwhelming. An emergency manager once described it as "trying to solve a puzzle while the pieces keep changing shape." Under these conditions, decision fatigue can develop, causing leaders to rely on habitual responses or delay action in search of clarity. Without proper support—such as decision triage, delegation, and clear communication protocols—even the most capable minds can stumble.

Emotional strain adds another layer. Leaders must absorb others' fears, grief, and uncertainties while managing their own reactions. This load is often invisible but deeply felt. A hospital director recalled, "I had to be the calm voice in the room, even when I was breaking inside." The weight of responsibility, especially when lives are at stake, can cause anxiety, guilt, and emotional exhaustion. These reactions are normal responses to extraordinary demands. But if ignored, they can reduce empathy, cloud judgment, and isolate leaders from their teams. Organizational friction makes the challenge even harder. Even the most emotionally resilient and mentally agile leaders can be slowed down by systemic barriers—unclear authority, siloed communication, outdated protocols, and conflicting priorities. One respondent noted, "We had the right people, but the wrong structure. Decisions got stuck in the hierarchy." In a crisis, time lost to bureaucracy is time taken away from resolution. Leaders must navigate not only the crisis itself but also the institutional barriers that slow action. This calls for political skill, strategic adaptability, and the ability to cut through procedural clutter without alienating stakeholders.

These burdens are real—they are not just theories. And they don't operate separately. Cognitive strain can heighten emotional fatigue; emotional exhaustion can make organizational barriers seem insurmountable. The leaders who succeed are those who recognize these dynamics, prepare for them, and build support systems around them.

Crisis leadership isn't just about competence; it's about capacity. Building that capacity requires more than grit; it calls for insight, empathy, and a commitment to leading through complexity with clarity and care.

Cognitive Overload: The Collapse of Clarity

In crisis situations, information spreads quickly—but rarely accurately. Leaders often must make high-stakes decisions with incomplete data, changing conditions, and conflicting priorities. The mental effort needed to process, interpret, decide, and act can become overwhelming fast. This is cognitive overload: a state where clarity drops, decision fatigue kicks in, and the ability for strategic thinking starts to break down. One emergency manager described it vividly: "It felt like trying to play chess while the board was on fire. Every move mattered, but nothing stayed still."

This challenge isn't just psychological—it's neurological. Under intense stress, the brain's executive functions, which handle reasoning, planning, and impulse control, begin to shrink. The prefrontal cortex, which is responsible for conscious thought, gives way to the limbic system, which favors instinct and quick reactions. Leaders may struggle to tell signal from noise, fall back on habitual responses, or delay action trying to get perfect clarity. A hospital administrator recalled, "I kept waiting for more data, but the situation didn't wait. I missed the window."

In crisis, hesitation can be just as costly as rushing. Tunnel vision is a common cognitive distortion under pressure. Attention narrows to the most immediate or emotionally charged stimuli, causing leaders to overlook bigger context, alternative options, or long-term effects. This narrowing focus can lead to reactive decisions that fix the wrong problem or create new ones. One logistics officer shared, "We focused so hard on one supply route that we missed a faster, safer option. We were solving the crisis we saw—not the one we had." Cognitive overload doesn't just slow thinking—it warps it. Effective crisis leaders develop strategies to lessen these effects. They use delegation to lighten mental load, decision triage to prioritize urgent choices, and structured communication protocols to cut down on confusion. These tools help save mental energy and prevent paralysis. A public safety official noted, "Our leader had a rule—three priorities, no more. That kept us focused when everything felt urgent." These practices are not just tactics; they are protective, shielding leaders from the damaging effects of overwhelm. But even the most capable minds can falter under too much pressure, too fast. That's why organizational support is key. Leaders need access to trusted advisors, clear decision frameworks, and environments that allow for pauses and recalibration. Mental clarity isn't automatic—it must be cultivated. And in the heat of crisis, the ability to think clearly isn't just a skill; it's a survival trait.

Emotional Strain: The Weight of Responsibility

Crisis leadership is emotionally demanding in unseen ways.

Leaders must absorb fear, uncertainty, and grief—sometimes from dozens of people at once—while keeping their composure and clarity. They carry the burden of others' safety, morale, and trust, all while managing their own internal feelings. This emotional strain can show up as anxiety, guilt, isolation, or burnout. One hospital director recalled, "I had to tell families we were out of ventilators. I had to keep my team focused while I was falling apart inside." These moments aren't just about operations—they are deeply human.

The emotional toll of leadership under stress doesn't just impact well-being; it affects judgment. Leaders may become reactive, withdraw from their teams, or overcompensate by resorting to rigid control. Empathy can fade, and decision-making may become more defensive than collaborative. A school superintendent shared, "I didn't sleep for three days after the lockdown. I kept replaying every decision, wondering if I missed something." If left unaddressed, these internal struggles can ripple outward—affecting team cohesion, morale, and trust.

Building emotional resilience isn't a luxury, it's a key leadership skill. Leaders who practice reflection, seek peer support, and establish recovery routines are better suited to sustain performance over time. One emergency manager described a simple but effective habit: "After every shift, I wrote down three things I did right. It helped me stay grounded." Organizations need to normalize emotional processing and create space for leaders to decompress, recalibrate, and reconnect with their purpose.

Organizational Friction: The Drag on Execution

Even highly capable leaders can be slowed down by the systems around them. Organizational friction refers to internal barriers that delay response, weaken authority, and create confusion. These include unclear roles, siloed communication, outdated protocols, and conflicting priorities. In a crisis, time lost to bureaucracy is time taken away from solving the problem. One respondent described a multi-agency drill where "everyone had a plan, but no one had a shared language." Another noted, "We had the right people—but the wrong structure. Decisions got stuck in the hierarchy."

This friction doesn't just slow down action—it erodes trust and weakens coordination. Teams start questioning leadership, duplicate efforts, or disengage entirely. Leaders need to manage these systemic challenges while maintaining momentum. This requires strategic flexibility and political skill to align stakeholders, clarify authority, and cut through procedural clutter. A logistics officer shared, "She didn't wait for permission—she built consensus, got what we needed, and kept us moving." In a crisis, leadership isn't just about vision, it's about velocity.

To reduce organizational drag, leaders must push for streamlined protocols, cross-disciplinary communication, and flexible decision-making structures. They need to challenge legacy systems and bridge silos. Because in high-stakes environments, execution depends not just on individual skill, but on institutional readiness. And the leaders who succeed are those who can lead people and systems through complexity.

Mental and Emotional Strain

Crises provoke intense psychological stress, often pushing individuals to their emotional and cognitive limits. The combination of danger, uncertainty, and rapidly changing conditions creates a perfect storm for anxiety, fear, and emotional exhaustion. Those in high-pressure roles, whether making urgent decisions, managing limited resources, or witnessing human suffering, frequently operate in a state of constant tension. One respondent, a disaster response coordinator, described it as "living in a fog where every decision feels like a gamble and every mistake feels personal."

This ongoing state of heightened alertness drains mental resources. As the brain works overtime to assess threats and make quick decisions, fatigue sets in. Judgment becomes cloudy, focus weakens, and emotional regulation falters. Emotional exhaustion often occurs, marked by frustration, helplessness, or numbness. These reactions act as temporary defense mechanisms, helping individuals keep functioning—but they come with a cost. Empathy may diminish, interpersonal bonds can weaken, and the ability to connect meaningfully with others can erode. A hospital administrator shared, "I stopped feeling. Not because I didn't care, but because I couldn't afford to anymore."

Most importantly, these effects don't end when the crisis does. Post-traumatic stress, depression, and burnout are common among those exposed to repeated trauma or lacking adequate recovery time. The psychological impact can linger, affecting relationships, decision-making, and overall performance. One emergency manager reflected, "Months after the incident, I still couldn't sleep. I kept replaying the choices I made." These unseen wounds can fracture team cohesion and reduce long-term organizational resilience if left unaddressed.

Understanding these dynamics is vital for leaders. Mental strain isn't a sign of weakness—it's a natural response to extreme demands. Leaders need to normalize conversations about stress, create space for emotional processing, and actively support recovery. Providing psychological first aid, encouraging stress management techniques, and ensuring rest and de-stressing are not optional—they're vital strategies. As one respondent noted, "She didn't just ask how we were doing—she made sure we had time to breathe. That's what kept us from breaking."

Leadership during a crisis involves protecting the minds and hearts of those who serve. By fostering a culture of care, leaders help individuals stay grounded, focused, and resilient—both during and after the storm. The ability to lead through emotional strain is not just compassionate, it's operationally essential. Because when the pressure mounts, it's not just the plan that matters, it's the people who carry it.

Physiological and Cognitive Effects

In moments of crisis stress, the body's natural physiological responses are activated. Adrenaline, cortisol, and other hormones flood the system, preparing individuals for immediate action. Heart rate increases, blood pressure goes up, and energy levels spike—enhancing short-term physical readiness. This response is evolutionary, evolved (naturally selected) to help us survive sudden threats. However, when this heightened state lasts too long, it starts to impair performance. One responder, a paramedic during a mass casualty event, described it as "running on fumes with your foot still on the gas." Prolonged activation of stress systems can overwhelm the body and hinder brain function. Cognitive overload occurs, making it harder to process information, remember details, and stay focused. Problem-solving becomes scattered, and decision-making shifts from careful to reactive. A public safety official recalled, "I knew the protocol, but I couldn't recall it. My brain just locked up." These physiological effects are not signs of weakness—they are expected outcomes of ongoing stress. Without intervention, they can weaken leadership effectiveness at crucial moments.

Tunnel vision, which is widely reported in my collected data, is one of the most common ways people's thinking gets distorted under pressure. Attention narrows to just a few stimuli, often the most urgent or emotionally charged, causing individuals to overlook broader context and other options. This can lead to quick decisions that prioritize speed over strategy. One emergency manager shared, "I focused so hard on one threat that I missed a bigger one developing behind it." In a crisis, leaders need to be trained not only to act but also to recognize when stress is skewing their perception.

These effects vary widely among individuals. Experience, training, personality, and emotional state all affect how people react. Experienced crisis leaders often develop their own strategies to spot and reduce these reactions. They learn to pause, reset, and proceed with clarity. A hospital administrator shared an observation about an emergency-disaster response coordinator for the medical center, "She had a routine—three deep breaths before every major decision. It wasn't just calming; it was centering." These small practices become essential tools for staying calm and flexible under pressure.

Dealing with physiological and mental challenges requires intentional effort. Techniques like controlled breathing, mindfulness, structured decision-making methods, and stress inoculation training can help leaders manage their responses, regain clarity, and make better decisions. Organizations must make these practices routine—not just wellness perks, but essential parts of operations. Because in high-stakes environments, the ability to control stress isn't just a personal skill; it's a leadership essential.

Ethical Dilemmas and Moral Distress

Crises often compel leaders to make ethically complex decisions under conditions of uncertainty, urgency, and limited resources. Whether it involves triaging medical care, balancing public safety with civil liberties, or choosing between competing risks, these moments carry profound moral weight. The stakes are high, and the options are rarely clear-cut. One respondent, a hospital administrator during the early COVID-19 surge, recalled, "We had one ventilator and three patients who needed it. There was no right answer—just the least wrong one." These decisions are not just operational—they are deeply human.

Leaders facing crises may experience moral distress —the psychological pain of knowing the right action but being unable to take it due to institutional constraints, policy limitations, or resource constraints. This internal struggle can leave emotional scars, especially when decisions cause harm despite good intentions. A public health official shared, "I knew the lockdown would hurt vulnerable families, but we had no other way to slow the spread. I still carry that weight."

Moral distress is not a sign of weakness—it signals ethical awareness. However, without support, it can weaken resilience and lead to burnout. The pressure increases under public scrutiny. Leaders must explain their choices to a diverse group of stakeholders—victims' families, media, regulatory agencies, and their teams—while balancing personal values and professional responsibilities.

The emotional toll of these dilemmas can be intense, often worsened by second-guessing, public criticism, and hindsight. One emergency manager noted, "We made the best call we could with the information we had. But months later, people wanted to know why we didn't do more. That's hard to carry." Ethical leadership during a crisis is not just about making decisions; it's also about accepting their consequences. Addressing ethical challenges requires more than personal resolve. It calls for structured preparation: training in adaptive decision-making, open team communication, and access to counseling and peer support. Leaders must be equipped not just to make tough decisions but to process their impact with integrity and resilience. Organizations should normalize ethical reflection, provide safe spaces for debriefing, and foster cultures that recognize moral complexity rather than avoid it. As one respondent explained, "We started including ethics rounds in our crisis simulations. It changed how we think—and how we lead."

In high-stakes environments, ethical clarity is essential. The ability to navigate moral complexity is a key test of crisis leadership, requiring courage, humility, and transparency. It also requires preparing leaders not just to act but to reflect, recover, and grow. Because in the crucible of crisis, the accurate measure of leadership lies not only in decisions made but in how you bear the weight of those decisions.

Prolonged Stress Exposure and Burnout

Prolonged crises and repeated trauma exposure take a cumulative toll—physically, emotionally, and cognitively. Over time, relentless pressure can cause burnout —a state of chronic fatigue, reduced energy, and emotional exhaustion. This isn't just tiredness—it's a deep erosion of resilience. One respondent, a hospital shift supervisor during the COVID-19 surge, described it as "waking up exhausted, going to work numb, and coming home unsure if anything I did made a difference." Burnout hampers focus, motivation, and decision-making, weakening the very abilities that leaders and teams rely on in high-stakes settings.

Emotional numbness often develops as a psychological defense. It helps individuals keep functioning amid overwhelming stress by dulling emotional intensity. But over time, this way of coping can backfire. It reduces empathy, flattens emotional engagement, and strains relationships—both within teams and with the communities served. Compassion fatigue becomes a real and present threat. A public safety official shared, "I stopped feeling. Not because I didn't care, but because I couldn't afford to anymore. That's when I knew something was wrong." When empathy diminishes, so does the bond of trust and cohesion.

Motivation also diminishes. The sense of purpose that initially drives people into crisis roles can erode under constant pressure. Individuals might start questioning the impact of their work or feel powerless in the face of the scale of the challenges they face. Initiative falls, problem-solving slows, and team cohesion begins to break down. An emergency manager reflected, "We started strong, but after months of nonstop response, people stopped volunteering ideas. They just wanted to get through the day." This loss of engagement isn't laziness—it's a sign of emotional exhaustion.

The risks go beyond performance. Long-term exposure to trauma significantly raises the chances of developing serious mental health issues, including depression, anxiety disorders, and post-traumatic stress disorder (PTSD). These conditions can impair cognitive functions, emotional regulation, and physical health. If left unaddressed, they may lead to absenteeism, long-term disability, or the departure of key personnel. The cost isn't only human—it's operational. A logistics coordinator noted, "We lost two of our best planners to burnout. It wasn't sudden—it was slow, and we missed the signs."

To mitigate these effects, organizations must invest in thorough support systems. This includes regular psychological debriefings, access to mental health professionals, peer support networks, and mandated rest and recovery periods. Training programs should focus on resilience-building, stress management, and early identification of burnout signs. But more than systems, leadership must get involved. Protecting the well-being of crisis responders isn't just compassionate, it's strategic. Consistent effectiveness in extreme conditions requires more than grit—it demands genuine care, proactive support, and a culture that values recovery as much as readiness.

Team Dynamics Under Stress

Stress not only affects individuals but also changes the social fabric of a team. In high-pressure moments, even small misunderstandings can grow into major conflicts. Strong emotions like frustration, anxiety, and fear can skew perception, reduce patience, and hinder communication. One logistics coordinator during a wildfire response recalled, "We were all exhausted. A simple scheduling mix-up turned into a shouting match. It wasn't about the task—it was about the tension." When clarity is most needed, it's often the first to be affected by stress. Trust—the foundation of effective teamwork—becomes fragile under pressure. Team members may start questioning each other's motives, decisions, or competence, especially when mistakes happen or accountability is unclear. This erosion of trust can trigger a downward spiral: less cooperation, more errors, and further breakdowns in communication. A hospital administrator shared, "We started second-guessing each other. Not because we didn't care, but because we were scared and overwhelmed." In crises, the absence of trust doesn't just slow progress—it fractures teams.

However, stress doesn't always cause division. Shared adversity can strengthen bonds. When teams face hardship together, they often develop a "we're in this together" mindset that boosts morale, empathy, and mutual respect. One emergency manager described a moment during a prolonged flood response: "We were soaked, tired, and behind schedule. But someone cracked a joke, and suddenly we were laughing. That moment reminded us we were a team." Teams that handle stress well tend to become more cohesive, resilient, and dedicated to one another and to the mission.

This variability highlights the vital role of intentional leadership. Leaders who promote psychological safety, model calm and compassionate behavior, and foster open communication can guide teams toward unity rather than division. Training in emotional intelligence, active listening, and conflict resolution helps leaders identify and manage interpersonal tensions before they escalate. As one respondent said, "She didn't ignore the tension—she named it, addressed it, and helped us move forward. That's what kept us together."

Stress is a double-edged sword. It can tear teams apart or bring them closer. The outcome depends not just on the stress itself, but on how leaders respond. By creating conditions that foster emotional stability, shared purpose, and mutual respect, leaders can turn adversity into alignment. In crises, team dynamics are not incidental—they are crucial. Leaders who understand this are the ones who convert pressure into performance.

Conclusion: Meeting the Moment

Leadership in a crisis isn't about titles, credentials, or organizational charts; it is demonstrated through behavior in moments of pressure, when clarity is limited, time is tight, and stakes are high. The challenges discussed in this chapter—ambiguity, urgency, ethical dilemmas, emotional strain, and team dynamics—are not abstract ideas. They are real experiences of those leading during emergencies, disasters, and critical incidents. As one respondent, a public health director, said, "The moment the phones lit up, it wasn't about who had the most degrees—it was about who could lead with calm and conviction." These factors shape the landscape of crisis leadership. They are not signs of personal weakness—they are conditions leaders must navigate. Recognizing them is the first step in preparing leaders to face them with clarity, composure, and courage. This goes beyond technical skill. It requires emotional intelligence, adaptability, moral bravery, and a strong commitment to others' well-being. A fire chief noted, "We didn't need someone who knew the manual—we needed someone who could read the room, make the call, and keep us together." The most effective crisis leaders are those who can interpret chaos, make sound decisions under pressure, and guide their teams with steadiness and compassion. They do more than manage events—they shape outcomes. They don't just react, they respond purposefully. And they don't lead from above— they lead from within. Their influence is earned through presence, not position. As one emergency manager said, "She didn't have the loudest voice, but she had the clearest one. That's who we followed."

This chapter highlights the pressures that test leadership in crisis. But recognizing these challenges is just the start. The next step is to rethink what leadership should look like in these moments—not through hierarchy or tradition, but through human performance. We need to move beyond outdated models that prioritize rank and resumes and start building a framework that reflects the behavioral traits leaders truly need when the margin for error is gone.

In Chapter 3, we begin that journey. We will explore why traditional leadership models—often based on fixed hierarchies, positional authority, and technical credentials—fall short in fast-paced, high-stakes settings. We will examine the behavioral traits that repeatedly appear among top crisis leaders and begin to create a new paradigm—one rooted in human factors, emotional resilience, and ethical integrity. This isn't about abandoning structure—it's about emphasizing substance. It's about shifting from control to connection, from command to calmness, and from status to service. Because the leaders shaping the future are not the ones with power, but those who earn trust. The next chapter starts the conversation about such redefinition—where we consider that leadership is no longer a *title* to hold, but a *practice* to live.

CHAPTER 3

RETHINKING LEADERSHIP

Most traditional leadership models are designed for predictable, routine organizational environments. Such models offer valuable insights for day-to-day operations, but their relevance diminishes when applied to non-routine, high-stakes situations, especially those involving crises, emergencies, and disasters. These environments demand a different mindset, skill set, and operational framework than conventional leadership literature typically emphasizes.

This reframing doesn't dismiss established principles—it builds on them. It expands foundational concepts to prepare leaders with the resilience, decisiveness, and adaptability needed when usual rules no longer apply, and critical decisions must be made quickly. Crises challenge individuals, teams, and organizations in profound and often unpredictable ways. They create intense psychological and operational pressures, requiring quick decisions, emotional stability, and flexibility in the moment. Even seasoned professionals, such as emergency responders, crisis managers, and disaster response teams, can find their mental clarity and emotional control weakened under extreme stress. During tough times, leadership becomes essential. A leader's ability to stay effective under pressure can determine whether there is unity or chaos, resilience or failure. Recognizing and cultivating the traits that support strong leadership in crises is not just strategic—it's fundamentally human. These qualities—emotional intelligence, decisiveness, judgment, stress tolerance—must be intentionally incorporated into how we select, evaluate, and develop leaders. Effective crisis leadership isn't accidental; it is teachable, measurable, and essential.

Traditional Models vs. Human Performance Models

Historically, leadership has been defined by formal authority, positional power, and technical expertise. In many industries, especially operational, emergency, and technical fields, leadership potential has been assessed based on rank, credentials, and years of experience. These traditional frameworks focus on structural competence: knowledge of policies, standard operating procedures (SOPs), chain of command, and system operations. While these elements are essential, they only represent part of the whole picture. In high-stakes, fast-paced situations, pre-planned responses often aren't enough. What matters most isn't just what leaders know, but how they perform—how they think, respond, connect, and influence others under pressure.

Human performance models shift the focus from static qualifications to dynamic behaviors. They highlight adaptability, emotional regulation, communication, and real-time decision-making. These qualities are not just helpful; they're essential in environments where uncertainty, urgency, and emotional volatility are common. Real-world case studies show consistently that frontline supervisors often perform better than senior executives during crises—not because of their rank, but because of their situational awareness, emotional control, and earned team trust. In these moments, performance—not titles—takes precedence.

Many organizations still rely on outdated methods for selecting and evaluating leaders. This chapter questions that approach and proposes a new primary framework—one that emphasizes and develops the traits, skills, and behaviors that really matter when the stakes are highest.

The Limitations of Traditional Standards

Traditional methods for choosing leaders tend to overemphasize degrees, certifications, tenure, and technical skills. While these credentials provide a foundation, they are poor indicators of leadership success in chaotic, high-pressure situations. In crises, leadership isn't shown by what's on a résumé—it's demonstrated through actions. One senior emergency manager said, "We had leaders with impressive titles, but when the pressure hit, it was the ones who could stay calm and connect that made the difference." Technical knowledge is essential, but it can't replace human skills under stress. A degree may show knowledge, but it doesn't guarantee emotional stability, empathy, or the ability to inspire trust. Experience can also be misleading. What worked in one crisis might be useless—or even harmful—in another. A hospital administrator shared, "He kept referencing what worked during the last outbreak, but this one was different. We needed someone who could adapt, not just repeat."

Leadership readiness should be judged not just by what someone knows, but by how they act when the stakes are high. Rank and seniority, often seen as signs of authority, can sometimes hinder the development of crucial traits during a crisis—such as humility, openness to feedback, and willingness to reflect and adapt—from emerging. Leaders at the top may feel pressured to seem confident, even when they are unsure. This can lead to rigidity, defensiveness, and missed opportunities to change course. One respondent said, "He was too proud to admit the plan wasn't working. We lost time we couldn't afford."

Conversely, leaders who show vulnerability and seek input build trust and adaptability. Practical knowledge and formal training are essential, but they must be balanced with human qualities such as emotional intelligence, flexibility, humility, and mental agility. These traits determine whether leaders can unite teams, make wise decisions, and maintain morale under pressure. They're not just "soft skills"—they are essential for survival. As one public safety official said, "She didn't have the longest résumé, but she had the strongest presence. That's who we followed when things got," hard." Leadership during a crisis isn't about titles or seniority; it's about how people think, act, and lead when clarity, courage, and connection are most needed. Our standards for leadership should change to match this reality. We need to look beyond credentials and focus on the behavioral traits that genuinely matter. Because when the next crisis hits, it won't ask for a transcript—it will ask for a leader.

Why Human-Centered Competencies Matter Most

In environments characterized by ambiguity, urgency, and emotional volatility, traditional qualifications—such as titles, degrees, and certifications—often prove insufficient. What truly matters is how leaders behave under pressure: how they connect with others, adapt to changing circumstances, and guide teams through uncertainty. These moments reveal not just what a leader knows, but who they are. As one respondent, a crisis response coordinator, shared, "We didn't follow him because of his résumé—we followed him because he stayed calm, listened, and made us feel like we could handle it."

Human-centered traits are not just abstract ideals. They repeatedly appeared in the Marks of a Leader research project, where respondents emphasized behavioral and interpersonal qualities over formal credentials. What truly mattered was not past achievements but present engagement, how leaders show up in the moment, inspire confidence, make decisions, and foster cohesion. A hospital administrator recalled, "She didn't have the most experience, but she had the most empathy. That's why we trusted her when things got hard." These traits—emotional intelligence, adaptability, situational awareness, and ethical judgment—are the real currency of leadership during a crisis.

As crises become more complex and interconnected, these skills provide a solid foundation for assessing and developing leadership. They are not just "nice to have"—they are essential. Training programs, evaluation methods, and organizational cultures must adapt to this reality.

Leaders need to be equipped not only with technical knowledge but also with behavioral agility to navigate disruption. One emergency manager observed, "We've trained for procedures. Now we need to train people on how leaders behave when the plan breaks down."

Importantly, these human-centered skills can be taught. They can be cultivated through coaching, simulation, feedback, and experience. Organizations that focus on developing these traits prepare leaders not only for daily operations but for moments that genuinely test character and skill. A public safety official shared, "We started including emotional regulation and team dynamics in our leadership training. The difference in performance during real incidents was dramatic." These traits don't just enhance leadership—they sustain it when everything else feels unstable.

The next crisis won't wait for a résumé review. It will demand presence, clarity, and connection. Leaders who embody these human-centered skills will be the ones others trust, follow, and remember. And organizations that prioritize these traits will be better equipped—not just to respond but to lead with integrity and impact when it matters most.

Developing Human Performance Skills

To prepare leaders for crisis situations, leadership development must shift from compliance-based approaches to capability-focused ones. This means going beyond checklists and credentials to focus on how leaders perform—especially under pressure.

Effective development strategies include:

> - Simulation-based training: Realistic, scenario-driven exercises that emulate the uncertainty, emotional stress, and time pressure of actual crises. These experiences enable leaders to practice decision-making, communication, and adaptability in controlled yet challenging environments.
> - Coaching and mentoring: Organized relationships that enhance self-awareness and develop psychological resilience. Through reflection and dialogue, leaders learn to control emotional triggers, improve interpersonal skills, and build confidence.
> - Constructive feedback: Ongoing input from peers, subordinates, and mentors helps refine behavior and strengthen leadership presence. Feedback is not a one-

time event—it's a continuous process that encourages growth and accountability.

➢ Behavioral assessments: Evaluating how leaders respond under stress, communicating during uncertainty as well as ambiguity, and supporting others during complex operations. These assessments focus on observable actions, not just theoretical knowledge.

Leadership is earned, not given or certified. It reveals itself in critical moments when adrenaline is running high, the stakes are real, and people look for someone they can trust. By intentionally developing human performance skills, organizations build leaders who are ready not just for routine tasks but also for the unpredictable challenges of crisis.

The Case for Reframing "Leadership"

Tomorrow's crises won't give us a warning. They will disrupt systems, challenge assumptions, and demand more than just technical skills. During those moments, titles and certificates won't comfort a frightened team or help make flexible decisions. What will? Presence. Clarity. Courage. Compassion. These aren't just ideals—they are actions we must take. As one senior emergency planner said, "When the alarms went off, no one asked for credentials. They looked for someone who could lead." Human-centered skills—like emotional intelligence, adaptability, situational awareness, and ethical judgment—are not optional. They are vital for leading effectively in unstable times. These qualities help leaders build trust, understand complex situations, and act swiftly. And importantly, they can be learned. Through simulations, coaching, feedback, and experience, leaders at every level can develop these skills. One hospital administrator shared, "We trained for procedures, but what saved us was behavior—how our leaders showed up, listened, and made decisions under pressure."

Rethinking what it means to lead is no longer just a theory; it's a practical necessity. Organizations must develop leaders who can rise, respond, and rebuild. Success will be judged not by credentials or charm, but by how many people will follow when it really matters. One respondent described a leader who "didn't have the most experience but had the most composure. That's who we trusted."

In a crisis, leadership isn't assigned; it's earned through actions. This new way of thinking requires a profound mindset shift. Leadership isn't given by rank or resume; it's demonstrated through actions when systems collapse, and people seek someone they can trust. By focusing on human performance, we prepare leaders not just to survive crises but to lead with integrity and impact. It's about valuing how leaders behave, not just what they know. It's about presence training, not just skill. The Marks of a Leader framework is built on this new perspective. It offers a behavioral blueprint for resilient, adaptable leadership rooted in human connection. It challenges us to move beyond old models and focus on traits that make leadership effective when the margin for error disappears. Because the next crisis won't ask for your résumé—it will ask if you're prepared. And being ready starts with leading differently.

Conclusion: Leadership Revealed by Action

Crises do not respect rank, résumé, or reputation. They strip away pretense and expose the essence of leadership—revealing character, clarity, adaptability, and the ability to inspire others when the stakes are highest. In these moments, leadership is not assigned; it is earned. It manifests through behavior, decision-making under pressure, and emotional presence that steadies teams and rebuilds trust.

This chapter challenges traditional ideas about what makes a leader effective in a crisis. We've learned that technical skills and authority matter but are not enough. What counts most is how leaders act when time is limited, information is scarce, and stakes are high. The ability to navigate chaos, communicate with empathy, and act with honesty becomes the true sign of leadership.

When organizations intentionally cultivate these human-centered skills, they do more than prepare individuals to shape culture. These traits serve as force multipliers: aligning teams, boosting morale, and speeding up recovery. They influence how people respond, how systems adapt, and how communities heal. In times of disruption, authentic leadership isn't about titles—it is demonstrated through character, built through action, and remembered for the impact it creates when everything is at stake.

This behavioral perspective redefines leadership as an ongoing practice—one that must be observed, developed, and supported. However, to move from understanding to action, we need a framework. We need a way to identify, teach, and measure the traits that characterize effective crisis leadership.

Chapter 4 introduces the Marks of a Leader project—a multi-phase research effort aimed at that goal. It started with a foundational survey to identify traits that practitioners, educators, and crisis-tested leaders repeatedly see as essential. The framework was then refined through workshops, seminars, interviews, focus groups, graduate student research, and the development of real-world training curricula.

The next chapter traces the evolution of the project—from its academic roots to practical uses. We'll examine how the *Marks* were validated, challenged, and expanded through conversations with leading experts. And we'll start to develop a shared language to understand what leadership looks like when it's tested—not just in theory, but in real-world practice.

Because leadership is demonstrated through action, understanding those actions—and the traits behind them—is the first step toward developing genuinely prepared leaders.

CHAPTER 4

IDENTIFYING THE 15 MARKS OF A LEADER

To understand what distinguishes effective leadership in high-pressure environments, Dr. J.D. Wallace and I launched a 26-month longitudinal study: *The Marks of a Leader Survey* research project. Our goal was to explore how experienced professionals perceive leadership during crises—across disaster response, emergency management, business continuity, law enforcement, and crisis operations.

The Marks of a Leader Project

That research survey was the first step of systematically explore the ideas about leadership that had been brewing in my mind since my CATTS observations of Battalion Command Group leadership decisions during simulated battle scenarios a decade earlier. My thinking was that if successful leadership in crisis is both essential and revealed through human behavioral processes, then the next logical step is to understand which behaviors matter most—and how we can identify, develop, and support them. That question became the driving force eventually behind the overall *Marks of a Leader Project*: a multi-phase long term research-tested application initiative aimed at capturing the key human performance traits that consistently distinguish effective leaders under pressure which has led to the book you are now reading. This chapter traces the beginnings of the journey of that project—including from its academic beginnings to its practical applications and uses.

It started with a basic survey tool designed to collect insights from practitioners across fields: emergency managers, healthcare workers, military officers, educators, and business leaders. The aim was straightforward yet ambitious: to find out which traits people trust when everything is at stake.

The initial survey instrument asked respondents to reflect on the most effective leader they had ever worked with during a crisis (and correspondingly an ineffective leader in similar circumstances). What did that person do? How did they behave? What traits stood out? Which aspects did the respondents ceem as important to the outcomes (either successful or unsuccessful). The responses we collected were rich, specific, and deeply human. They described leaders who stayed calm in chaos, who communicated with clarity and compassion, who made timely decisions without all the facts, and who earned trust through presence—not position!

From that survey data (the results which we published and I

later drafted into a White Paper for FEMA), the project expanded over the following years. Workshops, seminars, graduate student research, and focus groups helped refine the emerging framework. Interviews with crisis-tested leaders added nuance and depth. Training curriculum development and post-session feedback loops tested the applicability of the traits in real-world settings. Sessions at professional and academic conference generated feedback, suggestions, insights, anecdotes, stories, and much more – some of which are included in this book. Each phase over the years sharpened the focus, revealing patterns of human performance that transcended sector, rank, and role.

What emerged was not just a list of desirable qualities; it was a behavioral blueprint. A set of 15 distinct traits slowly emerged as related but important marks, each observable, teachable, and essential to leadership in high-pressure environments. These became the *Marks of a Leader* framework grounded in both research and reality.

In the pages ahead, we'll explore how these Marks were defined, validated, and translated into actionable knowledge, skills, and abilities (KSAs). We'll examine how they've been used to shape training programs, guide leadership selection, and build cultures of resilience. And we'll begin to understand how a shared language of leadership—rooted in behavior, not bureaucracy—can transform how we prepare for the next crisis.

Because if leadership is revealed by action, then the Marks of a Leader are the traits we must learn to recognize, cultivate, and reward.

The Original Survey Study

At the heart of the *Marks of a Leader* project was the qualitative, experience-based *Marks of a Leader Survey* designed to capture real-life leadership experiences under pressure. Distributed through national conferences, professional associations, and practitioner networks, the survey reached over 1,200 participants from both public and private sectors. These weren't just abstract respondents; they were professionals with direct experience in disaster recovery, emergency operations, contingency planning, and crisis leadership. Many had led teams through hurricanes, wildfires, cyberattacks, mass casualty events, and institutional breakdowns.

Instead of relying on theoretical constructs or predefined leadership models, the survey asked participants to recall specific incidents in which leadership either enhanced or hindered the response. Using open-ended prompts, they describe traits, behaviors, decisions, and interpersonal dynamics that impacted outcomes. This narrative approach offered rich, story-based insights from real-world experiences.

One respondent, a regional emergency manager, recalled a

leader who "walked into the command post, didn't raise his voice, didn't issue orders—he just asked the right questions. Within minutes, the room was focused." Another, a hospital administrator, described a colleague who "kept the team calm during a mass casualty surge. She didn't just manage logistics— she managed morale."

These types of shared reflections became the raw material for a deeper understanding of what leadership looks like under pressure.

Method

To ensure clarity and relevance, the survey instrument was pilot tested with a small group of practitioners before full deployment. The final version included open-ended prompts that encouraged honest reflection, allowing respondents to describe leadership in their own words—free from leading questions or rigid categories. Informed consent was obtained, and confidentiality was strictly maintained throughout the study. I continue to protect and respect that confidentially pledge in what I share with the readers of this book.

Responses were carefully reviewed, coded, and grouped into bipolar categories: effective versus ineffective leadership traits. Whenever possible, balanced pairs—such as decisiveness vs. indecisiveness, clarity vs. confusion, empathy vs. detachment—

were used to represent contrasting dimensions of leadership behavior for which we were receiving corresponding opposite sides of the same aspect. This emergent, qualitative approach required some interpretive effort but produced nuanced patterns that reflected what practitioners truly observe, value, and remember during high-stakes leadership moments.

Instead of imposing a theoretical framework, the study let the data speak for itself—highlighting the traits that consistently made a difference when it mattered most.

Key Findings and Implications

One insight stood out with remarkable consistency even this early in the project: technical expertise and formal credentials, while valuable, were seldom identified as the main qualities of effective crisis leadership. Instead, respondents heavily highlighted human-centered skills, for example, emotional intelligence, adaptability, communication, and sound judgment. Ineffective leaders were often seen as indecisive, rigid, emotionally distant, or poor communicators. These traits eroded trust, hindered coordination, and led to operational failures. In contrast, effective leaders displayed clarity, composure, empathy, and the ability to inspire confidence even under pressure.

The implications for leadership development were immediately striking and profound:

- ➢ Training should prioritize behavioral traits identified in the study—not just technical skills or procedural knowledge.
- ➢ Learning formats should be flexible and accessible, especially for field-based professionals who operate in dynamic, unpredictable environments.
- ➢ Barriers to participation, such as time constraints, lack of contextual relevance, and overly academic framing, must be addressed to ensure meaningful engagement.

This base line research offered a practical roadmap for improving how we select, develop, and evaluate leaders in crisis and continuity management. It shifted the focus from credentials to conduct—from what leaders know to how they lead when it matters most. This set the course for the following stages of this project.

Limitations

As with any exploratory study, the initial *Marks of a Leader Survey* as well as much of the subsequent interview and group feedback research project data collections, had limitations that must be acknowledged. These boundaries do not diminish the value of the findings, but they do help contextualize the framework's scope and applicability. Transparency about these constraints is essential for responsible interpretation and future refinement.

First, this stage of the project's geographic scope was primarily North America, with most respondents from the United States and Canada. While this provided useful insights into leadership behaviors within Western institutions such as healthcare, education, emergency management, and the corporate sector, it may have limited the cultural diversity of leadership expectations.

Leadership is not a universal, uniform concept; regional norms, historical backgrounds, and societal values shape it. As one international respondent mentioned, "In my country, leadership is more communal and less individualistic. We look for harmony, not just decisiveness." Future versions of the framework will likely include broader global participation to better understand these cultural differences. I am eager to explore how effective crisis leadership is consistent or varies across cultural context.

Second, the data collected were subjective. Respondents shared personal reflections, observations, and lived experiences — not empirical causation or statistically controlled results. This deliberate qualitative approach aimed to uncover behavioral patterns and practitioner wisdom. However, it means that the findings reflect perceived effectiveness rather than measurable performance metrics. One respondent, a crisis communication director, said, "I can't prove he saved lives—but I know his calm presence kept us from unraveling." These insights are powerful but inherently interpretive.

I concede that we are nearing the point where some empirical research could (might) narrow down these marks and their relative importance. On the other hand, the composite model in my thinking at this point that we are looking at overlapping and interconnecting knowledge, traits, skills, and characteristics and most likely the relative importance of specific marks may well *vary* by crisis event/situation, purpose, people involved, and setting-context. I discuss this idea later at the end of this chapter.

Third, the sampling method for the survey was non-random. Participants were recruited through professional networks, academic affiliations, and conference invitations. While this approach ensured relevance and depth—by involving experienced professionals in high-pressure roles—it also introduced selection bias. The data reflect thematic patterns rather than statistically generalizable conclusions. As one workshop attendee noted, "We're the kind of people who think about leadership all the time. That shapes how we respond." The framework, therefore, should be viewed as a conceptual model based on practitioner experience, not a universal solution.

Fourth, the fifteen traits identified in the study are not ranked by importance. Mention frequency on the open-ended items does not indicate priority or significance. Some traits—like decisiveness or composure—were mentioned more often, but this may reflect the urgency of crisis situations rather than their inherent value. Others—like humility or psychological safety— appeared quietly but held deep meaning. As one respondent shared, "She wasn't flashy, but she made us feel safe. That's why we followed her." The traits are presented as a constellation rather than a hierarchy.

Despite these limitations, the foundational study provided a useful and actionable framework. It captured practical knowledge from experienced professionals and translated it into a behavioral model for leadership development in high-stakes environments. The Marks of a Leader are not definitive; they are guiding. They point toward the behaviors that earn trust, inspire action, and sustain performance when it matters most. They also encourage ongoing dialogue, testing, and refinement as leadership challenges evolve.

Continuous Refinement and Growth of the Marks

Since the initial publication of this project's early findings 25 years ago in a professional journal and a white paper for FEMA, the framework has continued to evolve. It didn't stay confined to the page; it spread into classrooms, training centers, coaching sessions, and public forums. Each setting became a testing ground, offering new insights and valuable feedback. Graduate students questioned definitions, practitioners applied them in real-world situations, and educators tailored the traits to different learning environments. These ongoing cycles of use and reflection improved the model's clarity, relevance, and usefulness.

Over the years, I've integrated emerging traits into various leadership development settings, from executive coaching and crisis management workshops to graduate seminars and organizational retreats. Each experience revealed a new nuance. For example, in a healthcare leaders' workshop for the Hospital Association of Southern California, participants stressed the importance of emotional resilience and coordination during surge events. Conversely, corporate financial services management leaders in a disaster recovery planning seminar focused more on decisiveness and prioritization. These differences did not weaken the framework; they enriched it, demonstrating its versatility across sectors and stressful situations.

The traits discussed in this book are more than mere theories. They are rooted in real-world experience and supported by expert insights. Respondents consistently emphasized that these behaviors—clarity, composure, empathy, and adaptability—are what set effective leaders apart when mistakes have serious consequences. One emergency manager explained, "We've trained for procedures, but what saved us was behavior—how our leaders showed up, listened, and led." These traits are designed to help leaders succeed under stress, manage uncertainty, and lead with clarity, courage, and compassion.

Notably, the framework has evolved through academic rigor and ongoing dialogue. Public speaking events, conference panels, and small-group interviews have shared stories that challenged assumptions and expanded the model's boundaries. A fire chief once told me, "You nailed decisiveness—but don't forget the quiet ones who recalibrate the team when no one's watching." That insight prompted a deeper exploration of behavioral facilitation and psychological safety, now vital parts of the framework. The Marks have grown because field leaders have helped shape them.

A Common Question, A Complex Answer

When I train, teach, or present the Marks of a Leader framework, one question always arises: "Which Mark is the most important for successful or effective leadership?" It's a fair question—

intuitive, even. I understand people seek clarity, hierarchy, and a shortcut to understanding what matters most or what should be their priority. But the truth is, this question can't be answered definitively using the research methods used in this project. The data are qualitative, exploratory, and based on reported lived experiences—not meant to rank or measure traits in isolation. The findings suggest that these human performance factors are not separate skill silos; they overlap, reinforce, and interact dynamically. Coordination, for example, inherently involves communication, clarity, and prioritization. Decisiveness is shaped by situational awareness, emotional regulation, and adaptability. Psychological safety is built through empathy, listening, and behavioral consistency. These traits are not standalone competencies; they are interconnected parts of a broader leadership skill set. As one interview respondent told me when I asked the question so often posed to me: "You can't separate them. The best leaders don't just have one trait—they behave in ways that combine them." Moreover, the relative importance of each trait may vary depending on the nature of the crisis. In a fast-moving emergency, decisiveness and composure might take center stage. In a prolonged disruption, adaptability and emotional resilience could be more critical. In a politically sensitive situation, communication and ethical clarity may be paramount. But across all scenarios, every trait has its moment—its role in shaping outcomes, earning trust, and sustaining performance. As another respondent noted, "It's not about picking one—it's about knowing which to lean on when." As work on this project continues, I expect the original list of 15 traits will evolve. New data, broader participation, and deeper reflection will likely reveal additional human performance factors—especially those often dismissed as "soft skills," but which prove essential under pressure. Traits such as humility, curiosity, and cultural intelligence may become vital contributors to effective leadership in increasingly diverse and complex environments. The framework is not static; it is a living model, shaped by the realities leaders face and the wisdom they share. This book, then, is not meant to be the final word on the Marks of a Leader. It is a way station—a moment of synthesis and guidance for those who lead, those who train leaders, and those who seek to understand what makes leadership work when it matters most. Taken holistically, the Marks provide a powerful lens for describing the qualities practitioners consider essential. They help us move beyond credentials and charisma toward behavior—toward the observable, teachable, and repeatable actions that define leadership under stress. And perhaps that's the honest answer to the question: the most important Mark is not a single trait—it's the ability to integrate them. To lead with clarity, courage, and compassion. To adapt, decide, coordinate, and connect. To show up when it counts, and to do so in ways that others can trust, follow, and learn from. In the chapters ahead, we will examine each of the fifteen Marks in detail. I will try to define their behavioral essence, translate them into practical knowledge, skills, and attitudes (KSAs), and explore how they can be developed across roles, sectors, and experience levels. These traits are not fixed; they are dynamic, trainable, and measurable. They offer a roadmap for preparing leaders not just for ideal conditions, but for the realities they face. Because when the next crisis arrives, it won't ask to see your title, certifications, or credentials; it will demand to see your readiness. And readiness begins with choosing to lead differently.

The Surprising Emphasis on Human Traits

One of the most critical findings from this project was the rarity with which respondents mentioned technical knowledge, certifications, or academic credentials as indicators of effective leadership during a crisis. Although these qualifications were recognized as necessary, they were not the main qualities respondents focused on when describing leaders who earned trust, motivated action, and performed well under pressure. Instead, they consistently emphasized human attributes, mindsets, behaviors, decision-making styles, and emotional intelligence as the true differences.

This trend reveals more than just basic competence. It uncovers a fundamental truth: when stakes are high and the environment is unpredictable, human-centered skills often surpass technical expertise. One respondent, a senior emergency manager, bluntly said, "We had plenty of experts. What we needed were leaders who could listen, adapt, and keep us united." Another, a hospital administrator, noted, "Degrees don't help when the oxygen runs out. What matters is how you treat people, how you think under pressure, and whether you can lead without losing your humanity."

Traits such as resilience, adaptability, communication, empathy, and accountability were repeatedly highlighted across industries. These qualities help leaders build trust, promote teamwork, handle uncertainty, and make sound decisions quickly. They are not considered "soft skills"—they are essential survival skills. In fact, many respondents outright rejected the term "soft," arguing that these traits are harder to teach, more difficult to fake, and more crucial than ever. As one public safety official said, "He didn't know everything, but he knew how to keep us calm and focused. That's what made him a leader."

My understanding is that these human qualities also act as behavioral anchors during uncertain times. When protocols are unclear, resources are limited, and emotions are intense, a leader's mindset and presence influence how the team responds. Leaders who remain calm, communicate clearly, and show empathy help create psychological safety, allowing others to speak up, take initiative, and stay engaged. One respondent described a leader who "walked the floor, asked how we were doing, and made space for feedback. That wasn't in the manual—but it kept us going."

My message is clear: leadership development must focus on these human traits. Selection processes, training programs, and performance reviews should reflect the reality that technical knowledge alone isn't enough. We need to invest in the behavioral skills that make leadership effective when conditions are far from ideal. Because in a crisis, the question isn't just what you know, it's how you lead when everything is on the line.

The Antithesis: Ineffective Leadership Traits

While this book highlights the aspirational traits of effective crisis leadership, it is equally important to examine their behavioral opposites—the traits that consistently undermine trust, cohesion, and performance. Poor leadership rarely stems from a single flaw. More often, it's a convergence of blind spots, ego-driven decisions, and unchecked behaviors that erode credibility and destabilize teams. Respondents across sectors were candid in describing the traits they associated with leadership failure. These "antithesis marks" serve as cautionary signals—behaviors that, if left unaddressed, can derail even the most well-intentioned efforts.

➢ Disoriented and Unfocused

Instead of fostering clarity and coordination, ineffective leaders often drift. They lack direction, fail to prioritize, and confuse activity with progress. Meetings become repetitive, communication breaks down, and morale declines as frustration replaces confidence. One respondent, a senior operations manager, recalled, "He kept changing the plan mid-meeting. We spent more time reacting to his confusion than solving the actual problem." In a crisis, where clarity is essential, disorientation breeds chaos. Teams need leaders who can steady them, not add to the chaos.

➢ Reactive, Not Decisive

Another standard failure mode is the inability to make timely, informed decisions. Indecisive leaders hesitate, waiting for perfect information that never comes. Reactive leaders, on the other hand, act impulsively, driven by emotion rather than strategy. Both behaviors cause instability. Plans change unpredictably, and teams lose confidence in leadership. A public safety official shared, "He froze when we needed action, then overcorrected with a rash decision that made things worse." Decisiveness isn't just about speed; it's about clarity, timing, and the courage to commit.

➤ Narrow-Minded and Overconfident

Narrow-mindedness and overconfidence often go hand in hand. Rigid leaders mistake certainty for wisdom. They resist feedback, dismiss dissent, and surround themselves with agreement rather than insight. Several respondents noted that overconfidence frequently masked deeper insecurity. "He acted like he had all the answers," one healthcare leader said, "but he couldn't handle being questioned. That's when we stopped speaking up." This echo-chamber effect stifles innovation and prevents teams from surfacing critical information. In crisis, humility is not weakness—it's strategic awareness.

➤ Disconnected and Oblivious

Perhaps the most damaging trait is disconnection. Ineffective leaders are often out of touch with both the situation and the people they lead. They miss signal shifts in morale, emerging risks, or signs of fatigue—and rely on outdated assumptions. This tone-deafness erodes trust and alignment. A logistics coordinator recalled, "He kept referencing last year's playbook, even though the conditions had completely changed. We felt invisible." Leadership requires presence—not just physical, but emotional and cognitive. Disconnection breeds disengagement, and disengagement undermines performance.

Recognizing these antithetical traits is essential for developing self-awareness, fostering accountability, and building cultures where leadership can thrive. These behaviors are not just ineffective—they are actively corrosive. They diminish trust, fracture teams, and compromise outcomes. By naming them, we create space for reflection, growth, and recalibration. Because leadership is not just about what we aspire to, it's also about what we must avoid.

From Insight to Action

The Marks of a Leader framework is built on the real experiences of professionals who have led—and been led—through crises. These insights come not just from theory but from practice: from hospital corridors during mass casualty events, from mobile command units during hostage situations, from classrooms, boardrooms, and disaster zones. The voices of respondents shaped every trait, nuance, and behavioral marker in this model. What resulted is a framework that highlights what truly matters when pressure is high, uncertainty is constant, and outcomes are unpredictable.

The fifteen traits that follow are not abstract ideals or slogans. They are practical, observable, and teachable behaviors that shape how we select, train, and support leaders who must perform during critical moments. One respondent, a senior emergency manager, plainly said: "We don't need perfect leaders—we need prepared ones. People who know how to listen, decide, coordinate, and adapt." Each chapter will introduce one trait, define its core behavior, illustrate its impact with real-world examples, and offer strategies for growth, assessment, and application. Together, these traits form a blueprint for leadership that is resilient, adaptable, and rooted in human connection.

This book isn't just about presenting a leadership framework—it's a call to action. It challenges us to rethink how we prepare leaders for a world that's becoming more volatile and complex. It urges organizations to invest in traits that make leadership authentic, relevant, and reliable when every moment counts. And it invites readers—whether trainers, executives, educators, or frontline leaders—to use this framework as a tool for transformation. As one respondent noted, "We've trained for procedures. Now we need to train for behavior."

We start with the trait that makes all others possible: Coordination Facilitator. In a crisis, even the most capable teams can falter without alignment. Coordination acts as the behavioral glue that connects people, priorities, and processes to a shared mission. It turns fragmented effort into unified action. The next chapter will explore how leaders facilitate coordination under pressure—clarifying roles, removing barriers, and enabling performance when margins for error vanish.

CHAPTER 5

COORDINATION FACILITATOR

Effective crisis leaders are consistently described as those who foster team cohesion, promote coordination, and facilitate integration across functions and roles. In high-pressure environments, success rarely hinges on individual brilliance; it depends on the team's collective capacity. Leaders who understand this reality actively create a united, focused, and collaborative operational environment.

Survey respondents used words such as "steady," "approachable," "fair," and "dependable" to describe leaders who excelled at coordination. They recalled how these leaders "kept everyone connected" and "always knew how to bring people together." These leaders listen before deciding, value every contribution, and communicate clearly and purposefully. They calm tensions, resolve conflicts, and ensure that each team member feels supported and accountable. They are organized yet adaptable, balancing structure with empathy and guiding through collaboration rather than commands. Their effectiveness doesn't come from control but from seamlessly integrating roles, perspectives, and priorities. They connect silos, encourage open communication, and ensure information flows smoothly in both directions. To their teams, they are seen not just as authority figures but as trusted leaders whose interpersonal and organizational skills enable success that is both achievable and meaningful.

Facilitating Teamwork Under Pressure

Facilitation in crisis leadership is more than just a technique; it's a mindset based on intentionality, humility, and strategic awareness. Leaders who facilitate under pressure do more than direct actions; they shape group dynamics, clarify roles, and reinforce shared goals. This behavioral approach improves performance, lifts morale, and builds a resilient team culture. In high-stakes situations, where confusion and urgency often clash, facilitation becomes a stabilizing force—transforming reactive efforts into coordinated action.

Effective crisis leaders guide their teams through structured steps such as brainstorming, analysis, prioritization, and collaborative problem-solving. Instead of defaulting to top-down orders, they promote inclusive dialogue and shared input. One respondent, a logistics coordinator during a hurricane response, recalled, "Our leader didn't just issue orders—he asked, 'What are we missing?' That question opened the floodgates. Suddenly, everyone was contributing, and we found a workaround that saved hours." This kind of facilitative leadership yields more informed, balanced, and innovative solutions, especially when time is limited and resources are scarce.

Facilitation also promotes psychological safety, which is essential for team performance under stress. When team members feel heard, respected, and valued, they are more likely to speak up, take initiative, and stay engaged. A public health official shared, "She made space for disagreement. That's why we trusted her. Even when we didn't have consensus, we had clarity." Trust, constructive dialogue, and emotional stability serve as performance boosters—helping teams navigate uncertainty without falling apart. Facilitative leaders don't just manage—they empower. They create conditions that allow people to contribute fully, adapt quickly, and stay connected to the mission.

In chaotic environments, facilitation often makes the difference between fragmentation and cohesion. It enables leaders to tap into their teams' complete cognitive and emotional resources. It turns pressure into purpose. And it guarantees that leadership isn't just a solo act, but a collective effort. As one emergency manager said, "He didn't just lead the team—he built the team while leading it." That's the core of facilitation: guiding others not just toward a solution, but toward a stronger, more resilient way of working together.

Task Facilitation and Coordinated Performance

In a crisis, success depends on people—not just plans, protocols, or technology. Even the most advanced tools can fail when human coordination breaks down. Disjointed efforts and isolated decisions, despite good intentions, quickly unravel under pressure. That's why effective leaders focus not only on what needs to be done, but also on how it's accomplished—by uniting people, priorities, and resources around a shared goal. Coordination turns chaos into progress. One emergency manager described a flood response where multiple agencies arrived with overlapping mandates but no unified plan. "We had boats, medics, and logistics teams—but no one knew who was in charge. It wasn't until a county official stepped in, clarified roles, and set priorities that we started saving lives." In daily operations, teams may accept ambiguity. But in crises, even minor confusion can stall momentum, lead to duplicate efforts, or risk safety. Leaders must clarify roles, define interdependencies, and ensure every team member understands how their task fits into the mission.

Effective task facilitation starts with assigning roles based on capabilities. Leaders assess who is best suited—by training, position, or temperament—to manage specific duties. They clearly communicate expectations, cover all essential functions, and empower team members to act confidently within their scope. One respondent, a hospital incident commander, shared, "We didn't just assign tasks—we matched people to pressure. The nurse who stayed calm under fire got triage. The logistics lead, who knew the system inside out, handled the supply chain. That alignment made all the difference."

A clear command structure ensures tasks flow smoothly from strategy to execution. Leaders make key decisions and delegate authority, enabling others to carry them out. They utilize tools such as briefings, task boards, and incident management systems to keep clarity and focus. These tools do more than organize information; they reinforce accountability and maintain rhythm. As one fire captain said, "The whiteboard wasn't just a checklist—it was our heartbeat. It kept us focused, synchronized, and moving." In high-stakes situations, coordination isn't optional; it's lifesaving. Leaders who facilitate it effectively turn fragmented efforts into unified action.

Supporting Execution and Removing Barriers

Facilitation in crisis leadership isn't about micromanagement; it's about empowerment. Effective leaders don't try to control every step of the process; instead, they create conditions that allow others to succeed. This involves removing obstacles, sharing crucial information, tracking progress, and inspiring teams, especially when exhaustion, fear, or frustration threaten morale. One respondent, a logistics officer during a wildfire response, shared, "Our leader didn't hover—he cleared the path. He made sure we had what we needed and let us run." That kind of support transforms reactive effort into coordinated action.

Relational communication and awareness are the foundations of this facilitative approach. Leaders encourage real-time, two-way communication that keeps teams aligned and adaptable. They hold regular check-ins, seek feedback from the ground level, and use clear, straightforward language to prevent misunderstandings. Feedforward and feedback loops help maintain situational awareness and enable quick adjustments. As one emergency manager said, "Effective communication is the circulatory system of crisis response. It delivers vital information, aligns intentions, and supports informed decisions." Without it, even the best strategies falter. With it, teams remain connected, agile, and focused.

Facilitative leaders also tend to handle the human side of a crisis. Under stress, judgment can decline, tempers can flare, and relationships can become strained. Leaders who notice signs of fatigue, anxiety, or disengagement—and respond with empathy and clarity—help maintain team cohesion and performance. A hospital administrator recalled, "She saw we were burning out. She didn't just push harder; she paused, acknowledged the strain, and gave us space to regroup. That moment restored our focus." Emotional intelligence isn't a luxury in a crisis; it's a stabilizer. It helps leaders keep unity and momentum even under relentless pressure.

Ultimately, supporting execution means leading with purpose and reducing friction. It's about empowering others to act confidently, adapt quickly, and stay connected to the mission. Facilitative leaders don't just oversee tasks; they manage energy, clarity, and trust. They recognize that in high-stakes environments, success depends not only on what gets done but also on how people feel during the process. By removing barriers—both operational and emotional, they allow teams to perform at their best when it counts most.

Building Cohesion and Promoting Psychological Safety

Facilitating performance in crisis leadership goes far beyond assigning tasks — it involves building a team culture where individuals feel connected, supported, and psychologically safe. Effective leaders promote peer support, emphasize a shared mission, and establish conditions where people feel secure enough to speak up, admit mistakes, and offer ideas. This sense of safety is not a luxury — it's essential for resilience and creativity under pressure. As one respondent, a disaster response coordinator, mentioned, "The moment I knew we'd be okay was when someone said, 'I think we missed something,' and no one flinched. We listened, adjusted, and moved forward." These practices are crucial — not optional. In high-stakes environments, emotional support directly impacts operational success. Leaders who foster belonging and trust unlock their team's full potential, helping teams shift from compliance to commitment — moving from merely following rules to fully embracing the mission. A public health official recalled, "Our leader reminded us that mistakes were part of the process. That permitted us to be honest, and that honesty saved us from repeating errors." When people feel safe, they are more likely to take initiative, challenge assumptions, and collaborate confidently. Psychological safety isn't about comfort — it's about performance. It enables teams to work more agilely, share real-time insights, and adapt to changing conditions. In a crisis, where decisions must be made quickly and information is often incomplete, the ability to raise concerns without fear of repercussions is crucial. One emergency manager observed, "He didn't just tolerate dissent — he invited it. That's how we caught a blind spot in our evacuation plan." Leaders who model openness and humility signal that every voice matters, especially when the stakes are high. Cohesion and psychological safety also serve as buffers against the emotional toll of crises. When stress increases and fatigue sets in, teams that feel connected are more likely to support one another, maintain morale, and stay focused on the mission. Facilitative leaders notice when someone struggles and responds with empathy rather than judgment. They create rituals of connection — briefings that start with check-ins, debriefs that include reflection, and informal moments that reinforce shared purpose. By doing so, they build not only operational capacity but also human resilience. In the crucible of crisis, that resilience sustains performance even when everything else is strained.

Managing Transitions and Sustaining Performance

Crises are not static; they unfold in stages, fluctuate in intensity, and demand continuous adjustment. Effective leaders anticipate these changes. They recognize that strategies that work initially might fall short during extended efforts or recovery. They prepare their teams by discussing potential scenarios, rotating shifts to prevent burnout, cross-training staff for flexibility, and adjusting team structures as the crisis progresses. One emergency planner said, "We didn't just plan for the first wave—we built in pivot points. That's what kept us from collapsing when the second wave hit."

During the early stages of the COVID-19 pandemic, healthcare leaders faced overwhelming patient surges, supply chain disruptions, and constantly changing public health guidance.

Success wasn't measured solely by clinical expertise; it also depended on leaders' ability to coordinate exhausted teams, reassign roles quickly, and keep morale high amid uncertainty. Hospitals that practiced proactive transition management—such as rotating leadership roles, conducting mental health check-ins, and staging recovery teams—reported lower burnout and improved patient outcomes. As one hospital administrator reflected, "We didn't just manage beds—we managed people. That's what kept us going."

Sustaining performance under pressure requires more than operational agility; it demands emotional intelligence, foresight, and a deep commitment to team well-being. Leaders who manage transitions well don't just keep operations running; they keep people grounded. They recognize when fatigue is setting in, when communication needs to shift, and when the mission must be reframed. A public safety official shared, "He knew when to push and when to pause. That rhythm kept us from burning out." This kind of leadership creates continuity—not just in logistics, but in trust and cohesion.

Ultimately, managing transitions is about respecting the human aspect of crisis. It involves preparing for change, communicating clearly, and maintaining performance through empathy and adaptability. Leaders who master this skill help their teams navigate uncertainty confidently. They don't just get through the crisis—they grow from it. In doing so, they demonstrate the kind of resilience others can follow.

Conclusion: Coordination as Leadership

Effective crisis leaders are more than just strategists or decision-makers; they are enablers of performance. They don't simply issue directives; they foster clarity, cohesion, and capability. By defining roles, communicating expectations, and removing barriers, they turn individuals into unified teams capable of responding with agility and strength. One respondent, a regional emergency coordinator, expressed it this way: "She didn't just tell us what to do—she made sure we could do it, together." That's the core of coordination: it's not about control, but about connection.

During disruptions, coordination becomes the stabilizing force that transforms scattered efforts into synchronized action. It's the behavioral glue binding people, processes, and priorities to a shared mission. Leaders who embody this don't just manage complexity, they orchestrate it. They ensure each component contributes to forward movement. A logistics officer recalled, "We had dozens of teams, each with their own mandate. Our leader didn't micromanage—he aligned us. That's why we moved fast and stayed focused."

Coordination makes collective action possible when time is tight and stakes are high. The role of the coordination facilitator is not a luxury but a necessity. It supports every other leadership trait that follows. Without alignment, even the most talented teams falter.

Coordination creates the foundation for trust, clarity, and execution. But once that foundation is set, the next step requires something more: decisiveness. In a crisis, alignment without action leads to inertia. Teams need leaders who can make timely, confident decisions that turn strategy into movement. In high-pressure situations where uncertainty is widespread and time is limited; decisiveness becomes the next milestone of effective leadership. It marks the behavioral shift from planning to action. Leaders who hesitate risk losing momentum; those who decide with clarity and conviction drive teams into motion. The next chapter explores this vital trait, Decisiveness, and how leaders can develop the courage, clarity, and timing needed to lead when the margin for error vanishes.

CHAPTER 6

DECISIVENESS

Effective crisis leaders are consistently described as those who can analyze complex situations under pressure, filter through conflicting or limited data, and make informed, goal-directed decisions. This ability does more than resolve immediate challenges—it reduces organizational paralysis, enhances operational outcomes, and reinforces the leader's credibility.

When respondents described decisive leaders, their language conveyed confidence, respect, and a tangible sense of relief. These leaders were praised for their ability to "make the hard calls," "stand by their decisions," and "not hesitate when it mattered." One respondent recalled a leader who "cut through the noise and made the call no one else wanted to make." Another noted, "She didn't wait for perfect information—she acted, and we followed." Even when outcomes weren't perfect, the leader's willingness to take responsibility and move forward built trust and eased anxiety.

Decisive leaders were described as "anchors in the storm," "clear voices in the fog," and "the ones who gave us something to rally around." Their actions provided clarity when others were confused and offered direction during chaos. One team member shared, "He didn't just make decisions—he made us feel like we could move again." Another said, "Her decisiveness gave us permission to act, even when everything felt uncertain." This trait—Decisiveness—is not about impulsiveness or bravado. It's about timely, confident action rooted in purpose. In high-stakes environments, where hesitation can increase risk, decisive leaders serve as catalysts for coordinated responses and forward movement. Decisiveness isn't just about acting quickly; it also involves having a clear purpose, confidence under pressure, and the ability to turn uncertainty into coordinated action.

What Decisiveness Looks Like

In crisis leadership, coordination sets the foundation, but Decisiveness yields results. When people and processes are synchronized, the crucial moment comes when a leader must decide. Not later. Not perfectly. But now. Decisiveness turns readiness into action by enabling quick, confident choices even in the face of uncertainty and incomplete information. In high-stakes moments, hesitation can be costly. Effective leaders understand that action—even if imperfect—is often better than hesitation. Decisiveness isn't reckless; it's informed courage. It's what propels teams forward when time is tight, stakes are high, and clarity is scarce.

Decisiveness is not impulsiveness. It's the ability to make clear, firm, and timely decisions after considering relevant factors. It's a balance—acting quickly enough to maintain momentum, but carefully enough to ensure good judgment.

Respondents described four key attributes that define decisive leadership:

> ➤ Clarity: Knowing what needs to be done and choosing a course of action with purpose.
> ➤ Confidence: Trusting one's judgment without excessive second-guessing.
> ➤ Timeliness: Acting without unnecessary delay, especially when time is compressed.
> ➤ Commitment: Following through on decisions unless new evidence warrants adjustment.

Impulsiveness, by contrast, is acting without forethought—often driven by emotion, urgency, or external pressure. While both traits involve speed, they differ in process and outcome. Decisiveness is quick thinking; impulsiveness is quick action without reflection. Decisive leaders are remembered not for rashness but for steadiness. They act with conviction, take responsibility, and adapt when necessary—without wavering or losing momentum.

Decisiveness and Team Dynamics

Decisive leaders do more than make choices; they generate momentum. Their clear sense of direction fosters team unity, accelerates performance, and builds trust. Meetings become focused, decisions are communicated openly, and expectations are clearly defined. Teams move forward confidently, aware of their destination and purpose.

Importantly, decisiveness does not mean authoritarianism. Effective leaders seek input, respect different perspectives, and make decisions that teams can understand and follow. This inclusive approach boosts morale and encourages shared ownership. Even when team members disagree, they often appreciate the leader's willingness to act, explain, and adjust when necessary.

In high-pressure situations, this kind of decisiveness acts as a stabilizing force. It reduces ambiguity, coordinates efforts, and demonstrates leadership from the front.

The Costs of Indecision

Respondents often identify indecisiveness, hesitation, delays, or avoidance as key leadership flaws. In crisis situations where time is limited and information is incomplete, waiting for perfect clarity can have negative results. Progress stalls, uncertainty grows, and trust decreases. Teams rely on leaders for guidance.

When that direction is missing, individuals become disengaged, frustrated, and unsure of their roles. Opportunities are missed, resources are wasted, and confusion replaces coordination. Decisive leaders act despite uncertainty. They depend on training, experience, and intuition to inform their judgment. Their readiness to make timely decisions—even if imperfect— sets structure, creates momentum, and provides reassurance. In contrast, indecision raises risks and diminishes confidence.

Building Decisiveness Through Practice

Decisiveness is not an innate trait — it is a skill that can be developed. Leaders enhance it through intentional preparation, organized reflection, and experience tested under pressure. Respondents emphasized several practical strategies:

- Simulation-based training: Tabletop exercises, role-playing, and scenario drills replicate the urgency and ambiguity of real crises. These experiences build confidence and sharpen judgment.
- After-action reviews: Reflecting on past decisions helps leaders refine their process, recognize blind spots, and improve future performance.
- Stress regulation techniques: Controlled breathing, mental rehearsal, and grounding exercises help leaders

manage physiological responses that can cloud judgment under pressure.

➢ Decision tools: Such as checklists, decision trees, and pre-established thresholds, reduce cognitive load, enabling faster and more reliable choices.

These practices help leaders remain clear and composed when it matters most. They turn hesitation into confidence and uncertainty into action.

Organizational Impact

Decisiveness not only affects teams but also advances entire organizations. When leaders make clear, timely decisions, they accelerate progress, reduce waste, and build trust. Projects remain on schedule, resources are used efficiently, and teams collaborate more effectively. The ripple effects are significant.

➢ Operational efficiency improves as decisions prevent bottlenecks and delays.

➢ Team culture strengthens through reduced anxiety, clearer direction, and higher morale.

➢ Agility increases as leaders adapt strategies in real time, responding to new information without losing momentum.

> Innovation flourishes when teams feel empowered to take initiative and explore bold ideas.

Decisive leaders foster a culture of responsibility and initiative. Their clarity spurs action, accelerates recovery, and attracts high-performing individuals who value progress and trust. Over time, this creates a resilient organization—one capable of facing future challenges with confidence and unity.

Conclusion: Decisively Making Critical Calls

In times of crisis, leadership often boils down to a single imperative: decide. Decisiveness is the pivotal point—where uncertainty turns into action, and confusion shifts to coordination. It's not about achieving perfection; it's about creating clarity in motion. The courage to act, especially when the path is unclear and the stakes are high, separates effective leaders from hesitant bystanders.

As one respondent said, "Decisiveness is the leader's response to uncertainty—the courage to act with clarity when hesitation could cost everything." That clarity doesn't come from knowing everything; it comes from knowing enough to act. Decisive leaders don't wait for perfect information or ideal conditions. They act intentionally, take responsibility for their choices, and adapt as new realities emerge. Their presence stabilizes the team, speeds responses, and builds trust.

One team member, in the survey's open-response section, recalled the following about an effective leader: "When she made the call, we stopped spinning and started moving." Another said, "He didn't just decide—he made us feel safe enough to follow." These moments demonstrate the power of decisiveness not just as a tactical skill, but as a relational force. It signals confidence, direction, and care.

But decisiveness alone is not enough. Action without insight can be reckless. The strength of a decision depends on the thinking that comes before it. In high-stakes situations, impulsiveness can be just as harmful as inaction. Leaders must not only act—they must think carefully about how and why they act.

That's why the next step in the Marks of a Leader framework is so crucial. Decisiveness must be combined with critical thinking and discernment. The ability to analyze thoroughly, foresee consequences, question assumptions, and prioritize effectively transforms quick decisions into well-founded ones. It's not just about speed; it's about substance.

In the next chapter, we explore the cognitive engine behind effective crisis leadership: Critical Thinking. We'll examine how leaders process complexity under pressure, avoid common mental traps, and develop judgments that are both quick and deliberate. We'll see how critical thinking helps leaders navigate ambiguity, balance competing risks, and make timely, trustworthy decisions.

Because in a world where crises arrive without warning, the

ability to think clearly is just as important as the ability to act decisively. Chapter 7 begins the journey into that discipline.

CHAPTER 7

CRITICAL THINKING

I n dynamic, high-pressure environments, critical thinking is the leader's compass. It enables the analysis of complex, ambiguous situations, the envisioning of practical solutions, the anticipation of consequences, and the evaluation of outcomes. Respondents consistently identified it as essential to successful crisis leadership.

What became clear to me that critical thinking (the ability to step back, consider all available information and perspectives, test assumptions, avoid bias and heuristic fallacies, and make evidence-based judgments when the situation is confusing or high-pressure) is an important mark of effective leadership..

During a crisis, action is crucial, yet not all actions are equally effective. Decisiveness can jump-start the response, but critical thinking ensures the action is impactful. Great leaders don't just act quickly; they think clearly. They pause, however briefly, to evaluate, question, and anticipate. In high-stakes situations where information is limited and consequences are severe, critical thinking becomes the leader's guiding tool. It helps them differentiate noise from necessary signals, challenge assumptions, and consider options without freezing. This skill doesn't slow leaders down; it sharpens their focus. It enables them to make decisions that are not only fast but also wise. When describing leaders with exceptional critical thinking, respondents often use words like sharp, insightful, thoughtful, and deliberate. These leaders are praised for their ability to "see things others didn't," "ask the right questions," and "never jump to conclusions." Their decisions are not reactive; they are grounded in logic, data, and disciplined evaluation. One respondent noted, "She didn't just think fast, she thought well." Another shared, "He had a way of pausing just long enough to make sure we weren't missing something critical." This mental steadiness builds trust. Teams feel confident that every move is deliberate and well-considered. One team member recalled, "When our leader spoke, it was clear he'd already run the scenario five different ways in his head." Another said, "Her questions made us rethink our assumptions—and that's what kept us from making a costly mistake." Critical thinking in a crisis isn't about overanalyzing—it's about maintaining clarity under pressure. These leaders didn't get lost in complexity; they navigated through it. They filtered noise from signals, challenged groupthink tendencies, and created space for reflection without losing momentum. Their presence allowed teams to slow down just enough to get it right. In situations where urgency might impair judgment, critical thinking acts as the safeguard. It's the sign that guarantees decisions are not only quick, but also wise.

Thinking That Builds Confidence

Colleagues recalled how critical-thinking leaders "made complex situations make sense," "could see three moves ahead," and "always considered second- and third-order effects." These leaders exemplified command thinking—a combination of strategic foresight, analytical accuracy, and practical judgment. They didn't just solve problems; they clarified them. They challenged assumptions, encouraged reflection, and turned uncertainty into clarity. Their thinking was precise, future-oriented, grounded in logic but adaptable. They asked questions that deepened understanding instead of issuing commands that shut it down. Terms like adaptive thinking, tactical intelligence, crisis reasoning, and mission-focused analysis all pointed to the same core quality: the ability to think clearly under pressure. By demonstrating this discipline, they made the team smarter, clarified the mission, and made the path forward more achievable.

Why Critical Thinking Matters in Crisis

Crises are unpredictable, uncertain, complex, and ambiguous—often called VUCA (Volatility, Uncertainty, Complexity, and

Ambiguity) environments. VUCA is an acronym describing conditions that are volatile (fast, unstable change with unknown duration), uncertain (future events and outcomes are hard to predict), complex (many interconnected variables and stakeholders), and ambiguous (situations are hard to interpret; cause–effect is unclear). It is my understanding that it first originated in the U.S. Army War College's post–Cold War analysis and has since been widely adopted in business, crisis management, and strategic leadership to frame operating environments and the demands they place on decision-makers. I think that it a useful diagnostic lens or framing device, for more fully understanding the importance of dynamic critical thinking skill sets for crisis leaders.

In these situations, leaders must interpret incomplete or conflicting data, avoid cognitive traps, and make decisions that balance urgency with long-term impacts.

Critical thinking enables leaders to:

> ➢ Identify root causes rather than just treating symptoms.
> ➢ Adapt strategically as conditions evolve.
> ➢ Make evidence-based decisions that avoid emotional or reactive pitfalls.
> ➢ Stay resilient, remain calm, and methodical under pressure.

Critical thinking also fosters innovation. Leaders who critically examine assumptions, encourage new perspectives, and create space for fresh ideas tend to be more effective. This enhances not only immediate performance but also long-term growth and adaptability.

Creating a Culture of Thoughtful Leadership

Critical thinking isn't just an individual skill—it's a cultural force. Leaders who demonstrate it foster environments that value inquiry, evidence, and open dialogue. Teams become more engaged, collaborative, and innovative.

This critical thinking mindset was reported to have encouraged:

> ➤ Asking "why?" and "what else could be true?"
> ➤ Challenging mental shortcuts and biases.
> ➤ Welcoming dissent and learning from failure.

One respondent described an effective leader who rewards thoughtful dissent and treats mistakes as opportunities to learn, which is a key sign of true critical thinking. This approach not only improves decision-making but also enhances trust, transparency, and team cohesion. When leaders think critically, they encourage others to do the same. The result is a culture where ideas are tested, assumptions are challenged, and solutions are refined—together. In a crisis, leaders need to learn to "slow down the moment" mentally—even when everything around them is moving faster. This means:

- ➤ Recognizing what's known, what's uncertain, and what's changed.
- ➤ Predicting ripple effects across interconnected systems—logistical, social, political, emotional.
- ➤ Shifting perspectives and integrating multiple frames of reference.
- ➤ Questioning assumptions and verifying inputs before acting.

This disciplined, analytical, and reflective approach leads to better judgment, more informed decisions, and greater legitimacy and trust. It enables leaders to respond clearly instead of reacting with confusion. During a crisis, critical thinking becomes the light that reveals what truly matters.

The Cost of Uncritical Thinking

Leaders who lack critical thinking are consistently seen as less effective in crisis situations—and for good reason. Not having disciplined analysis often results in predictable but harmful patterns:

- ➤ Over-reliance on routines or outdated experience, even when conditions have changed.

- ➢ Suppression of dissent, resulting in groupthink and missed alternatives.
- ➢ Cognitive biases, such as confirmation bias, distort judgment.
- ➢ Decisions that are unclear, inconsistent, or misinformed.

These missteps damage credibility, increase confusion, and extend recovery. Instead of lowering harm, poor thinking can make it worse—turning manageable challenges into cascading failures.

Critical Thinking As A Learned Skill

Critical thinking is not an inborn talent but a learned skill that can be strengthened over time through deliberate practice in questioning assumptions, analyzing evidence, and reflecting on one's own reasoning. Fortunately, critical thinking can be improved—and it's vital to develop it. Leaders strengthen this skill through deliberate practice, mindful reflection, and exposure to different perspectives. Effective strategies include:

- ➢ Simulation-based training: Crisis scenarios that require analyzing conflicting data, evaluating options, and justifying decisions under pressure.

- ➤ After-action reviews: Reflecting on previous decisions to reveal reasoning and learn from both successes and mistakes.
- ➤ Cross-disciplinary engagement: Broaden mental models by learning from fields such as law, medicine, logistics, media, and psychology.
- ➤ Red teaming and devil's advocacy: Stress-testing assumptions, identifying blind spots, and challenging groupthink.

Organizations also play a vital role. Building leadership teams that promote diverse thinking and reducing hierarchies during emergencies ensures frontline insights are acknowledged. When inquiry is encouraged and dissent is accepted, collective intelligence improves—and so does the quality of decisions.

Conclusion: Thinking That Leads

Critical thinking is not just a leadership trait; it is a core leadership skill. It serves as the lens through which effective leaders interpret chaos, distinguish signal from noise, and chart a clear course forward. In times of complexity and uncertainty, critical thinking transforms confusion into clarity. It empowers leaders to guide others not only with authority but also with understanding, confidence, and trust.

In high-stakes environments, the most influential leaders aren't always the ones who act first, they are the ones who think most carefully. They pause to evaluate, question assumptions, and anticipate potential outcomes. Their decisions aren't just quick, they are deliberate, resilient, and ethically grounded. As one respondent noted, "Critical thinking is the leader's lens—focusing on chaos, filtering signal from noise, and uncovering the wisest path forward when the stakes are highest."

Importantly, critical thinking is not innate. It is a learned and cultivated mental discipline—a skill set that must be developed through intentional practice. Respondents consistently emphasized that the most trusted leaders were those who had trained their minds to think under pressure. One shared, "She didn't just react—she had a mental framework that helped her see through the fog." Another noted, "He made critical thinking part of our drills. It wasn't just what he did—it was what he taught."

For current and future leaders, developing critical thinking is essential for readiness. Hope isn't a strategy, and instinct alone isn't enough. Leaders need to actively improve their cognitive skills through scenario planning, structured reflection, and disciplined analysis. Organizations must embed this skill into their culture—encouraging thoughtful inquiry, recognizing sound judgment, and creating space for reflection amid urgency.

Because when pressure mounts, clear thinking becomes the anchor. It steadies the team, sharpens decision-making, and guards against impulsive mistakes. But once clear thinking is in place, clarity of focus must follow.

The next chapter explores Prioritization—the leader's skill in identifying what's most important, allocating attention and resources effectively, and keeping everyone aligned when everything feels urgent. During a crisis, not all tasks are equal, and not all voices can be addressed at once. Effective leaders must make tough choices, clearly communicate priorities, and help their teams stay focused amid competing demands.

Because in the fog of a crisis, the question is not just what to do—but what to do first. Chapter 8 begins that exploration.

CHAPTER 8

PRIORITIZATION

I n a crisis, everything can seem urgent—but not everything holds equal importance. Effective leaders know how to cut through the noise, identify what truly matters, and direct their team's energy to where it counts most. Prioritization is the disciplined ability to stay clear about what matters most and act on it, even under intense pressure.

The capacity to set and continually update clear priorities is essential for an effective crisis leader because it directs scarce time, attention, and resources toward what most protects people, operations, and long-term viability. In contrast, a leader who lacks the ability to establish clear, ultimate priorities is easily overwhelmed by noise, reacts inconsistently, and leaves teams confused about what truly matters in the response.

Effective leaders understand that clarity of thought must translate into clarity of focus. Prioritization serves as a marker that helps leaders sift through competing demands, recognize what's most critical, and allocate attention, effort, and resources accordingly. It's not just about making lists; it's about making deliberate choices. In high-stakes situations, where time is limited and stakes are high, prioritization becomes a strategic act of triage. Leaders who master this skill don't just react—they respond with precision. They guide their teams toward meaningful actions, ensuring that the most vital tasks are addressed first and that distractions don't obstruct progress. Respondents consistently emphasized that effective crisis leaders don't only focus on the right actions. During overwhelming demands, these leaders demonstrate a rare ability to prioritize competing needs while maintaining strategic focus. They distribute attention, time, and resources thoughtfully, ensuring efforts are directed where they will have the most significant impact. One respondent noted, "She didn't chase every fire—she knew which ones threatened the whole building." Another shared, "He kept us focused when everything felt urgent. That's what made the difference." This focus—prioritization—is what keeps teams aligned, operations running smoothly, and results in achieving success. It's not about doing more; it's about doing what truly matters. Effective leaders resist the pull of reactive busyness. Instead, they clarify objectives, distinguish signals from noise, and steer their teams toward meaningful action. As one team member said, "Our leader gave us permission to ignore the noise and focus on what would actually move the needle." In high-pressure environments, prioritization becomes a key leadership skill. It's about the discipline to say no, the insight to say yes, and the courage to stay focused amid distractions. Leaders who embody this create clarity in the chaos of urgency. They help their teams breathe, align, and act with purpose.

What Prioritization Looks Like

Effective crisis leaders do not treat all tasks equally—they prioritize. They distinguish between what is urgent and what is essential, what requires immediate action and what can wait. Their focus is intentional, not reactive. In high-pressure situations, where everything competes for attention, prioritization guides the leader—directing teams toward what truly matters.

Respondents consistently praised leaders who demonstrated this clarity. They described them as having "a clear sense of what mattered," "never chasing distractions," and "always keeping the team aligned." One team member recalled, "She didn't just tell us what to do—she helped us understand why it mattered." Another noted, "He made it okay to let go of the noise and focus on the mission."

These leaders didn't just manage time; they managed purpose. Every decision reflected a hierarchy of importance centered on mission, impact, and feasibility. Their ability to prioritize built confidence within teams, reduced mental overload, and ensured energy was directed toward what mattered most.

Prioritization involves:

> Clarity of purpose: Knowing what the mission demands and aligning actions accordingly.

> Situational awareness: Understanding how conditions shift and adjusting priorities in real time.

> Resource discipline: Allocating people, time, and tools where they'll have the most significant effect.

> Team alignment: Ensuring everyone understands their priorities and works toward them together.

One respondent summarized it by saying, "Our leader didn't just keep us busy—he kept us focused. That's what made the difference."

This kind of leadership doesn't just keep things moving; it ensures they go in the right direction. It turns urgency into strategy and guarantees that every step forward is a step toward resolution. Crises compress time, stretch resources, and flood leaders with conflicting demands. In this environment, prioritization is not just a skill; it's a vital survival tactic. It's the mark that distinguishes motion from progress, activity from impact. Leaders who prioritize effectively don't just keep things moving; they make sure that what moves really matters. Respondents consistently highlighted that the most effective crisis leaders were those who could guide the team's focus to what truly matters. One explained, "She didn't chase every problem—she chose the right ones to solve." Another noted, "He helped us stop reacting and start responding." These leaders didn't give in to urgency; they shaped it. Their decisions reflected strategic intent rather than reactive impulses. Prioritization enables:

➢ Faster decision-making by eliminating distractions and narrowing the field of focus.

➢ Clearer communication about what matters most, reducing ambiguity and confusion.

➢ Better resource allocation in constrained environments, ensuring tools and talent are deployed where they'll have the most significant effect.

➢ Greater team cohesion through shared focus, aligned goals, and a common sense of purpose.

When everything feels urgent, prioritization helps leaders stay focused, conserve energy, and drive meaningful action. It's discipline that transforms chaos into coordinated effort.

How Prioritization Builds Trust and Momentum

When leaders prioritize effectively, they do more than just organize tasks; they create clarity. This clarity reduces anxiety, builds trust, and helps teams act confidently. People understand what matters, why it matters, and how their work fits into the bigger picture. Respondents remembered leaders who "kept us focused," "didn't let us get distracted," and "always made sure our energy went toward the right things." One team member said, "She made us feel like we weren't just busy—we were making progress." Another added, "His priorities became our priorities, and that's what kept us together." Prioritization also demonstrates accountability. When leaders clearly identify what is most important, they are more likely to follow through, track progress, and adjust when necessary. This consistency builds trust and encourages a culture of disciplined execution. It shows teams that their efforts are not only valued but also strategically directed. In a crisis, momentum is critical, and prioritization is how leaders generate momentum through one clear decision at a time.

Common Pitfalls of Poor Prioritization

When leaders fail to set priorities effectively, the repercussions spread rapidly—and often painfully. In crisis situations, where time is scarce and resources are limited, poor prioritization not only leads to inefficiency but also increases the level of risk. Respondents identified several common pitfalls that occur when leaders lack clarity or discipline in establishing priorities.

- ➢ Everything feels urgent: Without clear guidance, teams chase every issue, spreading their focus and draining resources. One respondent said, "It felt like we were putting out fires with no idea which one was closest to the fuel."
- ➢ Reactive decision-making: Leaders react to noise rather than strategy, driven by the loudest voices or recent disruptions. As one team member said, "We were constantly pivoting—not because the situation changed, but because someone new shouted louder."
- ➢ Misaligned teams: When departments lack shared priorities, they drift apart, causing confusion, redundancy, and inefficiency. A respondent observed, "We had five teams working hard—but not together. It was like rowing in circles."
- ➢ Wasted effort: Time and energy are used on low-impact tasks, leaving critical needs unmet. One leader reflected, "We spent hours chasing a minor issue while the real threat was gaining ground."

These patterns not only slow progress but also erode trust. Teams start doubting leadership's judgment, lose confidence in the mission, and disengage from the process. Momentum halts, and morale declines. In a crisis, poor prioritization can turn a manageable challenge into a cascading failure—where missed signals, wasted resources, and misaligned actions worsen the situation. Respondents made it clear: not having priorities isn't neutral — it's risky. One summed it up directly: "Without priorities, we weren't leading — we were reacting. And that's how things got worse."

Prioritization Examples Across Sectors

Healthcare Sector

> **Failure – Fragmented Response:**

During a regional hospital's response to a mass casualty incident, multiple department heads acted independently. The emergency department prioritized triage, the ICU focused on bed availability, and the communications team issued updates without clinical input. Without a unified prioritization strategy, resources were misallocated, ambulances were rerouted unnecessarily, and critical patients faced delays in care. A nurse later reflected, "Everyone was working hard, but we weren't working together. We needed someone to say, 'This is what matters most right now.'"

> **Success – Focused Response:**

In contrast, another hospital facing a similar surge activated a pre-established prioritization protocol. The incident commander quickly identified three main priorities: stabilize critical patients, ensure staff safety, and streamline communication. Roles were clarified, non-essential procedures were put on hold, and a single point of contact managed external messaging. As one physician noted, "We didn't have all the answers, but we had a clear focus. That made all the difference."

Education Sector

➤ Failure – Fragmented Response:

Following a school lockdown due to a nearby threat, administrators tried to address multiple issues at once—parent communication, student safety, media inquiries, and internal coordination. Without clear priorities, conflicting messages went to parents, teachers lacked guidance, and students stayed locked down longer than necessary. A teacher later said, "We were all waiting for direction, but it felt like no one was steering the ship."

➤ **Success – Focused Response:**

In a separate incident, a school district's crisis team used a tiered prioritization model. The superintendent first focused on student safety, then activated a communication sequence: internal staff, followed by parents, then the media. A designated liaison managed press inquiry, allowing leadership to concentrate on operations. "We knew exactly what to do and in what order," a principal shared. "That structure kept us calm and effective."

Corporate Sector

> Failure – Fragmented Response:

Following a significant data breach, a tech company's leadership team hurried to respond. Departments like legal, IT, marketing, and HR issued separate instructions. Some employees were told to shut down systems, while others were instructed to keep operations running. Customers received conflicting messages. The lack of clear priorities caused reputational harm and drew regulatory attention. An executive admitted, "We were reacting to everything at once—and solving nothing."

> **Success – Focused Response:**

In contrast, a financial services company facing a cyberattack activated its crisis playbook. The CEO assembled a cross-functional team and set three immediate priorities: contain the breach, notify regulators, and communicate transparently with clients. All other actions were postponed or delegated. "We didn't try to do everything," said the CIO. "We did the right things first—and that protected our credibility."

Public Safety Sector

> ➤ Failure – Fragmented Response:

During a wildfire evacuation, local agencies operated on separate radio channels without a unified command. Law enforcement focused on roadblocks, while fire crews aimed at containment. Evacuation orders were delayed in some areas and duplicated in others. Residents were confused and put in danger. A firefighter recalled, "We were all doing our jobs—but without a shared sense of what came first.""

> ➤ **Success – Focused Response:**

In a neighboring jurisdiction, a unified command structure allowed real-time prioritization. The incident commander identified life safety as the top priority, followed by property protection and resource staging. Agencies coordinated smoothly, and evacuation zones were cleared efficiently. "We had a common map, a common mission, and a clear order of operations," said the emergency manager. "That saved lives."

These examples highlight a key truth: in a crisis, everything may seem urgent—but not everything holds equal importance. Leaders who can prioritize under pressure create order out of chaos, unify teams around shared goals, and ensure that limited time and resources go where they are needed most.

Developing Prioritization Skills

Prioritization isn't just a mindset; it's a skill, and like any skill, it can be honed. Effective crisis leaders aren't born knowing what matters most; they learn to identify it through intentional practice, structured reflection, and disciplined decision-making. In high-pressure environments where urgency and complexity intersect, the ability to prioritize becomes a form of strategic literacy.

Respondents emphasized that the best leaders didn't rely solely on instinct; they trained for clarity. One shared, "Our leader ran drills where we had to choose between five urgent tasks. It taught us how to think under pressure." Another noted, "She used a simple framework that helped us cut through the noise and focus on impact."

Several strategies stood out across interviews and field reports:

> ➢ Scenario-based training: Simulated exercises with competing demands help leaders practice triage in real

time. These drills build muscle memory for making tough calls under pressure.

> Decision frameworks: Tools such as impact-effort matrices, priority grids, and mission filters offer structure. They clarify what warrants attention and assist leaders in justifying their decisions.

> After-action reviews: Reflecting on past decisions shows what was prioritized, why, and how it affected results. These reviews promote accountability and ongoing improvement.

> Team input: Engaging diverse perspectives reveals blind spots and improves collective judgment. One respondent said, "He always asked the team what they thought mattered most—and sometimes, they saw things he didn't."

Organizations play a key role in developing this skill. When environments foster focus, reduce distractions, and align priorities across teams, leaders can act with clarity. One respondent summarized it: "We didn't just learn to prioritize— we learned to prioritize together." When leaders and teams understand what matters most, execution improves, and smarter, more resilient prioritization shifts from an individual habit to a shared language of strategic action.

Conclusion: Focus That Leads

In crisis leadership, clarity isn't a luxury; it's a lifeline. And prioritization is the discipline that safeguards it. When everything seems urgent, and the stakes are high, effective leaders don't try to do everything. They focus on what matters most. They distinguish the essential from the noise, align their teams around shared goals, and turn urgency into strategy. As one respondent said, "The best leaders didn't just act fast—they acted on what mattered." Prioritization isn't just a tactical skill— it's a leadership multiplier. It channels energy, sharpens decisions, and builds trust. It reduces overwhelm, prevents fragmentation, and ensures limited time and resources are used where they will make the most impact. When leaders focus, teams follow. And even in chaos, progress becomes possible. But prioritization doesn't come from instinct alone. It is shaped by something deeper: experience and preparation. The ability to prioritize effectively often depends on a leader's exposure to past challenges, their readiness for future ones, and their capacity to reflect, learn, and adapt. Leaders who have been tested, who've trained under pressure, debriefed after failure, and learned hard lessons—are better equipped to make quick, focused, and effective decisions when it matters most. This shows an important truth: prioritization isn't just about what leaders do in the moment—it's about what they've done before the moment arrives. It results from mental rehearsal, organizational learning, and a culture that values preparation as much as performance. The next chapter looks at Experience and Readiness—two fundamental forces that shape how leaders respond under pressure. We'll explore how experienced leaders draw on past events to guide current decisions, how organizations can build readiness through training and reflection, and how experiential learning boosts the confidence and skills needed to lead through the unknown. Because in a crisis, the question isn't just what you know, it's what you've lived through, learned from, and prepared for. Chapter 9 starts that journey.

CHAPTER 9

EXPERIENCE AND READINESS

Experience isn't just a background detail—it's a defining asset. Respondents consistently emphasized that leaders who have "been there before" bring calm, clarity, and confidence to crisis situations.

Experience in crisis leadership is more than technical expertise or credentials; it is the readiness to apply that knowledge under real pressure, to adapt in unfamiliar conditions, and to perform reliably with and through other people. True readiness comes from deliberately learning from past events—successes, near-misses, and failures—so that each new situation benefits from accumulated insight rather than repeating the same human-performance mistakes.

Experience also serves as a visible badge of authority that others recognize and respect. It signals to team members, subordinates, and even superiors that the leader has earned credibility through past performance, not just formal position.

Their authority comes not from theory but from real-world experience in handling emergencies, conducting drills, and honing instincts through repetition and reflection. In crisis leadership, instinct alone is rarely enough. The ability to prioritize, decide, and coordinate under pressure is developed through experience and reinforced by preparedness. Leaders who excel in high-stakes environments often draw on a deep reservoir of past challenges where they have been tested, pushed, and refined. However, experience alone is not sufficient. Preparedness complements it as the proactive side: the drills, frameworks, and mental rehearsals that enable leaders to act before the storm arrives. Together, experience and preparedness form the foundation of confident leadership. They allow leaders to recognize patterns, anticipate outcomes, and respond clearly while others are still trying to catch up.

The Impact of Experience and Readiness

In moments of crisis, experienced leaders stand out—not just because of their actions but for how they inspire others. Respondents consistently described these individuals as confident, steady, and shaped by experience. They "never got rattled," "knew exactly what to do," and "brought order to chaos." Their presence was more than reassuring; it was transformative.

These leaders didn't just perform well under pressure; they also trained others to do the same. One respondent recalled, "She ran training that felt real—like we were already in the middle of a disaster." Another shared, "He pushed us hard, so we'd be ready. When the real thing hit, we didn't panic. Their commitment to preparedness was contagious. Teams absorbed their discipline, mirrored their focus, and rose to meet the challenge."

Experienced leaders made solid decisions quickly, communicated clearly under pressure, and stayed focused when others faltered. Their calm demeanor brought stability in chaos. One team member said, "When everything was falling apart, he was the one who kept us grounded." Another noted, "She didn't just lead; she made us feel like we'd trained for this our whole lives."

One respondent observed that during a regional flood response, an emergency operations director was commended for her ability to turn preparation into effective action. Months prior to the crisis, she had led a series of scenario-based drills that simulated infrastructure failure, supply chain disruptions, and mass displacement. When the floodwaters rose and communication systems failed, her team didn't panic or falter— they activated procedures and succeeded. "We didn't have to guess," the respondent wrote. "We had practiced this. She had guided us through every step, every contingency." Another added, "She was calm, focused, and decisive. That steadiness spread throughout the entire team."

Thanks to her foresight and training, shelters opened earlier than planned, supply routes were rerouted effectively, and public messaging stayed clear and consistent. Her experience didn't just guide the response—it raised its level.

These leaders also impacted team readiness. They "ran training that felt real," "pushed us hard so we'd be ready," and "made sure everyone knew the plan." Their commitment to preparation was inspiring. They didn't just prepare themselves; they helped others get ready, too.

Experience gave them foresight. They predicted problems before they escalated, noticed subtle changes in conditions, and responded effectively. Their authority came from action, not theory—and their teams trusted them because they earned it.

Experience and Readiness – Built Before the Storm

Readiness isn't innate, it's something you develop. The most effective crisis leaders don't wait for disruption to test them; they prepare for it. They build readiness through planning, disciplined practice, and continuous reflection. Their composure under pressure isn't just a personality trait, it's the outcome of purposeful effort. Respondents consistently highlighted that readiness is a key trait of trusted leaders. These leaders were described as experienced, steady, and battle-hardened. They "never got rattled," "knew exactly what to do," and "brought order to chaos." Their level of preparation affected team performance. One team member recalled, "She ran training that felt real—like we were already in the middle of a disaster." Another said, "He pushed us hard, so we'd be ready. When the real thing hit, we didn't panic; we executed!" A "ready" leader radiates confidence. They evaluate quickly, activate efficiently, and communicate calmly. They foresee issues rather than react, fostering trust within the team. Their presence signals, "We've prepared for this. Let's move." Readiness is built on more than just experience; it's shaped by structured development. Building readiness isn't left to chance—it results from deliberate practice and intentional design. Respondents emphasized several key strategies that help leaders build the capacity to perform under pressure and lead confidently. These practices aren't isolated efforts; they are integrated into the very fabric of resilient organizations. One fundamental method was training and simulation. Leaders who practiced under pressure—through drills, exercises, and immersive scenarios—built muscle memory and decision fluency. These experiences allowed them to rehearse critical thinking in real-time, sharpen their instincts, and gain confidence to act decisively when the stakes are high. As one respondent said, "Our best leaders weren't just thrown into the fire—they were trained to handle heat." Contingency planning also played a crucial role. This includes having a plan beyond the plan. By anticipating various scenarios and preparing tailored responses, leaders increased their foresight and strategic flexibility. They learned to think multiple steps ahead, adapt when circumstances changed, and lead their teams with clarity even amid uncertainty. Equally important was developing personal resilience. Leaders who built their physical, emotional, and mental strength were better able to handle stress and recover from setbacks. They showed steadiness, kept perspective, and supported their teams through long-term challenges. Finally, continuous learning became a key trait of effective leadership. Leaders who regularly reflected on past events—both successes and failures—could improve their future performance. They didn't just move on from crises; they analyzed them for insights. One respondent noted, "We didn't just learn to prioritize—we learned to prioritize together." That shared reflection fostered a culture of growth, in which every challenge became an opportunity to improve. Organizations that focus on these practices do more than build individual skills—they cultivate cultures of proactive resilience. They make sure that readiness is built into the way they operate, not just a reaction to crises. In doing so, they prepare their leaders to not only respond effectively but also to lead with clarity, confidence, and credibility.

Experience as a Core Leadership Trait

Real-world exposure not only boosts confidence but also shapes the core traits that define effective crisis leadership. Respondents consistently emphasized that experience was more than just a line on a résumé; it served as a testing ground. Leaders who faced challenges in dynamic, high-pressure situations developed a kind of leadership fluency that can't be gained from theory alone.

One of the most apparent traits which can be developed through experience is situational awareness. Experienced leaders learn to notice subtle cues, anticipate changes, and identify emerging threats before they escalate. Their ability to scan the environment and understand complexity helps them stay ahead, even during unstable conditions.

Communication under pressure is another essential trait. Skilled leaders communicate clearly and confidently when it matters most. They know how to transform chaos into clear messages, soothe nervous teams, and maintain credibility with stakeholders. As one respondent said, "She didn't just talk—she made sense when no one else could."

Strategic decision-making also improves with experience. Leaders learn to prioritize and adapt with limited data, making informed choices even when time is tight and options are unclear. Past outcomes shape their judgment, and their confidence stems from insights they've earned.

Experience also boosts team coordination. Leaders who have

faced real crises understand how to delegate effectively, allocate resources, and keep teams aligned. They recognize when to intervene, when to step back, and how to sustain momentum without micromanaging.

In complex settings, cross-functional collaboration becomes vital. Experienced leaders learn to bridge mandates across agencies, departments, and disciplines. They build trust across silos and foster cooperation where turf wars might otherwise impede progress.

Most importantly, experience fosters adaptability and resilience. Leaders who have faced adversity learn to pivot quickly without losing sight of strategy. They manage stress, recover from setbacks, and demonstrate emotional steadiness to their teams. Over time, these qualities become second nature—reflexes sharpened through repetition, reflection, and exposure to both real and simulated challenges. As one respondent said, "You could tell who had been through it. They didn't flinch—they led."

Real vs. Simulated Experience

Respondents consistently emphasized that both real-world and simulated experience are crucial for developing confident, capable crisis leaders. Instead of viewing them as opposing approaches, they see them as complementary—each providing unique but equally valuable contributions to readiness. Real-world experience builds emotional resilience and deep confidence. It exposes leaders to the raw complexity of crises, where decisions have real consequences and pressure is unfiltered. Leaders who have faced actual emergencies learn to navigate ambiguity, manage stress, and lead with conviction. One respondent vividly described this: "You can't fake the feeling of being responsible for lives. That changes how you lead." These moments shape judgment in ways that no classroom or manual can match. Meanwhile, simulated training develops mental models and prepares leaders for rare or emerging scenarios. High-quality simulations—interactive, time-sensitive, and sensory-rich—can rival real-world exposure in building readiness. They allow leaders to rehearse decision-making, test contingency plans, and experience the cognitive load of a crisis without real-world stakes. As one participant noted, "The drills were so intense, I forgot it wasn't real. That's how I knew I was ready." Together, real and simulated experience forms the foundation of confident leadership. They help leaders identify patterns, anticipate outcomes, and respond clearly, while others are still catching up. The most effective leaders draw from both—grounding their instincts in lived experience while sharpening their foresight through deliberate practice. In doing so, they build not just competence but credibility.

The Power of Both: Experience and Practice

The most effective crisis leaders don't rely only on what they've seen or done; they also deliberately prepare for what they haven't yet faced. They carry the weight of real-world experience combined with the discipline of ongoing, future oriented intentional practice. Together, this dual foundation builds the judgment, flexibility, and crisis intuition that separate merely competent leaders from truly exceptional ones.

Respondents consistently emphasized that the most trusted leaders were those who had "been through it" and "trained like it was real." These leaders didn't just survive past crises; they studied them. They didn't just run drills—they made them meaningful. One team member recalled, "She didn't just have experience—she made sure we were ready for what we hadn't yet faced." Another noted, "He treated every exercise like it mattered, and when the real thing came, it showed." This blend of exposure and preparation develops leaders who are confidently calibrated. They understand how to read a room, sense when something is wrong, and respond accurately. They can spot emerging threats early, adjust their course without losing momentum, and make decisions that balance urgency with strategic purpose. Their instincts are not impulsive; they are informed. Experience provides the raw material—memories of past crises, scars from tough decisions, lessons learned under pressure. Practice sharpens those instincts, embedding mental models and decision routes that can be activated in real time. Together, experience and practice develop leaders who are not just reactive but prepared leaders who don't just act but act wisely. In the words of one respondent: "The leaders we trusted most were the ones who had seen the worst—and still trained like the worst was yet to come."

Accelerating Experience Through Training

Experience takes time—but training can speed up its effects. While real-world exposure remains essential, respondents highlighted that organizations can significantly reduce the learning curve by merging operational immersion with high-quality simulation. The aim isn't merely to prepare for known threats but to develop the cognitive and emotional agility needed to confront the unknown. As one respondent said, "We didn't just wait for a crisis to teach us—we trained like it was already happening."

The most effective training programs mimic the intensity of real crises. Immersive simulations—featuring time pressure, sensory overload, and decision-making confusion—evoke authentic responses and compel leaders to face complexity directly. These exercises aren't just about ticking procedural boxes; they focus on developing judgment under stress. Leaders learn to prioritize, communicate, and adapt in environments that feel real enough to matter.

But simulation alone isn't enough. Structured reflection is what turns experience into insight. After-action reviews help teams identify blind spots, challenge assumptions, and refine their decision-making skills. Leaders review what went well, what went wrong, and why, creating a feedback loop that boosts future performance.

Cross training also plays a crucial role. By rotating through various roles and scenarios, leaders broaden their mental models and gain a wider understanding of how different functions work under pressure. This exposure encourages adaptive thinking and helps leaders collaborate across silos when the stakes are high.

Scenario diversity is just as important. Respondents emphasized the importance of training for a wide range of challenges—from cyberattacks to natural disasters, supply chain disruptions to reputational threats. This variety ensures that leaders aren't just prepared for the last crisis; they're ready for the next, no matter what form it takes.

This cycle—preparation, application, reflection—turns training into true transformation. Leaders don't just learn what to do, they practice how to think, decide, and lead under pressure. One respondent captured it perfectly: "The drills didn't just teach us procedures—they taught us how to lead."

The Experience Trap

Experience is undoubtedly powerful. It builds confidence, sharpens instincts, and provides leaders with valuable insight to rely on during crises. However, as several respondents warned, experience can also be a drawback, especially when it leads to overconfidence. Leaders who depend too much on past successes may fall into what many call the "experience trap": the belief that what worked before will work again, even if circumstances have changed.

One respondent vividly illustrated this: "He kept using the same playbook—even when the game had changed." In fast-paced, high-stakes environments, relying too rigidly on past strategies can cause mistakes, missed cues, and ineffective actions. The traits that once contributed to a leader's success can become blind spots if they are not balanced with reflection and adaptability.

Effective leaders avoid this trap by questioning their own

assumptions. They consider whether familiar solutions are still relevant, and they stay open to the idea that new situations require new strategies. They remain curious—consistently seeking new information, different viewpoints, and emerging best practices. Their confidence is not fixed; it grows and adapts with the changing landscape.

Adaptability is crucial. Leaders must recognize when the environment calls for a change in strategy, tone, or execution. They should be willing to rewrite the playbook, even if it means letting go of methods that once seemed reliable. This doesn't mean discarding experience — it means using it wisely, with discernment and humility.

True mastery involves knowing when to rely on experience and when to move beyond it. It's about respecting past lessons while staying open to new ones. As one respondent said, "The best leaders didn't just rely on what they knew—they kept learning, even in the middle of the storm." That mindset—focused on growth rather than ego—is what keeps leadership relevant, responsive, and resilient.

Stress Inoculation – Building Resilience

Experience not only builds skill—it also fosters resilience. In high-stakes settings, the ability to stay calm, think clearly, and make smart decisions under pressure isn't automatic; it's a skill that must be cultivated. Respondents explained how repeated exposure to stressful situations helps leaders distinguish important information from distractions, maintain high decision quality, and stay steady even when emotions run high. This developmental process—known as stress inoculation—works much like a vaccine. Controlled adversity, whether through intense training or real-world challenges, enhances a leader's capacity to perform under stress.

Over time, leaders exposed to increasing levels of stress begin to develop essential traits of effective crisis leadership. They gain emotional control, remain calm when others panic, and project a sense of stability that grounds their team. They improve cognitive clarity, focus, and the ability to process accurate information despite chaos, confusion, or incomplete data. They also enhance priority management, learning to focus on what matters most even when everything feels urgent. Additionally, they build decision-making stamina, maintaining sound judgment under prolonged stress without burning out or freezing up.

One respondent summarized this transformation: "He didn't just survive the pressure—he made decisions that moved us forward." Another said, "She had a way of slowing things down mentally, even when everything around us was speeding up." These leaders didn't just endure turbulence—they led through it.

Simulations with layered complexity, especially when combined with structured reflection, can accelerate growth. By immersing leaders in realistic, time-sensitive scenarios and guiding them through thoughtful debriefs, organizations help develop the psychological and physiological readiness needed for volatile conditions. Leaders learn to control their responses, recalibrate their focus, and keep their judgment, empathy, and mission intact—even when stakes are high.

Stress inoculation doesn't eliminate pressure—it prepares leaders to thrive in it. And during a crisis, that resilience is contagious. Teams look to leaders who stay calm, and that stability becomes a grounding force throughout the entire response effort.

Credibility and Trust – The Currency of Experience

Experience doesn't just shape a leader's performance; it also builds their credibility. To their teams, experienced leaders wield a different kind of influence. Their decisions are grounded in real-life experience rather than just theory. This foundation fosters trust, encourages teamwork, and reduces the second-guessing that can paralyze teams during challenging moments. Respondents consistently noted that trust in a leader was mainly based on demonstrated readiness. It wasn't about charisma or authority—it was about composure and competence. One team member said, "He didn't have to raise his voice—we trusted him because he'd been there before." Another recalled, "She earned our confidence by staying calm and making sense when everything else felt chaotic." These leaders didn't just speak about leadership—they demonstrated it when it mattered most. Their credibility came not from titles or authority, but from their actions. They remained calm and capable even under high pressure. They fostered psychological safety by modeling steadiness, enabling their teams to focus, speak up, and perform without fear. Their authority wasn't imposed—it was earned. Teams followed them not out of obligation, but because they believed in them. In a crisis, trust acts as a force multiplier. When teams believe in their leader, they move faster, coordinate more easily, and recover more quickly. Trust reduces friction, enhances coordination, and sustains morale. As one respondent said, "We didn't just follow orders—we followed someone we believed in." That belief doesn't develop overnight. It's built through consistent actions, tested under pressure, and strengthened with each decision made in the crucible of crisis. Experience provides leaders with that foundation, and trust is the structure that rises from it.

Conclusion: Experience Is Indispensable

Experience—whether acquired in the field or developed through simulation—is a vital advantage in crisis leadership. It shapes judgment, hones instincts, and builds the confidence needed to lead amid volatility. However, experience alone does not ensure effectiveness. To truly make an impact, it must be combined with reflection, humility, and a commitment to continuous learning. Leaders who excel during crises don't just accumulate moments—they find meaning in them. They reevaluate decisions, challenge assumptions, and refine their approach with each new challenge.

As one respondent stated: "Prior experience transforms leadership from theory into trust—built through action, improved through reflection, and shown when the stakes are highest."

The most effective leaders don't rest on past achievements; they build upon them. They train intentionally, reflect diligently, and adapt quickly. They see every challenge as preparation for the next, and every setback as a lesson in resilience. Their readiness isn't reactive; it's deliberate. When the moment arrives, they are prepared—not just to respond but to lead with clarity, confidence, and credibility.

Experience and readiness lay the foundation, but leadership in crisis also demands clear direction. Without a strong sense of purpose, even the most skilled teams can lose their way. The next chapter explores Goal Orientation: how effective leaders stay focused on results, align teams around common goals, and ensure that every action supports a larger mission. In high-stakes environments, having clarity of destination is just as crucial as clarity of response.

CHAPTER 10

GOAL ORIENTATION

In crisis leadership, goal orientation isn't optional, it's essential. Respondents consistently identified leaders who set clear short- and long-term goals as more capable of navigating complexity, uncertainty, and pressure. These leaders assign tasks with clarity, define measurable objectives, and develop actionable strategies—even when plans must evolve.

A goal-orientation mindset in a VUCA situation means staying relentlessly focused on the few outcomes that matter most, even as conditions shift, information changes, and plans must be rewritten on the fly. It is essential because clear goals anchor decision-making, keep teams aligned, and prevent leaders from being consumed by noise, confusion, and constant tactical firefighting.

Leading with Purpose in Crisis

In the chaos of a crisis, it's easy to lose sight of the goal. Urgency pulls attention in all directions, and without a clear sense of purpose, even well-meaning efforts can scatter. Goal-driven leaders resist that drift. They anchor their teams to key outcomes, ensuring every action supports a bigger mission.

These leaders don't just react directly. They turn complexity into clarity, align efforts with their intentions, and keep momentum connected to meaning. Respondents consistently emphasized that the most effective leaders are those who hold the mission at the forefront. One shared, "She never lost sight of the objective, even when everything else was shifting." Another remembered, "He kept us focused on what mattered. No matter how noisy it got, the goal stayed clear."

These leaders are remembered not just for their decisiveness but for their unwavering sense of direction and larger purpose. Their clarity of purpose, confidence, and unity. Meetings, decisions, and actions were tied to outcomes—not just routine bureaucracy or reactive moves. One team member noted, "Every time we hit a wall, she reminded us of why we were doing this. That kept us going." Another added, "He didn't just give instructions—he gave us a reason to care."

Goal-driven leaders create alignments where fragmentation usually happens. They ensure that teams aren't just busy— they're effective. Their skill in linking daily actions to strategic results turns activity into impact. In high-pressure situations, this trait becomes a steady force. It keeps teams grounded, focused, and moving forward—even when conditions are unstable. Ultimately, these leaders are remembered as focused, purposeful, and results oriented. They don't just lead during a crisis—they lead toward something. And in doing so, they turn uncertainty into progress.

Focus That Cuts Through Chaos

In the chaotic swirl of crisis, goal-focused leaders stand out for their ability to cut through the noise. They simplify complexity, avoid distractions, and pivot when necessary—without losing sight of the mission. Their clarity functions as a compass, guiding teams through uncertainty with purpose and precision. Respondents consistently described these leaders as the ones who "didn't chase shiny objects," "cut through red tape," and "had a gift for making the impossible feel manageable."

These leaders don't confuse activity with progress. They resist the urge to react to every disruption or chase after every new idea. Instead, they evaluate decisions through a clear lens of purpose. One team member recalled, "She had a way of asking, 'Does this serve the mission?'—and if it didn't, we moved on." Another noted, "He didn't just keep us busy—he kept us aligned."

Goal-oriented leaders see plans as tools rather than limits. They understand that strategy must be adaptable, especially in unpredictable environments. When conditions change, they adjust—but always stay focused on the core purpose. Their disciplined flexibility builds trust, unity, and real success. Teams feel confident to improvise, knowing the goal remains clear.

Respondents admired how these leaders-maintained focus under pressure. One shared, "She could take a dozen competing priorities and boil them down to one clear path." Another said, "He didn't just lead meetings—he led momentum. Every conversation moved us closer to the goal."

Even when everything else feels uncertain, goal-oriented leaders offer steady guidance. They don't just keep teams moving; they ensure they're heading in the right direction. Their presence brings clarity amidst chaos, and their leadership transforms scattered efforts into strategic impact.

Strategic agility and creative problem-solving

Goal-oriented leaders don't just follow plans—they make things happen. Respondents described them as leaders who "saw opportunities others missed," "weren't afraid to take calculated risks," and "knew how to get results."

These leaders combine discipline with innovation. They respect procedures but are not controlled by them. When obstacles arise, they find ways around, over, or through—always guided by a clear sense of mission. Their leadership fosters a culture where adaptability is valued, initiative is supported, and results come from thoughtful action. They lead with clarity, courage, and creativity—fueling innovation and resilience through deliberate effort.

Why Goal Orientation Matters

In a crisis, goals go beyond simple targets—they act as lifelines. When pressure mounts and uncertainty clouds judgment, goal-focused leaders provide the clarity teams need to stay grounded. Respondents highlighted that these leaders offer direction when chaos overwhelms, motivation when morale drops, and alignment when teams risk drifting apart. Their focus becomes a stabilizing force, helping others navigate complexity without losing sight of what truly matters.

Goal orientation allows leaders to block out distractions and concentrate efforts on high-impact results. It transforms scattered activities into strategic movements. These leaders inspire their teams by establishing a shared purpose—reminding everyone not just of what they are doing but why it matters. They turn strategy into coordinated action, making sure roles, resources, and decisions align with key objectives. They also foster accountability—not through strict supervision, but by tracking progress and intentionally adjusting plans.

Respondents consistently described goal-oriented leaders as those who not only managed tasks but also guided purpose. One said, "She turned setbacks into momentum. Every challenge became a reason to refocus." Another noted, "He helped us move forward with clarity, even when everything else felt uncertain." These leaders didn't just keep teams busy—they kept them purposeful.

From Plans to Purpose

Goal-oriented leadership isn't about simply ticking off a checklist; it's about delivering results. During a crisis, plans often break down. Conditions evolve. Assumptions turn out to be wrong. But the mission remains the same. Effective leaders understand that flexibility is essential, but clear direction is critical. They adapt tactics without losing sight of the goal.

Respondents commended leaders who "kept the mission in focus," "used plans as guides—not scripts," and "responded with intentionality." These leaders didn't confuse process with progress. They recognized that a perfect plan was less important than having a clear purpose. When the playbook no longer fit the moment, they improvised with discipline, grounding every decision in what mattered most.

This capacity to navigate uncertainty while staying on course sets goal-oriented leaders apart. They don't just react; they recalibrate. They don't merely adjust—they realign. In doing so, they help teams advance with confidence, coherence, and conviction.

The Anchor in Chaos

In high-stress environments, goal orientation is more than just a leadership trait—it's the stabilizing force that keeps teams united. Respondents consistently called it the "anchor in chaos," a mindset that blocks out distractions, manages competing demands, and aligns teams across different disciplines, jurisdictions, and operational silos.

When everything feels urgent, goal-oriented leaders help others focus on what's truly important. Their clarity spreads, allowing teams to concentrate, prioritize, and act with purpose. These leaders bring clarity amid confusion. They don't just give orders, they clarify direction. One respondent recalled, "She helped us see through the fog. When everything felt chaotic, her focus gave us something to hold onto." By simplifying complexity into clear priorities, they help teams focus on what matters most. They also generate momentum through micro-wins—small, achievable short-term goals that boost morale and reinforce progress. These tiny victories become emotional fuel, especially when the bigger mission feels distant or overwhelming. As one team member said, "He gave us goals we could reach, and every time we did, it reminded us we were moving forward." Perhaps most importantly, goal-oriented leaders foster unity of effort. They align diverse teams and agencies around shared objectives, creating coherence where fragmentation might otherwise prevail. Their goals become the organizing principle that turns turbulence into coordinated progress. In their presence, teams don't just work, they work together.

Cultivating Goal-Oriented Leadership

Goal orientation is not just a personality trait — it's a skill you can develop. Respondents highlighted that effective leaders foster this mindset through intentional practice, structured reflection, and active engagement with their teams. It's not about strict adherence to plans; it's about adaptable focus, rooted in purpose.

One essential strategy is clarifying the "why." Leaders who define mission-critical outcomes and explain why they matter foster a shared sense of purpose that goes beyond just completing tasks. They help teams understand not only what to do but also why it is important. This clarity boosts motivation and resilience.

Effective leaders also set goals that are specific, measurable, achievable, relevant, and time bound. These SMART goals provide structure without rigidity, enabling teams to monitor progress and adjust as needed. Tiered goals — combining strategic vision with tactical steps — ensure that long-term aims are supported by immediate action. Consistent communication is vital. Goal-oriented leaders emphasize the mission's "North Star" throughout the response, continuously reminding teams of the destination even as conditions change. They adapt with discipline, re-evaluate goals when necessary, but never lose focus. Their flexibility is deliberate, not reactive. Importantly, these leaders include their teams in the process. They co-create milestones, track progress together, and celebrate achievements as a team. This shared ownership increases commitment, improves cohesion, and fosters a culture of purpose-driven performance. In times of crisis, goal orientation is more than just a leadership style — it's a lifeline. When intentionally cultivated, it becomes the force that transforms uncertainty into unity, confusion into clarity, and motion into meaningful progress.

Embedding Goal Orientation in Training

Goal orientation isn't just a concept to be taught; it's a discipline to practice. Respondents highlighted that leadership development must mimic the pressure, ambiguity, and urgency of real crises to foster this mindset. Leaders don't gain clarity of purpose simply by reading about it—they achieve it through experience, reflection, and repetition in environments that reflect the seriousness of actual emergencies. Effective training immerses leaders in fast-paced, unpredictable scenarios that require prioritization and mission-focused action. These simulations challenge participants to make decisions under pressure, filter distractions, and stay focused on outcomes rather than just tasks. One respondent said, "The best exercises didn't just test our procedures—they tested our purpose." Intent-based planning is another key element of goal-oriented development. Leaders learn to communicate desired outcomes instead of micromanaging every step. This approach allows teams to adapt while remaining aligned, promoting initiative without losing coherence. Post-incident reviews reinforce this mindset by assessing decisions based on goal alignment—not just procedural compliance. Leaders reflect not only on what was done, but why it was important.

Mentorship also plays a crucial role. Pairing emerging leaders with experienced mentors during real-world events speeds up learning and embeds goal orientation through lived experience. These mentors model how to lead with intent, improvise with discipline, and stay focused when conditions change.

Cross-training further broadens this view, allowing leaders to see how goals influence decisions across roles, functions, and disciplines. Collectively, these practices help leaders internalize goal orientation as a reflex. They learn to guide teams by purpose, not just process—to lead with clarity, not just urgency.

Conclusion: Leading with Purpose

Goal-oriented leaders do more than just give orders; they provide direction. In moments of crisis, when urgency threatens to scatter attention and complexity clouds judgment, these leaders anchor their teams to meaningful outcomes. They align actions with intent, keep teams focused, and turn chaos into coordinated progress. Their leadership is characterized not only by decisiveness but also by clarity, consistency, and conviction. They ask the essential question: "What are we trying to achieve?" and ensure that every decision, resource, and moment bring the team closer to that goal. Their presence transforms confusion into clarity and movement into momentum. One respondent captured it perfectly: "A goal-oriented leader keeps the horizon in view, steering through chaos with purpose so that every action, however small, moves the team closer to what matters most."

These leaders are remembered not for reacting quickly but for responding wisely. They don't just manage tasks; they guide intent. They help teams prioritize when everything feels urgent and model how to adapt without losing direction.

Their goals become the guiding principle that sustains morale, fosters unity, and drives meaningful results. However, even the clearest goals must be communicated effectively. Purpose without communication is like a compass without a map. The next chapter explores Communication and Listening—how leaders share information, adapt messages, listen with empathy, and build trust through every word and action. Because in a crisis, what leaders say—and how they say it—can either reinforce clarity or deepen confusion. When stakes are high, communication becomes not just a skill but a lifeline.

CHAPTER 11

COMMUNICATION AND LISTENING

In high-pressure environments, communication isn't just a skill—it's a lifeline. Respondents consistently identified effective communication as a defining trait of successful leaders. These leaders don't just transmit information; they create understanding, foster trust, and guide action through clarity, empathy, and presence.

Most leaders instinctively think of "good communication" as sending clear messages: explaining decisions, giving updates, and issuing instructions. That matters—but in crisis it is only half the job. Equally critical is the leader's presence as an open, attentive receiver: listening actively, asking sharp, honest questions, and genuinely processing others' concerns, questions, and expertise. When leaders stay receptive, curious, and inquiry-driven instead of defensive, they create a climate where people feel safe to speak up, surface bad news early, and challenge assumptions—exactly the kind of communication culture that keeps organizations safer and smarter under pressure.

Building Trust, Clarity, and Connection

In a crisis, communication is more than just a tool—it's a lifeline.

It's not only about conveying information or issuing clear instructions. True leadership communication is relational, adaptive, and deeply human. It influences how teams interpret events, how they feel about their roles, and how they respond under pressure. The most effective leaders don't just speak clearly; they connect meaningfully.

Respondents highlighted that communication in high-stakes environments involves much more than just words. It comprises tone, timing, presence, and intent. It includes meta-communication, the unspoken signals that shape how messages are received and how relationships are built. It also involves listening—not as a passive activity but as an active show of respect, empathy, and strategic understanding. Additionally, it encourages relationship-building interactions, the ongoing effort to earn trust, foster psychological safety, and create space for honest dialogue. One respondent said: "The best leaders didn't just tell us what to do, they communicated in a way that made us feel heard, even when they had to move fast." Another shared, "Her tone mattered as much as her message. We trusted her because she spoke with care, not just clarity."

In this chapter, we explore how communication acts as a leadership multiplier—strengthening purpose, enhancing cohesion, and building trust during uncertain times. We will examine how effective leaders customize their messages to different audiences, listen intentionally, and use every word and gesture to reinforce mission, values, and connection. Because in a crisis, communication isn't just about what leaders say, it's about how they lead.

Clarity, Connection, and Confidence

Across numerous survey responses, focus groups, and one-on-one interviews, respondents highlighted communication as a key factor in a leader's success. It wasn't just about giving instructions; it was about creating clarity, building trust, and maintaining momentum. The leaders who stood out were those who "made things clear," "kept everyone informed," and "turned complexity into focus." Their messages were concise, purposeful, and easy to understand. They didn't rely on jargon or hide behind vague generalities; they communicated in ways that made people feel informed, empowered, and aligned.

These leaders established a routine of regular updates, which became a stabilizing force in unpredictable environments. One respondent shared, "Even when the situation kept changing, we never felt lost. She kept us in the loop, and that made all the difference." Another noted, "He didn't just communicate—he created a rhythm. We knew when to expect updates, and that gave us confidence to act." This predictability reduced anxiety and helped teams stay focused, even when external conditions were chaotic.

Importantly, no one operated in an information vacuum. Effective communicators made sure everyone understood what was happening, why it mattered, and how their role contributed to the mission. They didn't just broadcast information—they connected. Their communication fostered a sense of belonging, purpose, and shared responsibility. One team member reflected, "She made us feel like we were part of something bigger. Her words reminded us that our work mattered."

This kind of communication also builds relational trust. Leaders who communicated openly and consistently were seen as credible, approachable, and dependable. They didn't just talk; they listened. They created space for questions, acknowledged uncertainty, and responded with empathy. As one respondent said, "He didn't pretend to have all the answers—but he made sure we were never in the dark."

In a crisis, communication transcends mere skills—it becomes the defining hallmark of leadership. It shapes how teams interpret chaos, trust their leaders, and perform under pressure. Done right, it transforms raw information into unbreakable alignment and alignment into decisive action.

Two-Way Dialogue and the Listening Orientation

Effective crisis leaders don't just speak; they connect. Their communication style is rooted in genuine engagement, not a one-way monologue. In high-stakes moments, when time is limited and emotions run high, these leaders remain approachable, authentic, and easy to talk to. Respondents often described them as individuals who made others feel heard, even under pressure. Their empathy wasn't just for show — it was evident in how they acknowledged concerns, invited input, and treated questions as opportunities for dialogue rather than interruptions to their plans.

This wasn't about being soft — it was about being present. These leaders understood that communication is a two-way street, and listening is its most critical lane. They paid full attention, suspended judgment, and asked clarifying questions to ensure understanding. They didn't merely give orders from afar; they actively sought frontline perspectives, recognizing that insight often comes from those closest to the action. One respondent recalled a leader who, amid a chaotic emergency response, paused to ask, "What are we missing?" That simple question unlocked critical feedback that shifted the team's strategy and improved outcomes.

This type of listening — where leaders genuinely want to hear rather than just be heard — fosters psychological safety. It shows respect, builds trust, and encourages open dialogue. When people feel genuinely listened to, they contribute more freely, collaborate more effectively, and stay engaged even when the way forward isn't clear. Listening becomes a stabilizing force, especially when other systems are strained.

In a crisis, listening isn't passive; it's an act of leadership. It involves paying attention to both spoken words and unspoken signals: body language, emotional cues, and the energy in the room. Leaders who listen deeply exhibit humility and curiosity. They demonstrate that they value others' experiences and perspectives, even when those views challenge their own assumptions. They don't just accept dissent — they embrace it as a source of insight.

This approach to dialogue fosters a culture where people feel safe to speak up, share concerns, and contribute ideas. It replaces defensiveness with curiosity and transforms uncertainty into shared understanding. In high-stakes environments, that shift can be the difference between division and unity, confusion and clarity. Over time, in leadership, it's what separates compliance from genuine commitment.

Intellectual Humility

One of the most remarkable traits of effective crisis leaders is their ability to ask the right questions at the right moments. When others default to giving directives or making declarations, these leaders choose to inquire instead. Respondents often recalled leaders who "asked the questions no one else thought to ask"—not to assert control, but to spark insight. Their questions weren't meant to showcase authority; they aimed to clarify complexity, reveal hidden risks, and harness collective wisdom. These leaders didn't rely solely on statements to guide their teams. They used inquiry as a tool for clarity, collaboration, and growth. Their questions were intentional—not rhetorical or performative. They challenged assumptions, uncovered blind spots, and encouraged deeper thinking. In doing so, they demonstrated intellectual humility: a willingness to admit what they didn't know and a curiosity about others' perspectives. This attitude didn't weaken their credibility; it strengthened it. It showed that they saw leadership as a shared effort, where good decisions often come from diverse viewpoints and open dialogue. One respondent described a leader who, amid a rapidly unfolding crisis, paused to ask, "What are we missing?" That simple question shifted the room's tone. It prompted reflection, uncovered overlooked details, and ultimately improved the response.

Another team member recalled, "She didn't pretend to have all the answers. She asked questions that made us think harder—and that made us trust her more." By asking insightful questions, these leaders fostered a culture of curiosity. Dialogue replaced defensiveness. Team members felt safe to speak up, share ideas, and reevaluate their own views. The leader's willingness to be challenged promoted accountability and encouraged critical thinking throughout the organization. It wasn't just about collecting input, it was about developing a mindset where learning mattered more than ego, and insight mattered more than certainty. In high-stakes settings, this kind of questioning becomes more than just a communication technique, it becomes a leadership approach. It indicates that the leader is not only directing actions but also actively shaping understanding. It encourages others to participate, turning passive recipients into engaged contributors. It changes command into collaboration. Ultimately, strategic questioning demonstrates wisdom, not weakness. It shows a leader's ability to handle ambiguity with curiosity and to lead with both confidence and humility. In crisis situations—where conditions change quickly, information is often incomplete, and decisions are critical—that mindset can be crucial.

Strategic Questioning

In high-stakes environments, stakeholder tensions are inevitable. Competing priorities, limited resources, and divergent perspectives can cause friction even among well-intentioned teams. The most effective crisis leaders don't suppress these tensions, they engage them. And they do so not by asserting authority but by asking the right questions. Respondents described leaders who used inquiry as a bridge across divides. When departments clashed or external partners disagreed, these leaders didn't rush to judgment or impose top-down solutions. Instead, they asked questions that reframed the conflict and encouraged collaboration. One respondent recalled a leader who, during a tense interagency coordination meeting, simply asked, "What does success look like for each of us?" That question shifted the tone from defensiveness to shared purpose. It allowed stakeholders to express their goals and discover areas of alignment that had previously been hidden by urgency and emotion.

Strategic questioning also helped leaders identify constraints and adjust plans in real time. In quickly changing situations, assumptions often break down and strategies must evolve. Leaders who asked, "What's changed since our last decision?" or "What are we not seeing yet?" created space for reflection and flexibility. These questions weren't just rhetorical; they were catalysts. They encouraged teams to reevaluate, reframe, and respond more accurately. Importantly, this approach demonstrated intellectual humility. Leaders who asked questions showed they didn't have all the answers—and didn't need to. They valued insight over ego and welcomed dissent as a means of gaining clarity. One team member shared, "She didn't just ask for updates—she asked for challenges. She wanted to know what wasn't working, and that made us trust her more." This kind of inquiry changed how stakeholders interact. Instead of reinforcing silos, it encouraged shared ownership. Instead of increasing tension, it promoted dialogue. And instead of inflexible execution, it supported an adaptive strategy—where plans evolved based on new information and decisions reflected collective intelligence. In a crisis, strategic questioning is more than just a communication skill; it's a leadership posture. It transforms conflict into cooperation, uncertainty into understanding, and complexity into coordinated action. In the hands of a capable leader, a well-placed question can achieve what no directive ever could: unlocking the group's wisdom and advancing the mission.

Adaptability and Audience Awareness

One of the most consistently admired traits of effective crisis leaders is their ability to tailor their communication style to different audiences. Respondents repeatedly described these leaders as people who "knew how to talk to anyone"—whether briefing senior executives in a boardroom, coordinating logistics with field responders, or calming a worried public during a press conference. They didn't rely on a one-size-fits-all approach. Instead, they adjusted their tone, vocabulary, and delivery with skill, empathy, and strategic purpose.

This adaptability wasn't about performance—it was about connection. These leaders recognized that different audiences have distinct needs and tailored their messages accordingly. For example, a technical team might require detailed data and operational specifics, while a community group might need reassurance, clarity, and emotional support. Instead of expecting others to conform to their style, these leaders met people where they were. They simplified complex information into accessible language, used stories to communicate purpose, and highlighted shared goals to foster unity among diverse groups.

Most importantly, they did all this without losing authenticity. Their messages remained genuine and sincere, even as they changed formats and phrasing. Respondents noted that these leaders didn't "code-switch" to manipulate—they adapted to connect. Their ability to be flexible while staying true to their values helped them bridge divides—between departments, disciplines, and personalities. One team member recalled, "She could speak to engineers in the morning and community volunteers in the afternoon—and both felt like she understood them."

This skill helped resolve misunderstandings, build consensus, and motivate action. It wasn't just about being articulate; it was about being attuned. These leaders listened before they spoke, gauged the emotional temperature of the room, and chose words that resonated. They understood that communication isn't just about transmitting messages; it's about ensuring they are received. In crises, where confusion and fragmentation are common, this kind of audience awareness becomes a strategic advantage.

It ensures that messages land with clarity and impact, regardless of who's listening. It enables leaders to unify teams, ease tensions, and gather support across sectors. It also emphasizes the leader's role not just as a messenger but as a unifier—someone who brings people together through thoughtful, intentional communication. In environments where every word matters, adaptability becomes a form of leadership intelligence—and audience awareness becomes a bridge to trust.

Empathy, Calm, and Transparency

During a crisis, communication must do more than just relay facts; it needs to reach both the mind and the heart. The most effective leaders understand that in high-pressure situations, people aren't only looking for information—they want reassurance, clarity, and connection. During these times, empathy becomes the bridge between urgency and understanding, turning communication from a simple task into a profound human act of leadership.

Respondents described these leaders as emotionally aware and grounded. They didn't shy away from the emotional weight of the moment. Instead, they recognized fear, fatigue, and frustration without diminishing or dismissing them. Their words validated others' lived experiences, offering comfort without false promises. One respondent recalled, "He didn't sugarcoat anything, but he made us feel like we could get through it together." These leaders conveyed hope and purpose not through slogans or spin, but through a shared sense of humanity and mission.

This kind of empathetic communication builds psychological safety. It shows that the leader recognizes the individuals behind the roles, understands their concerns, and cares about their well-being. As a result, it boosts morale, cohesion, and trust—key elements for team resilience under pressure. When people feel acknowledged and supported, they are more likely to stay engaged, speak up, and keep going through uncertainty. Equally important was the leader's calm presence. In chaotic moments, they avoided escalating tension with reactive language or erratic tone. Instead, they communicated with deliberate composure. Their clarity cut through confusion, and their steadiness helped others find their footing. Whether briefing a team, addressing the public, or managing interagency relationships, they projected confidence without arrogance and urgency without panic. One team member remarked, "Her voice was steady, even when everything else was shaking. That steadiness gave us something to hold onto."

Transparency also became a key trait. These leaders didn't pretend to have all the answers. They were honest about what they knew, open about what they didn't, and clear about the reasons behind their decisions. They shared evolving information without defensiveness and admitted when plans needed to change. This openness didn't weaken their authority—it strengthened it. It gained credibility and built trust, even when outcomes were uncertain or timelines weren't clear. As one respondent said, "He didn't hide the hard stuff. That's why we believed him when he said we'd get through it."

In a crisis, empathy, calm, and transparency are not optional; they are essential. They turn communication from a simple exchange into a meaningful act of leadership. They remind people that they are not alone, that their experiences matter, and that their leaders walk beside them, not above them. And in the toughest moments, that shared sense of humanity becomes the foundation for collective strength.

Supportive Communication and Psychological Safety

In crisis leadership, support isn't just a sentiment—it's a strategy. The most effective leaders understand that psychological safety isn't a luxury reserved for calm environments; it's a necessity for high performance under pressure. When stakes are high and the way forward is unclear, people need more than just guidance—they need to feel safe to speak, ask questions, and admit uncertainty. That safety doesn't happen by chance. It's cultivated through intentional, supportive communication that shows respect, trust, and shared commitment.

Respondents consistently described these leaders as accessible and responsive. They didn't hide behind closed doors or layers of hierarchy. Instead, they remained visible and engaged, walking alongside their teams rather than above them. They recognized contributions, acknowledged effort, and made space for honest dialogue. Their presence conveyed a powerful message: every voice mattered—not just the loudest, most senior, or most confident. One team member recalled, "He made time for everyone. You didn't need a title to be heard."

These leaders encouraged honesty without fear of reprimand. They normalize uncertainty, making it clear that not having all the answers is not a failure; it's a reality of complex, changing situations. By doing so, they reduce the pressure to be perfect and boost the willingness to report issues early, share emerging concerns, and work together on solutions. Their communication style promotes openness rather than defensiveness. One respondent noted, "She didn't punish mistakes—she used them to help us learn faster."

Supportive communication also involves offering emotional and psychological care. These leaders checked in with their teams not just on deliverables but on well-being. They noticed when someone was struggling, showed empathy, and provided resources when needed. This wasn't about being soft—it was about being human. In high-stakes environments, that human touch strengthened, made teams more resilient, and made them more cohesive. It fostered a culture where people felt seen, valued, and supported—not just as professionals, but as individuals.

The climate these leaders established allowed for quicker problem-solving and more precise reporting. People didn't hold back or conceal mistakes—they spoke openly, knowing they would be heard and supported. That transparency, based on trust, became a strong asset in managing uncertainty and responding efficiently under pressure. It transformed reactive teams into proactive ones and turned isolated individuals into cohesive collaborators.

In a crisis, supportive communication isn't just a side note; it's a foundation. It builds trust that drives coordination, safety that promotes innovation, and resilience that helps teams endure through long periods of disruption. When leaders speak with care, listen intentionally, and lead with empathy, they don't just manage crises—they transform them.

Communication Pitfalls to Avoid

Even the most experienced leaders can stumble under pressure. During a crisis, when quick decisions are needed and emotions run high, communication mistakes can have serious consequences. Trust can break down, confusion can spread, and team performance can decline. Participants in this study pointed out several common pitfalls—behaviors that, although often unintentional, consistently reduce leadership effectiveness and strain team relationships. One of the most common issues was over-talking. Leaders, eager to assert control or feel uncomfortable silence, sometimes overwhelmed their teams with a flood of directives. This tendency to dominate the conversation can drown out valuable frontline insights and discourage participation. One respondent noted, "He talked so much we stopped trying to contribute. It felt like there was no room for us." In moments when collaboration is most needed, over-talking can unintentionally silence the very voices that hold critical information. Equally harmful is under-listening. When leaders ignore dissenting voices or dismiss perspectives that challenge their assumptions, they create a disengaged environment. Team members may start to self-censor, withholding concerns or observations that could influence decisions or improve outcomes. This breakdown in dialogue results in blind spots and missed opportunities. As one respondent said, "She didn't hear us until it was too late. We had flagged the issue, but no one followed up." Mixed messaging also became a common concern. Inconsistent or conflicting communication—whether in tone, content, or timing—confuses teams and erodes confidence. When messages change without explanation, people start to question the leader's clarity and trustworthiness. This uncertainty can cause hesitation, misalignment, and a breakdown in coordinated action. One team member said, "We got three different versions of the plan in one day. It made us doubt everything."

Another subtle but powerful disruption is emotional misalignment. Leaders who communicate with flat affect or volatile intensity risk alienating their teams. A lack of emotional resonance can make leaders seem disconnected or indifferent, while excessive emotion can escalate anxiety and undermine confidence in their leadership. The tone of a message often carries more weight than its content. When leaders fail to match their emotional delivery to the situation, they risk sending mixed signals about urgency, empathy, or control.

Withholding information, even unintentionally, fosters speculation and distrust. In a crisis, transparency is crucial. When leaders fail to share what they know—or explain their reasons for certain decisions—they create a vacuum that others will fill with assumptions, often inaccurate or harmful. Respondents stressed that even partial updates, when delivered honestly, are better than silence. One said, "He didn't have all the answers, but he told us what he could. That made us trust him more." Finally, information overload can be just as damaging as silence. Bombarding teams with too much detail, especially during stress, overwhelms cognitive capacity and hinders decision-making. Leaders who fail to prioritize and simplify information risk hiding the critical message in the noise. Effective communicators know how to provide clarity instead of complexity, guiding teams with focused updates that promote action rather than paralysis.

Listening Under Pressure: The Cost of Missed Signals

During my data collection while I was at Illinois State, I spent many Saturday mornings gathering leadership data from SWAT team members—experienced professionals who had led and participated in high-risk operations. These conversations shaped my understanding of leadership in crisis, not through theory but through real experience. One story has stayed with me for decades. It was shared quietly, without bravado, but its lessons were profound. During the hostage situation, the SWAT commander was inside a mobile command vehicle, coordinating tactics while his team handled various tasks. One subordinate was responsible for monitoring the audio feed—whether from a microphone or a live phone call, I can't recall—but what happened next was unforgettable. The hostage taker issued a frightening ultimatum: he would kill the hostage in 30 seconds if his demands weren't met immediately. The subordinate relayed this message to the commander, who was intensely focused on planning the next tactical move. But the urgency of the message didn't register. The commander continued strategizing, seemingly unaware of the time-sensitive threat unfolding in real time. The subordinate repeated the warning. Still, no response. As the seconds ticked down, he had to confront the commander physically—get in his face—to break through the mental fog and make him listen. Only then did the commander realize the seriousness of the situation and quickly change his strategy. The team later saw this moment not as a tactical failure but as a breakdown in communication. The commander wasn't negligent; he was overwhelmed. But during a crisis, listening isn't optional. It's mission critical.

The Leadership Implications

This story emphasizes an important truth: in high-pressure environments, listening becomes a vital skill for survival. It is not passive but active, intentional, and often requires effort. Leaders need to listen attentively, interpret urgency, and respond appropriately. When cognitive load is high and adrenaline is flowing, even critical messages can be missed. That's why listening should be practiced, reinforced, and protected.

In crisis leadership, listening serves multiple functions:

➢ Situational Awareness: It helps leaders detect shifts in threat, urgency, and opportunity.

➢ Team Trust: It signals respect and responsiveness, encouraging subordinates to speak up.

➢ Decision Calibration: It ensures that tactical choices are informed by real-time intelligence.

➢ Emotional Regulation: It allows leaders to absorb stress signals and respond with empathy.

As one SWAT member subsequently said, "The best leaders don't just hear, they listen through the noise. They know when to stop planning and start paying attention."

Listening as a Leadership Discipline

Listening under pressure is not innate; it's a behavioral skill. It requires leaders to manage their own mental capacity, create space for input, and stay open to information that may challenge their current plan. It also means empowering teams to speak up—even forcefully—when something critical is at stake. This story reminds us that leadership isn't just about giving commands—it's also about listening to them. It's about knowing when to pause, when to pivot, and when to let someone else's voice influence the direction. In the chapters ahead, we'll explore how leaders can develop this discipline through training, feedback, and organizational culture. Because in a crisis, the ability to listen can mean the difference between escalation and resolution.

Recognizing these pitfalls is the first step to avoiding them. By understanding the patterns that weaken communication, leaders can make intentional choices to stay grounded, responsive, and clear—even under pressure. In a crisis, every word counts. When communication breaks down, leadership must readjust—not just to be heard, but to earn trust. Listening is not a passive trait, a skill you develop. It requires learning, practice, and continuous refinement. In high-pressure situations, where clarity is brief and outcomes happen quickly, listening becomes a vital behavior. It's not innate; it's a deliberate act. Effective crisis leaders know that listening isn't just about hearing words, it's about interpreting urgency, reading emotional cues, and responding precisely. It demands cognitive bandwidth, emotional control, and behavioral discipline. It must be regarded as a core part of leadership development—not a soft skill, but as a strategic asset. In the chapters ahead, we'll discover how leaders can strengthen this discipline through immersive training, structured feedback, and organizational culture. Because in a crisis, the ability to listen can determine whether a situation escalates or is resolved. It's the key to situational awareness, team cohesion, and ethical decision-making.

The Pitfalls of Poor Listening

Recognizing listening failures is the first step to preventing them. When leaders become distracted, overwhelmed, or overly focused on their own plans, they risk missing critical signals. These failures are not always obvious—but their consequences often are.

> - Missed urgency can delay response.
> - Dismissed input can erode trust.
> - Fragmented communication can fracture teams.

By recognizing patterns that weaken communication—such as

tunnel vision, emotional detachment, or hierarchical filtering—leaders can make intentional choices to stay grounded, responsive, and clear. Listening isn't just about being heard; it's about earning trust through listening. In a crisis, every word matters. As one SWAT team member later reflected on a leader with good listening skills, "He didn't just listen to the facts, he listened to the fear behind them. That's what made his decisions feel human."

Recalibrating Through Listening

When communication breaks down in a crisis, leadership must do more than react—it must recalibrate. This recalibration begins with listening. Not passive hearing, but active, intentional engagement. It requires leaders to pause, absorb, ask clarifying questions, and create space for others to speak. It means recognizing that authority does not guarantee awareness—and that the best leaders remain open to input, especially when the pressure is high.

Listening isn't a sign of hesitation; it's a sign of strength. It shows that a leader is present, attentive, and willing to adapt. It demonstrates humility, responsiveness, and trustworthiness. Plus, it helps build the kind of relational capital teams need to follow—not just because they're told to, but because they truly believe in the person leading them.

One respondent, a fire chief, described a moment during a multi-agency response when a junior officer flagged a critical safety concern. "The incident commander was locked into the plan. But when he stopped and really listened, he realized we were about to send a crew into a compromised structure. That pause saved lives."

Another hospital administrator recalled a tense moment during a mass casualty surge: "We were overloaded. One nurse kept saying we needed to reroute incoming patients. The leader didn't hear it the first time. But when she repeated it with urgency, he stopped, recalibrated, and made the call. That decision changed the course of the whole night." These stories reflect a consistent theme: listening is the key point between misalignment and recovery. It's the moment when leaders shift from executing a plan to adapting it. And it's often the difference between escalation and resolution. Respondents emphasized that recalibrating through listening requires behavioral discipline. One shared, "He had a habit of asking, 'What am I missing?' That question opened the door for honest input." Another noted, "She didn't just listen to the loudest voice—she listened for the quiet ones who saw what others missed." In high-stakes environments, recalibration isn't a luxury; it's vital. It helps leaders absorb new information, adjust their course, and regain clarity. It also demonstrates to the team that their insights matter, their voices are valued, and leadership is a shared responsibility. When leaders recalibrate through listening, they do more than change strategy—they strengthen trust. They show that leadership isn't about being infallible but about being responsive. And they model a presence that steadies teams in a storm. Because in a crisis, the most powerful words a leader can say may be: "Tell me what you see."

Communication as Leadership in Action

During times of crisis, communication isn't just a leadership skill; it's the core of leadership itself. It shows how leaders present themselves, stabilize the environment, and guide people forward when the way isn't clear. Respondents consistently emphasized that the most effective leaders didn't just communicate well; they led through their communication. Every message, every moment of listening, and every tone of voice carried meaning. In their hands, communication became a tool for alignment, reassurance, and progress.

These leaders didn't rely solely on authority. They earned trust by being present—physically, emotionally, and intellectually. They paid close attention not just to what was said, but how it was said. They observed body language, noted emotional cues, and listened not just to reply but to understand. Their attentiveness demonstrated respect. It built psychological safety, allowing others to speak openly, raise concerns, and share ideas without fear of dismissal or retaliation. One respondent shared, "He didn't just hear us—he made us feel heard. That changed everything."

When delivering high-stakes briefings, these leaders were deliberate and precise. They avoided jargon, sidestepped vague generalities, and resisted overcomplicating. Instead, they outlined priorities, explained next steps, and answered questions with calm authority. Their language was grounded and accessible, designed not to impress but to guide. In doing so, they reduced anxiety and fostered clarity—two essential ingredients for effective action under pressure.

Emotional intelligence played a key role in their communication. These leaders had a keen sense of timing and tone. They knew when their team members needed reassurance, when individuals needed encouragement, and when the moment called for firm leadership. They adjusted their messages based on emotional cues, not just operational details. They recognized fear without fueling it, strengthened resilience without downplaying hardship, and helped their teams stay focused and united through tough times.

Inclusive communication was another vital trait. These leaders created space for diverse voices, purposefully seeking input from different roles, levels, and perspectives. They understood that valuable insights often come from the edges of the organization, not just the top. By encouraging broad participation, they fostered shared ownership of the mission and showed humility through their actions. One respondent recalled, "She made it clear that everyone had something to contribute. That made us all more invested."

Most importantly, they built trust through transparency. They didn't pretend to have all the answers or give false reassurances. Instead, they were honest about challenges, open about what was still being developed, and transparent about the reasons behind their decisions. This honesty didn't undermine their authority. It gained them credibility and boosted team cohesion, even amid deep uncertainty. As one team member said, "He told us the truth, even when it was hard to hear. That's why we followed him."

In a crisis, communication isn't just part of leadership at its core. It connects people to purpose, keeps them grounded in reality, and provides the clarity needed to act. Effective leaders don't just give orders; they foster alignment, shared understanding, and unity through their communication. It is through their words—and their listening—that they lead. In doing so, they remind us that leadership isn't only about making decisions; it's about creating meaning.

Communication as a Core Learned Competency

Communication is not an innate gift reserved for natural articulation; it is a skill, refined through study, practice, and reflection. The most effective crisis leaders view communication not as a soft skill but as a core operational competency. They understand that clarity, composure, and connection under pressure are not luck-based traits—they come from intentional development and disciplined rehearsal.

Respondents in this project over the years consistently emphasized that strong communication skills are built through structured learning and deliberate practice. These leaders didn't just "pick it up" naturally—they put in effort to grow. They studied key principles like message prioritization, adapting to their audience, and active listening. They learned to state their intentions clearly, anticipate how their messages would be received, and adjust their tone to match the emotional and operational needs of each situation.

But knowledge alone wasn't enough. Guided practice turned theory into habit. Organizations that emphasized communication created immersive experiences where leaders could apply their skills in high-pressure simulations. In one emergency management training, participants had to brief multiple audiences, media, public, and response teams—with different needs and expectations. Leaders needed to clarify their messages quickly, adjust their tone as required, and stay composed while answering tricky questions in real time. These exercises didn't just test knowledge—they built muscle memory for moments when clarity and calm are most crucial.

The third pillar—feedback-driven refinement—proved essential for sustainable growth. Leaders reviewed video recordings of their briefings, received structured peer feedback, and participated in coaching debriefs. These reflective practices fostered self-awareness and accelerated skill development. Leaders saw firsthand how body language, pacing, and tone affected understanding. They learned to be more intentional, grounded, and practical—not just in what they said, but in how they expressed it.

Research across sectors—from healthcare to aviation to emergency management—supports the importance of communication training. Programs like Crew Resource Management (CRM) and TeamSTEPPS have become standards because they reduce errors, improve coordination, and lead to better outcomes. The evidence is clear: when leaders are trained to communicate under pressure, performance improves. Communication isn't a luxury—it's a critical component of operational success.

For organizations committed to developing crisis leaders, communication training must be viewed as fundamental infrastructure. It's not a one-time workshop or just a checkbox in a leadership program; it's an ongoing cycle of learning, practicing, receiving feedback, and applying lessons in increasingly complex situations. Over time, these cycles develop leaders who can command a room, connect authentically, and rally teams when it matters most.

Embedding Communication in Leadership Development

If communication is the lifeblood of effective leadership, then it must be central to leadership development—not merely an optional addition. The most successful organizations recognize this and intentionally include communication training in their leadership pipelines, especially for those preparing to lead in high-stakes environments.

Respondents in this project emphasized that communication excellence does not happen naturally. Instead, it is developed through immersive, repeated experiences that mirror the complexity and pressure of actual crises. Leaders need opportunities to practice, reflect, and improve their communication skills in environments that challenge their adaptability, emotional intelligence, and clarity under stress.

High-impact programs use scenario-based simulations that require leaders to brief diverse audiences—from internal teams to external stakeholders with different concerns and expectations. These exercises push participants to adapt tone, prioritize messages, and respond to evolving situations in real time. For example, a simulated chemical spill might require a leader to calm a panicked community, then work with technical experts, and finally update elected officials—all within a tight timeframe and with shifting facts. These layered challenges build agility and improve strategic awareness.

To reinforce learning, organizations include listening labs where leaders practice reflective responses, empathy coaching to boost emotional attunement, and structured feedback sessions using PIR (Post-Incident Review) or AAR (After-Action Review) formats. These tools help leaders internalize lessons, identify blind spots, and develop habits that lead to confident, compassionate communication under pressure. The goal isn't perfection—it's progress. And when sustained, progress becomes transformation.

Over time, these experiences shape leaders who can command a room with confidence, connect genuinely during tense moments, and unite teams around a shared purpose. They become communicators who lead not just with words but with presence, empathy, and trust. In a crisis, that kind of leadership doesn't just inform — it inspires.

Conclusion: Communication as a Lifeline

In times of crisis, communication is not just a leadership skill—it is the lifeline that connects people to purpose, clarity, and each other. It is through communication that leaders convey strategy, foster collaboration, and build resilience. When the stakes are high and the path ahead is uncertain, the ability to speak clearly, listen deeply, and respond empathetically becomes the leader's most vital tool.

Throughout this chapter, we've seen that effective communicators do more than transmit information—they create understanding. They foster trust, align efforts, and guide teams through complexity with presence and precision. Their words carry weight not because they are loud or frequent, but because they are intentional, grounded, and human. They know that tone shapes perception, that listening builds safety, and that clarity is a form of care.

The leaders who stand out in crisis are those who treat communication as a craft. They invest in their growth, practice under pressure, and seek feedback to refine their skills. They understand that communication is not a one-time activity, it is a continuous discipline. And in moments of fear and fragmentation, their voice becomes the anchor that stabilizes the team, the signal that cuts through noise, and the bridge that turns confusion into clarity, fear into trust, and isolated effort into unified action. But even the clearest message depends on knowing what's truly happening. Communication and listening are inseparable from awareness. A leader's ability to connect meaningfully is only as strong as their ability to perceive the moment accurately. What's unfolding? What's shifting? What's being said—and what's being left unsaid?

The next chapter explores the leadership trait of Situational Awareness, the ability to perceive, interpret, and respond to unfolding dynamics with clarity, agility, and informed judgment. We'll examine how leaders read the room, scan the horizon, and make sense of complexity in real time. Because in crisis, awareness is not just a cognitive skill; it's a strategic imperative. And when paired with communication, it becomes the foundation for wise, adaptive leadership.

CHAPTER 12

SITUATIONAL AWARENESS

I n crisis leadership, clarity is not a luxury—it's a necessity. The ability to perceive what's happening, interpret unfolding dynamics, and anticipate what comes next is what separates reactive leaders from responsive ones. This capacity is known as situational awareness, and respondents consistently identified it as one of the most vital competencies for leading effectively under pressure.

Situational awareness is the leader's real-time ability to perceive unfolding events, understand their implications, and anticipate how they will evolve amid incomplete or conflicting information. In crises, it is vital because it enables proactive decisions, prevents surprises from escalating, and keeps teams one step ahead of the chaos rather than reacting to it.

Perceiving, Interpreting, and Responding with Precision

In a crisis, leaders constantly navigate an ever-changing landscape. Conditions shift, information updates, and decisions become more urgent. In this environment, situational awareness is not just a helpful trait; it becomes an essential skill. It's the leader's ability to perceive what's happening, interpret its significance, and respond with clarity and speed. Without it, even the best strategies can fail. With it, leaders gain the insight needed to act decisively and adapt effectively.

Situational awareness goes beyond just observing. It involves combining multiple inputs—such as environmental cues, team dynamics, operational data, and emotional undercurrents—into a clear understanding of the situation. It's the difference between simply reacting and honestly responding, between being caught off guard and being prepared. The most effective crisis leaders don't just see what's directly in front of them; they sense what's developing, anticipate what's coming next, and adapt their approach accordingly.

Respondents in this study described these leaders as "tuned in," "always scanning," and "able to read the room and the horizon at the same time." They noticed what others missed — not because they had more information, but because they paid better attention. They tracked subtle shifts in tone, tempo, and tension. They asked, "What's changing?" and "What does this mean?" — not just once, but continuously.

This chapter examines situational awareness as a key leadership trait: a combination of knowledge, skills, and attitudes (KSAs) that enable leaders to stay grounded while remaining flexible in their responses. We'll explore how leaders develop this awareness, how they apply it to make decisions, and how it enhances other leadership skills—from communication and coordination to prioritization and critical thinking.

Because in a crisis, awareness isn't passive. It's not just about seeing, it's about understanding. And the leaders who master it don't just survive the moment—they shape it.

Situational awareness is more than just noticing—it's about understanding. It involves scanning the environment, gathering input from diverse sources, and synthesizing that information into a clear picture of reality. Effective leaders don't rely solely on instinct or experience; they actively seek out data, listen to frontline perspectives, and stay open to new insights, even when those insights challenge their assumptions.

Respondents described leaders with strong situational awareness as "always one step ahead," "able to see the whole field," and "quick to adjust when things changed." These leaders didn't just react to events—they anticipated them. They recognized patterns, identified emerging risks, and made decisions based on a dynamic understanding of context. Their awareness kept them grounded as they navigated uncertainty, and it gave their teams confidence that someone was truly paying attention. In moments of volatility, the ability to see clearly is not just helpful, it's transformative.

The Three Levels of Situational Awareness

Situational awareness isn't just a single moment of insight; it's a layered process of perceiving, interpreting, and anticipating. In high-stakes environments, leaders need to do more than just observe what's happening; they must understand it and predict what could happen next. This process occurs across three levels: perception, comprehension, and projection. Together, these form the foundation of adaptive leadership in crisis.

> ➢ **Level One: Perception**

At its core, situational awareness starts with perception—the ability to recognize and interpret essential cues in the environment. This includes physical details (such as weather conditions, resource availability, or personnel movements), emotional signals (like stress, fatigue, or morale), and operational indicators (such as timelines, disruptions, or emerging threats). Effective leaders are attuned to both obvious and subtle signs. They notice what others overlook, not because they have more data, but because they pay closer attention. One respondent described a leader who "could walk into a room and immediately sense what wasn't being said." That kind of perceptual sharpness is the first step toward informed action.

> ➢ **Level Two: Comprehension**

Perception alone is insufficient without comprehension—the

ability to interpret what those cues mean within the context. This step involves combining various signals into a clear understanding of the situation. Leaders must ask: What's happening? Why is it happening? What does it mean for our mission? Comprehension requires pattern recognition, contextual knowledge, and emotional intelligence. It's where leaders connect the dots, recognize risks, and grasp the implications of unfolding events. In a crisis, comprehension helps leaders distinguish between noise and signal, urgency and importance.

> ➤ **Level Three: Projection**

The highest level of situational awareness is projection—the ability to anticipate future states based on current understanding. Leaders must look ahead and ask: What's likely to happen next? How will this evolve? What decisions will position us well for what's coming? Projection is not prediction—it's informed foresight. It helps leaders stay ahead of the curve, prepare contingency plans, and guide teams proactively rather than reactively. Respondents praised leaders who "always seemed two steps ahead," not because they had perfect information, but because they cultivated the habit of thinking forward.

Together, these three levels form a dynamic cycle. Perception influences comprehension, comprehension facilitates projection, and projection enhances future perception. Leaders who grasp this cycle are better equipped to handle ambiguity, address complexity, and lead with clarity during crises. They don't just react to what is visible; they respond to what is developing. In doing so, they transform situational awareness from passive observation into a strategic advantage.

Anticipation and Readiness to Act

Situational awareness starts with perception, but it doesn't stop there. Effective leaders not only observe their surroundings; they also analyze these cues and anticipate what might happen next. This layered process—seeing, understanding, and predicting—enables them to stay ahead of unfolding events rather than being caught off guard. In a crisis, when time is limited and stakes are high, anticipation can be the key difference between being prepared and being reactive.

Respondents described outstanding leaders as those who were "always scanning the horizon," "quick to spot shifts," and "able to connect the dots before others even noticed a pattern." These leaders didn't rely solely on instinct. They developed a disciplined approach to gathering information, drawing insights from on-the-ground team members, technical experts, external partners, and even informal observations. They combined these inputs into a clear understanding of the situation by asking insightful questions, challenging assumptions, and staying open to new information, even when it disrupted their initial plans.

This mindset requires both humility and discipline. Leaders must resist the urge to jump to conclusions or cling to outdated mental models just because they once worked. Instead, they adopt a curious mindset, viewing every new development as a data point to analyze. They realize that in a crisis, yesterday's facts may no longer be relevant—and that clarity is not a fixed goal, but a moving target that demands ongoing learning and adjustment.

Anticipation is the final and most strategic layer of situational awareness. Leaders with this skill don't just respond to what's happening; they think ahead. They assess second- and third-order effects, predict how stakeholders might react, and develop contingency plans that offer flexibility without losing sight of the goal. This future-oriented mindset enables them to guide their teams with confidence, even when the situation is uncertain and the timeline is tight. One respondent recalled a leader who, "always had a Plan B—and a Plan C—before anyone else realized Plan A might fail."

In high-pressure environments, perception without interpretation is just noise. Interpretation without anticipation causes delays. But when all three are present—when leaders see clearly, think critically, and act proactively—they create the conditions for effective, adaptable leadership. They don't just navigate the crisis—they shape its course. In doing so, they give their teams both direction and a sense of preparedness.

Building Anticipation Skills

Anticipation isn't guesswork; it's disciplined practice. The most effective crisis leaders don't wait for uncertainty to catch them by surprise; they actively prepare for it. They build anticipation through structured exercises that challenge assumptions, expose vulnerabilities, and expand their thinking beyond the immediate. Key tools in this forward-looking approach include red teaming, pre-event reviews, and horizon scanning.

Red teaming involves intentionally adopting an adversarial or alternative perspective to evaluate plans, decisions, and assumptions. Leaders assign a specific group—or empower their teams—to act as challengers. The goal isn't to undermine the strategy but to strengthen it. By simulating dissent, uncovering blind spots, and stress-testing decisions, red teaming helps leaders anticipate potential failure points, stakeholder resistance, or external factors that could disrupt their plans. One respondent described a leader who "always asked someone to argue the opposite—just to make sure we weren't missing something." That habit of constructive challenge fosters resilience and agility.

Pre-event reviews offer a future-focused outlook. Unlike After-Action Reviews, which analyze failures after they happen, pre-event analysis asks teams to assume that a plan has already failed—and then examine why it might have or could have failed. This approach shifts the mindset from optimism to realism, encouraging teams to face uncomfortable possibilities before they occur. Leaders who run pre-reviews show humility and strategic foresight. They demonstrate that preparation involves planning for potential problems, not just hoping everything goes smoothly. As one respondent said, "She made us imagine the worst-case scenario—not to scare us, but to prepare us."

Horizon scanning broadens the outlook. It systematically observes emerging trends, signals, and changes across sectors, regions, and disciplines. Leaders who scan the horizon don't just react to immediate threats; they predict long-term outcomes. They look for weak signals that could become major disruptors, monitor policy changes, technological advances, and social shifts that might transform the environment. This strategic curiosity helps them position their teams ahead of the curve rather than fall behind.

Together, these practices foster a proactive mindset. They help leaders move beyond reactive tactics and develop strategic foresight. They cultivate the habit of asking tough questions, envisioning different futures, and preparing for complex situations before they occur. In a crisis, this kind of anticipatory thinking not only protects the mission but also empowers the team. It builds confidence, not because the future is inevitable, but because the leader has prepared for its uncertainty.

Staying Present and Scanning the Environment

Situational awareness isn't a sudden realization; it's an ongoing practice. During a crisis, the most effective leaders stay mentally engaged, actively observing their environment for new cues, subtle changes, and emerging trends. They resist the pull of tunnel vision, where initial beliefs become blind spots. Instead, they maintain a mindset of vigilance, flexibility, and openness to new information.

Respondents described these leaders as "always watching," "never caught off guard," and "able to pivot quickly when the ground shifted." This wasn't about paranoia—it was about vigilance. These leaders habitually check in with their teams, monitor external developments, and ask questions that keep their understanding fresh. They don't wait for problems to escalate; they spot early signs and act before issues become crises. One respondent recalled a leader who "could sense when something was off before anyone said a word—and she always asked the right question to surface it."

This kind of presence requires emotional discipline. In high-pressure situations, it's easy to become reactive, jumping from one urgent task to another, driven by adrenaline and stress. However, the most effective leaders slow down just enough to see the whole picture. They balance urgency with thoughtful reflection, action with awareness. They understand that rushing without clarity can lead to mistakes and that taking a moment to evaluate is essential, not optional.

They also know where to look. Situational awareness isn't just about noticing the obvious — it's about catching what others might miss. These leaders pay attention to informal conversations, changes in body language, shifts in morale, and subtle signs of operational friction. They listen to quiet voices, observe the energy in the room, and pick up cues that others might overlook. By doing so, they discover insights that lead to smarter decisions and more responsive leadership. One team member shared, "He noticed when people stopped asking questions—that's when he knew something was wrong."

Ultimately, staying present and scanning the environment is about cultivating a mindset of curiosity and care. It's about being attuned to the moment, aware of the context, and committed to leading with clarity—even when the path ahead is uncertain. These leaders don't just monitor—they interpret. They don't just react, they respond. And in doing so, they create a climate where awareness becomes collective, and leadership becomes a shared act of sensemaking.

Training Situational Awareness

Situational awareness may seem natural to some, but it is not an innate talent; it is a skill that can be developed through deliberate practice. The best crisis leaders view it as a vital ability to improve, not just a passive trait they possess. They develop habits that keep them alert, help them understand complexity, and enable them to anticipate changes—even under stress. In fast-paced environments, awareness isn't optional; it's a crucial aspect of leadership.

Respondents highlighted that successful leaders in this area didn't wait for clarity—they created it. They habitually scan their environment, consistently asking themselves and their teams: "What's happening now? What's changed? What don't we know?" These questions aren't rhetorical; they're part of a disciplined routine that keeps awareness sharp, responsive, and actionable.

Structured tools play a critical role. Leaders use SITREPs (Situation Reports), checklists, and decision templates to organize information and reduce cognitive overload. These frameworks help them prioritize what matters most, especially when time is limited and stakes are high. They also welcome dissent. Exercises such as red teaming and devil's advocacy challenge assumptions and reveal blind spots. Leaders ask, "What are we missing?" and encourage team members to consider both worst-case and best-case scenarios. This openness to different viewpoints strengthens understanding and improves decision-making.

Team-wide awareness is another essential element. Effective leaders promote upward communication, share real-time dashboards, and encourage cross-training so team members understand related roles. These practices build shared mental models—enabling teams to coordinate smoothly, even with limited guidance. When everyone shares the same evolving picture, coordination becomes instinctive, and friction decreases.

Simulation-based training ties everything together. Leaders practice in environments designed to simulate uncertainty, ambiguity, and changing conditions. These scenarios involve unexpected events, role confusion, and shifting variables, requiring adaptive responses. The goal isn't perfection; it's agility. Leaders learn to recalibrate on the fly, respond to incomplete information, and stay clear-headed under pressure.

Finally, self-awareness underpins the process. Leaders often ask themselves: "Am I overloaded? Am I rushing? Am I ignoring something that doesn't fit the narrative?" They monitor their own stress, fatigue, and bias, understanding that personal discipline is essential to maintaining clarity. Situational awareness begins with external scanning—but it depends on internal reflection to sustain it.

In my workshops, situational awareness training is a vital part of the CrisisMasters® leadership development series. Through immersive simulations, strategic foresight exercises, and reflective coaching, participants learn to build and sustain awareness in high-pressure situations. The program emphasizes not only what leaders see but also how they interpret, anticipate, and respond to what they observe.

Situational awareness isn't just about noticing; it's about remaining open, curious, and grounded. With the right tools, habits, and mindset, it can be learned, practiced, and mastered.

Situational Awareness in Leadership Development

Situational awareness is too critical to leave to chance. Organizations that train leaders for high-stakes environments must incorporate this skill into their development programs— not just as a theoretical concept but as a practical, trainable ability. Awareness should be viewed as a muscle that needs regular strengthening, not as a reflex to be taken for granted. Respondents emphasized that the most effective programs didn't just discuss awareness—they cultivated it. They immersed leaders in dynamic scenarios, changing conditions, and real-time decision-making challenges that mirrored the complexity of actual crises. These experiences helped leaders improve their perception, refine their judgment, and develop the mental agility needed to lead under pressure.

Training techniques varied, but several core practices emerged. Managing cognitive load was vital; leaders learned to recognize when their mental capacity was stretched and how to prioritize effectively. Scenario-based exercises with dynamic injections compelled participants to adapt quickly, respond to incomplete information, and recalibrate strategies as new variables appeared.

Field observations and post-incident reviews helped leaders connect theory to practice. By analyzing real-world events, they gained insight into how awareness influenced outcomes—and how lapses in awareness led to missed opportunities or costly mistakes. These lessons rooted abstract concepts in real experience.

Team-based workshops focused on shared mental models and adequate information flow. Leaders practiced maintaining collective awareness to ensure everyone on the team had access to the same evolving picture. This alignment improved coordination and reduced friction during fast-moving operations.

Reflection journals and learning debriefs added a personal dimension. Leaders tracked their own thought processes, identified patterns in their decision-making, and gained insight into how their perceptions evolved under stress. These reflective practices strengthened individual awareness and helped leaders become more intentional in how they scan, interpret, and respond to their environments.

Embedding situational awareness into leadership development isn't about creating perfect foresight—it's about fostering the habits, tools, and mindsets that help leaders stay grounded, curious, and adaptable. When organizations invest in this kind of training, they equip their leaders to navigate complexity effectively—and to guide their teams through uncertainty with confidence.

Conclusion: The Leader's Radar

Situational awareness is the leader's radar—constantly scanning, interpreting, and anticipating so decisions are grounded in reality, not assumptions. It is not a passive trait or a fleeting insight. It is an active discipline, cultivated through attention, reflection, and strategic curiosity. Leaders who master this skill are better equipped to detect weak signals, anticipate cascading effects, and guide their teams with clarity and foresight—especially when the stakes are high and the path ahead is unclear. In the fog of a crisis, situational awareness becomes the foundation for every other leadership skill. It guides communication by aligning messages with reality. It enhances decision-making by revealing context and consequences. It supports adaptability by signaling when conditions have changed. And it builds trust by showing that the leader is tuned in—not just to the mission but to the people carrying it out.

This mark of leadership isn't reserved for the naturally perceptive. It can be taught, practiced, and refined. Through immersive training, structured feedback, and deliberate habit-building, leaders can learn to see more clearly, think more broadly, and act more wisely under pressure. They can develop the skill to read both the room and the horizon, notice what others miss, and respond with grounded confidence. As one workshop participant said, "Situational awareness is the leader's radar—scanning the horizon, sensing the shifts, and guiding the team through uncertainty with clarity and calm." It is the quiet force behind decisive action and the steady lens through which complexity becomes manageable. But awareness alone isn't enough. Leadership during a crisis requires more than observation; it demands adaptation. The next chapter explores the hallmark of adaptability: the ability to pivot, adjust, and respond effectively as conditions change and new realities emerge. We'll see how leaders maintain flexibility without losing focus, turn setbacks into opportunities, and guide teams through change with resilience and resolve. Because during a crisis, the leaders who succeed are not just aware of what's happening, they are prepared to adapt to it.

CHAPTER 13

ADAPTABILITY

Adaptability is the mark of a leader who thrives in uncertainty. While situational awareness helps leaders perceive change, adaptability empowers them to respond—flexibly, creatively, and decisively. It is the ability to pivot strategies, reallocate resources, and rethink assumptions on the fly when new facts emerge or initial plans falter. In the unpredictable terrain of crisis leadership, this trait is indispensable because rigid adherence to a failing plan can turn manageable problems into disasters, whereas adaptive leaders turn chaos into opportunity by staying agile without losing sight of the mission.

Leading Through Change with Agility and Resolve

In a crisis, change isn't optional; it's inevitable. Conditions shift, plans unravel, and new variables emerge unexpectedly. The leaders who excel in these moments are not those who cling to rigid strategies but those who intentionally adapt. Adaptability demonstrates a leader's ability to pivot without losing sight of goals, adjust without compromising integrity, and respond calmly.

Adaptability isn't about improvising aimlessly — it's about purposeful flexibility. It's the capacity to handle disruption, reframe obstacles, and tweak strategies on the fly. Effective crisis leaders don't just accept change — they leverage it. They recognize when a plan no longer fits the situation and have the courage to shift direction while keeping teams aligned and focused.

Adaptability in Action

During a crisis, adaptability isn't a luxury; it's a necessity. The leaders who earned the most respect from respondents in this study were those who demonstrated the ability to pivot intentionally. They didn't rely on rigid scripts or outdated assumptions. Instead, they reexamined, adjusted, and shifted efforts without losing momentum. They made change manageable, helping teams see adjustment as progress, not disruption. Their flexibility was grounded in purpose, not indecision.

Respondents consistently praised adaptable leaders. They remembered individuals who were "quick to adjust," "calm in the face of change," and "able to find opportunity within disruption." These leaders didn't panic when conditions shifted; they paused, reassessed, and acted decisively. Their strength was not in having all the answers but in knowing how to change their approach when new information arose. One respondent said, "She didn't flinch when the plan unraveled. She just said, 'Okay, let's reframe,' and within minutes, we had a new direction."

Deliberate pauses and careful recalibration defined this type of adaptability. Leaders didn't rush to fix everything; they took time to listen, reflect, and reorient. Another respondent shared, "He didn't get stuck when things shifted unexpectedly. He asked the right questions, brought the team together, and moved us forward without losing momentum." That ability to slow down enough to see the full picture was a common theme among the most effective.

Adaptable leaders also show emotional stability. They didn't transfer their stress to the team. Instead, they maintained calmness and confidence, even in uncertain situations. One team member recalled, "She was honest about the uncertainty, but she didn't let it rattle her. That steadiness helped the rest of us stay grounded." During volatile moments, this emotional control served as a stabilizing force.

Importantly, these leaders didn't adapt alone; they involved others in the process. They sought input, welcomed dissent, and empowered their teams to develop solutions together. In one example, a respondent described a leader who "called an impromptu huddle when the plan started falling apart. He asked, 'What are we missing?' and within fifteen minutes, the team had a better path forward." That openness to collaboration turned disruption into innovation.

Adaptability also shows in how leaders reinterpret setbacks. Instead of viewing change as a threat, they see it as a signal—an invitation to rethink, retool, and respond. One respondent remarked, "She didn't see the delay as a failure. She saw it as a chance to strengthen the plan. That mindset changed how we all approached the challenge."

This chapter explores adaptability as a leadership skill rooted in mindset, approach, and emotional intelligence. We'll examine how leaders develop adaptive capacity, guide teams through uncertainty, and balance flexibility with consistency. Because in a crisis, adaptability isn't just a survival skill — it's a strategic advantage. The leaders who master it don't just respond to change; they lead through it.

Ultimately, adaptability isn't about being reactive — it's about being responsive. It's the ability to stay grounded in purpose while adjusting tactics. The leaders who exemplified this didn't just survive change — they shaped it. In doing so, they built cultures of resilience in which teams felt empowered to evolve, experiment, and succeed — even when the path ahead was uncertain.

The Cognitive and Emotional Foundations of Adaptability

Adaptability is more than just a behavioral trait; it is closely linked to how leaders think, feel, and manage themselves under pressure. The most effective crisis leaders demonstrate adaptability not because they are naturally flexible, but because they develop the mental and emotional skills to pivot with clarity and confidence.

Cognitively, adaptability begins with mental agility. Leaders need to shift perspectives, reframe problems, and adjust their assumptions as new information arises. This demands cognitive flexibility, the ability to consider multiple possibilities, suspend early judgments, and accept ambiguity. Respondents described leaders who "could change direction without losing focus" and "always had room for a better idea." These leaders didn't cling to a single story; they looked for patterns, questioned their own thinking, and stayed open to different interpretations.

Critical thinking also plays a vital role. Adaptable leaders assess risks, consider trade-offs, and forecast consequences in real time. They don't just react—they reason. One respondent recalled a leader who, during a rapidly changing crisis, said, "Let's slow down and think through the ripple effects before we act." That pause for analysis helped avoid costly mistakes and choose a more sustainable path forward.

Emotionally, adaptability is rooted in self-regulation. Leaders must manage their stress, remain calm under pressure, and prevent anxiety from spreading to their teams. Emotional intelligence, particularly the ability to recognize and adjust one's own emotional responses, is essential. Adaptable leaders aren't immune to frustration or fear, but they know how to handle those emotions productively. They appear steady, not because they feel no pressure, but because they've learned to manage it without letting it cloud their judgment.

Empathy also boosts adaptability. Leaders who are attuned to their teams' emotional states can better adjust their communication, pacing, and support. They notice when people need reassurance, when morale dips, and when a change in tone can restore unity. One respondent shared, "She could sense when the team was overwhelmed and changed the way she led that day. That made all the difference."

Together, these cognitive and emotional foundations build the internal structure of adaptive leadership. Mental agility helps leaders see the terrain clearly; emotional intelligence guides them through it with grace. When both are present, leaders respond to change not with panic or rigidity, but with clarity, compassion, and strategic purpose.

Adaptability in Strategy, Relationships, and Response

Adaptability in crisis leadership shows not only through

strategic shifts but also in subtle interpersonal interactions. The most effective leaders don't just change plans—they adjust their posture. They "read the room before responding," "knew how to talk to anyone," and tailored their tone and approach to meet people where they were. Whether delivering urgent instructions or providing quiet reassurance, they communicated with emotional intelligence and situational awareness. This responsiveness, built trust, encouraged collaboration, and fostered diverse perspectives. One respondent observed, "She could shift from briefing the board to calming a frontline team without skipping a beat. Everyone felt seen."

In problem-solving, adaptability involves quick thinking and mental agility. These leaders were described as "quick on their feet," "never locked into one plan," and "always willing to try a new approach if the old one wasn't working." They combined decisiveness with humility—able to make decisions when necessary but open to changing course when evidence called for it. They didn't take failure personally. Instead, they viewed setbacks as signals, using them to learn, improve, and innovate. This attitude fostered a culture of experimentation and resilience, encouraging teams to explore new ideas and adapt fluidly to emerging challenges. One team member reflected, "He didn't punish mistakes—he asked what we learned and how we'd adapt."

Adaptability also involves emotional stability. Leaders who stayed calm and composed under pressure helped ease anxiety and boost morale. Their presence signaled that change was not chaos—it was progress. They were described as "fluid yet firm," capable of adjusting without sacrificing integrity or focus. Whether working with executives, field teams, or external partners, they balanced multiple perspectives while keeping everyone aligned with common goals—their ability to stay grounded. At the same time, adapting fostered psychological safety and operational clarity.

During a crisis, adaptability is not optional; it is essential. It allows leaders to modify tactics quickly, reassign resources, shift priorities, and stay clear-headed amid chaos. In contrast, rigid leadership risks failure, missed opportunities, and increased stress. Adaptable leaders cultivate cultures that welcome change, foster innovation, and build resilience. They embody a mindset that says, "We may not control the disruption, but we can control how we respond.

The Mindset of Adaptability

Adaptability is more than just a behavior; it's a mindset—a way of thinking and leading that views change as a constant rather than an interruption. Effective crisis leaders don't merely react to shifting conditions; they engage with them intentionally, balancing flexibility with determination. This mindset helps them stay grounded in purpose while remaining open to new paths, perspectives, and opportunities. It's not about being indecisive or chasing after novelty; it's about responding to reality with clarity and courage.

Respondents consistently described adaptable leaders as intellectually agile and emotionally stable. These leaders are comfortable with ambiguity, willing to revise assumptions, and able to change strategies without losing focus. Their adaptability isn't impulsive; it's deliberate and thoughtful. They don't pivot just for the sake of movement or abandon plans at the first sign of resistance. Instead, they adjust their course when the evidence warrants it, demonstrating a rare mix of decisiveness and humility. One respondent noted, "She didn't need to be right—she needed to be effective. That's why we trusted her when things changed."

This mindset is built on several interconnected foundations. Cognitively, adaptable leaders show flexibility in their information processing. They consider multiple scenarios, update their mental models, and remain open to new data— even when it contradicts previous beliefs. They don't cling to certainty; they think in probabilities and possibilities, asking not just "What do we know?" but "What might we be missing?" This openness helps them navigate complexity without becoming paralyzed by it.

Behaviorally, they demonstrate a willingness to modify routines, tactics, and roles as circumstances evolve. They don't depend on a single playbook—they develop a set of strategies and know when to shift gears. Their agility isn't random. They adapt not because they're uncertain, but because they're attentive.

Emotionally, these leaders control their emotions. They stay calm and composed under pressure, refusing to let frustration or fear impair their judgment. Their stability acts as a calming influence for others. During uncertain moments, their presence signifies that change isn't chaos—it's progress. One respondent shared, "He didn't flinch when the plan unraveled. He just said, 'Let's rethink,' and we followed his lead."

Interpersonally, adaptable leaders tailor their communication and leadership style to fit the context and the people involved. Whether speaking to a technical team, a concerned community, or a skeptical stakeholder, they adjust their tone, language, and body language to foster trust and alignment. They don't stick to a script—they speak according to the situation.

Ultimately, adaptable leaders view uncertainty not as a threat but as a landscape to explore. They don't resist change; they embrace it. In doing so, they demonstrate a mindset that helps teams stay agile, innovative, and focused on their mission, even when the way forward is unclear. Their adaptability isn't just a reaction — it's a leadership philosophy that turns disruption into opportunity.

Assessing Adaptability: Evidence in Motion

Adaptability may seem intangible at first, but it can be measured with notable accuracy. The best crisis leaders aren't just flexible in theory; they show adaptability in practice, especially when the stakes are high and the path isn't clear. Participants in this study emphasized that adaptive leadership isn't about abstract traits; it's about how leaders think, react, and recover when conditions shift.

One clear sign of adaptability is recognizing inflection points— the moment when a plan fails and a new approach is needed. Adaptive leaders don't cling to outdated strategies out of pride or inertia. They notice early signs of misalignment, acknowledge when circumstances have changed, and pivot before wasting time and resources. As one respondent said, "She didn't wait for the wheels to fall off—she saw the curve coming and adjusted before we hit it."

Another key trait is the ability to generate alternatives under pressure. When faced with disruption, adaptable leaders don't freeze or stick to familiar paths. Instead, they think creatively, evaluate options quickly, and make wise choices. Their skill to produce multiple viable options—often on tight deadlines—

demonstrates both cognitive agility and strategic discipline. This capacity to reframe problems and find new solutions is a vital aspect of adaptive leadership.

Clear communication is also essential for successful adaptability. When a change is needed, adaptive leaders honestly and clearly explain the reason for the shift. They don't mask uncertainty with vague reassurances; they clarify what's changing, why it matters, and what will happen next. This transparency helps build trust, reduce confusion, and keep teams aligned during tough times. As one team member said, "He didn't just change direction—he brought us with him."

A successful pivot also requires realigning the team. Adaptive leaders understand that change isn't complete until everyone is reoriented. They quickly redefine roles, adjust priorities, and clarify expectations to maintain momentum. This ability to re-anchor the team after a shift transforms a simple adjustment into a coordinated effort.

Finally, staying calm under stress is a strong sign of adaptability. Feedback from peers and evaluators often highlights a leader's demeanor during disruptions. Calm, focused communication, especially when others are anxious, shows confidence and helps keep the team steady. Adaptive leaders don't hide their emotions, but they control them. Their presence demonstrates that, even with uncertainty, their leadership remains steady.

Together, these indicators shift the focus from whether a leader knows the "right answer" to whether they can lead flexibly as circumstances change. Adaptability isn't about being perfect; it's about being responsive, transparent, and resilient in action. It's the ability to stay true to your purpose while intentionally adjusting your course. When assessed by behavior rather than just beliefs, it becomes a tangible, trainable leadership skill.

Strengthening Adaptability Skills

Adaptability isn't just a personal trait—it's a strategic skill that organizations can cultivate. The mental and emotional skills supporting adaptive leadership—such as mental agility, emotional regulation, and reflective awareness—can be strengthened through intentional development. Organizations committed to building resilient leadership pipelines must go beyond mere encouragement and invest in practical, structured methods to help leaders develop these abilities under pressure. Coaching is one of the most effective tools for developing adaptive leaders. Skilled coaches help individuals identify their default thought patterns, challenge rigid assumptions, and improve emotional self-awareness. Through guided conversations, leaders learn to recognize when they're stuck in outdated mental models or reacting out of stress rather than strategy. One respondent described a coaching session where the leader realized, "I wasn't resisting change—I was resisting uncertainty." That insight became a turning point in how they approached future disruptions.

Coaching also provides a safe environment for leaders to explore discomfort, try new behaviors, and receive feedback on how they present themselves in dynamic settings. When combined with real-time observations such as shadowing during high-pressure meetings or debriefing after important decisions, coaching acts as a mirror that highlights both strengths and areas for growth. It helps leaders develop the internal discipline to pause, reevaluate, and pivot intentionally.

Reflection practices enhance personal growth. Journaling, structured debriefs, and peer learning sessions help leaders understand how their perceptions, emotions, and decisions shift under stress. Organizations can integrate reflection into daily routines—encouraging leaders to note moments of tension, identify cognitive biases, and observe when emotional triggers influence their responses. Over time, these habits build metacognition: the ability to think about one's own thinking. Leaders become more intentional, more aware, and better equipped to adapt in real time.

Scenario-based training boosts adaptability. Immersive simulations that replicate crisis conditions—featuring changing variables, limited information, and emotional intensity—allow leaders to practice adaptive behaviors in a controlled environment. These exercises encourage participants to make decisions under stress, respond to unexpected events, and modify strategies quickly. When paired with structured feedback and reflection, scenario training serves as a powerful tool for building adaptive capacity.

The most effective programs combine all three elements. For example, a leader might participate in a simulation involving a cybersecurity breach, receive coaching on managing ambiguity and team dynamics, and then reflect on how their emotional responses influenced their decision-making. This integrated approach turns adaptability from a vague goal into an evident, trainable skill.

Organizations serious about developing adaptive leadership must consider these foundations as essential skills—not optional extras. By investing in coaching, reflection, and scenario-based training, they prepare leaders to handle complexity with clarity, calmness, and confidence. In doing so, they foster cultures where change is not feared but welcomed as a driver for growth.

Training Adaptive Flexibility

Adaptability isn't just a trait; it's a skill that can be learned. The most effective crisis leaders don't just rely on instinct; they build adaptive capacity through intentional practice, reflective thinking, and exposure to complexity. Respondents highlighted that adaptability becomes second nature when leaders are immersed in environments that require it.

Training adaptive flexibility starts with dynamic simulations. These aren't scripted tabletop exercises; they're unpredictable, high-pressure scenarios with changing factors that force leaders to adapt instantly. A flood response might suddenly involve a chemical spill. A cybersecurity breach could escalate into a public misinformation campaign. These disruptions help leaders learn to think beyond straightforward plans and respond quickly and flexibly.

Progressive layering of complexity is a key strategy. Leaders start with simple challenges and gradually face more complex, interconnected crises. As complexity grows, for example, with multiple stakeholders, cascading failures, and conflicting priorities, leaders learn to stay calm, prioritize effectively, and adapt under pressure.

Role rotation and perspective-taking expand leaders' understanding. By taking on unfamiliar roles—such as a logistics officer serving as a public information lead—leaders develop empathy for other functions and lessen tunnel vision. This cross-functional experience enhances coordination and improves decision-making in real-world crises.

Reflective practice is where adaptability becomes a habit. After each exercise, leaders engage in structured reviews: What worked? What didn't? When should we have pivoted sooner? These decision audits develop metacognition—awareness of how they think—and sharpen their ability to recognize when a plan is failing and needs adjustment.

Time-pressure drills create urgency. Leaders must make quick decisions, delegate effectively, and adapt even with incomplete information. These exercises mimic the stress of real crises, helping leaders develop composure and confidence in fast-paced situations.

Together, these methods turn adaptability from a reactive instinct into a proactive discipline. Leaders learn not just to handle change, but to transform disruption into opportunity and guide their teams clearly through the unknown.

Embedding Adaptability in Organizational Culture

Adaptability doesn't thrive in isolation—it flourishes in cultures that value learning, experimentation, and flexibility. Organizations that handle disruptions effectively don't just train individual leaders to be adaptable; they embed adaptability into the core of decision-making, team operations, and the definition of success. In these environments, adaptability isn't just reactive; it's a strategic mindset.

Respondents in this study highlighted that adaptive cultures encourage initiative and reward thoughtful risk-taking. Leaders in these organizations aren't punished for pivoting—they're recognized for responding to real-world conditions. When plans shift or circumstances evolve, the ability to adapt is regarded as a strength, not a failure. Mistakes aren't stigmatized—they're seen as opportunities for insight. One respondent shared, "We didn't get in trouble for changing direction—we got praised for catching the shift early." This mindset transforms failure from something to avoid into a learning opportunity, fostering a climate where experimentation is not only allowed but expected.

Diverse perspectives are welcomed, not dismissed. Adaptive cultures promote dissenting opinions, understanding that challenges strengthen strategy. Leaders should listen, reconsider, and adapt—not only to external factors but also to internal feedback. This openness fosters psychological safety, improves team cohesion, and cultivates shared ownership. When people feel their insights matter, they become more committed to the mission and more willing to speak up when circumstances change.

Organizations that prioritize adaptability also change how they assess performance. Instead of rewarding strict adherence to plans, they recognize leaders who can effectively revise their course, communicate changes clearly, and keep their teams aligned during uncertainty. These behaviors signify success—not deviation from it. One respondent noted, "Our best leaders weren't the ones who stuck to the original plan—they were the ones who knew when to change it and how to bring everyone along."

Coaching and mentorship play vital roles in reinforcing adaptive habits. Pairing leaders with advisors skilled in learning agility helps develop the mental flexibility required. These relationships provide immediate feedback, challenge assumptions, and foster growth in complex contexts. They also exemplify reflective practice, turning experience into insights and insights into action.

Ultimately, embedding adaptability into culture means shifting from control to responsiveness—moving from static planning to dynamic learning. It involves creating systems that support flexibility, reward curiosity, and equip leaders to succeed when the road ahead is unpredictable. In such cultures, adaptability isn't just a backup plan—it's a core skill. When integrated into the organization's DNA, it becomes a source of resilience, innovation, and sustained performance.

Conclusion: Leading Through Adaptive Change

Adaptability is a leader's strength in action—deliberately

pivoting, clearly adjusting, and guiding teams smoothly through change without losing sight of their direction. In crisis, it's not the rigid who succeed—it's the flexible. Leaders who thrive are grounded in purpose while being adaptable in their approach, capable of shifting strategies, reframing challenges, and leading confidently through uncertainty. Their adaptability isn't reactive; it's intentional, based on judgment, and driven by mission.

As this chapter explains, respondents clearly emphasize that adaptability is not a luxury — it's essential. It helps leaders respond to changing conditions, maintain team unity, and seize opportunities amid disruption. It's the difference between simply reacting and responding effectively, between just surviving and truly leading. Adaptive leaders don't wait for clarity — they create it. They develop a mindset that views change not as an obstacle but as a crucial part of the journey.

But adaptability isn't just about external changes; it's about internal discipline. It requires humility to revise assumptions, courage to change course, and emotional stability to guide others through uncertainty. It's a mindset that sees change not as a threat but as an opportunity to grow, learn, and improve. These leaders show that flexibility isn't a weakness—it's wisdom in action.

Organizations that foster adaptability—through training, culture, and leadership development—embed resilience into their core. They prepare leaders not only to follow plans but also to think critically, act flexibly, and lead confidently amid uncertainty. In such environments, adaptability becomes a shared language, a collective strength, and a strategic advantage.

As one respondent noted, "Adaptability is a leader's strength in motion—pivoting with purpose, adjusting with clarity, and guiding teams through change without losing direction." It reflects a leader who can handle complexity calmly and lead transformation while maintaining trust.

Even the most adaptable leaders encounter moments that test their endurance. Change may be constant, but it isn't always easy. The next chapter explores Personal Resilience, the inner strength that helps leaders persevere through prolonged stress, setbacks, and uncertainty. We'll examine how resilient leaders recover, reflect, and stay grounded, and how they lead not just with stamina but with empathy. Because in a crisis, resilience isn't just about survival—it's about the ability to rise repeatedly, with purpose still strong.

CHAPTER 14

PERSONAL RESILIENCE

n crisis leadership, resilience is the quiet force that sustains momentum when everything else feels unstable. It is the leader's capacity to recover quickly from setbacks, maintain composure under prolonged stress, and lead with clarity despite uncertainty or repeated blows. While adaptability enables pivots, resilience ensures persistence—making it indispensable for crisis leaders who must endure chaos long enough to guide their teams to safety and success.

Endurance, Empathy, and the Inner Strength to Lead

In a crisis, leadership is tested not only by complexity but also by its duration. The pressure doesn't just spike; it remains constant. Plans break down, emotions surge, and the weight of responsibility grows heavier every hour. During these moments, personal resilience becomes the quiet force that keeps leaders moving—not just through the initial shock but throughout the long journey of recovery, adjustment, and renewal. Resilience surpasses stamina; it is the ability to manage stress, recover from setbacks, and lead with clarity and kindness. It involves staying grounded amid continuous change and providing stability to others even in uncertainty. The most resilient leaders don't just endure—they adapt, reflect, and rise. They lead not out of exhaustion, but from a deep sense of purpose that restores rather than drains. Respondents in this project described resilient leaders as "anchored," "emotionally present," and "able to carry the weight without losing their humanity." These leaders didn't pretend to be invulnerable; they acknowledged stress, sought support, and demonstrated healthy coping strategies. One team member recalled, "She was honest about how hard it was—but she never let it harden her." This combination of vulnerability and strength fostered a climate of trust and cohesion. This chapter examines personal resilience as a leadership hallmark rooted in emotional intelligence, reflective practice, and values-based endurance. We will explore how leaders sustain themselves through prolonged stress, develop empathy without burnout, and establish habits that protect their clarity, integrity, and ability to lead. Because in a crisis, resilience isn't just about survival — it's the foundation for sustained, compassionate leadership. Respondents described resilient leaders as "steady in the storm," "able to absorb pressure without passing it on," and "the emotional anchor for the team." These leaders didn't shy away from difficulty—they faced it head-on. They stayed focused when plans fell apart, remained grounded when emotions ran high, and helped others find strength when fatigue and frustration threatened to take over. Resilience was evident in how these leaders managed their own energy and emotions. They recognized when they were drained, took steps to recharge, and employed healthy coping strategies. They didn't pretend to be invulnerable; they showed that strength includes self-awareness and self-care. This honesty-built trust and allowed others to acknowledge their own limits without shame. But resilience wasn't just personal; it also involved relationships. These leaders cultivated environments where recovery was possible. They checked in with their teams, provided encouragement, and created space for reflection. They understood that resilience is contagious: when leaders show calm and resolve, teams mirror that steadiness. This chapter explores resilience as a leadership skill—not merely a personal trait but a strategic advantage. It examines how resilient leaders sustain performance under pressure, support their teams through challenges, and foster cultures that recover stronger after setbacks. Because in a crisis, resilience isn't just about surviving—it's about leading forward.

The Psychological Dimensions of Resilience

Resilience is often mistaken for toughness or stoicism, but its true strength lies not in resisting stress, but in the ability to recover, adapt, and stay emotionally whole amidst adversity. Essentially, personal resilience is a psychological trait—a dynamic mix of mindset, emotion, and meaning-making—that allows leaders to endure hardship without becoming hardened. One of the most vital aspects of resilience is emotional regulation. Resilient leaders aren't immune to stress, fear, or frustration; they experience these emotions deeply. What makes them different is their ability to manage these feelings effectively. They don't suppress or ignore what they're feeling; instead, they acknowledge it, work through it, and choose how to respond. This self-awareness helps them stay calm under pressure and serve as steady examples for their teams. As one respondent shared, "He never pretended things were easy, but he never let his stress spill onto the rest of us. That made all the difference." Another key facet is cognitive framing—the ability to interpret events in ways that maintain a sense of agency and purpose. Resilient leaders view setbacks not as personal failures but as challenges to understand and overcome. They ask, "What can I learn from this?" instead of "Why is this happening to me?" This shift from victimhood to control is subtle but powerful. It helps leaders keep a sense of control, even in chaotic situations. One leader described this mindset as "choosing to believe that every disruption has something to teach me, even if I can't see it yet." Optimism also plays a crucial role—though not the naive kind that ignores difficulty. Instead, resilient leaders adopt what psychologists call "realistic optimism"—the belief that while challenges are real, they can also be overcome. This mindset fuels perseverance and helps leaders inspire hope without false promises. It also sustains long-term motivation, especially when progress slows or setbacks happen often. Purpose serves as another psychological anchor. Leaders who are deeply connected to a sense of mission—whether it's protecting a community, supporting a team, or upholding core values—draw strength from that clarity. Purpose becomes a stabilizing force, reminding them why their effort matters, even when the work is exhausting. As one respondent said, "What kept me going wasn't the plan—it was the people. I couldn't quit on them." Finally, self-compassion is an often overlooked but essential part of resilience. Leaders who treat themselves with kindness acknowledge their limits, forgive their mistakes, and seek support when needed are more likely to recover and stay effective over time. They understand that resilience isn't about being unbreakable; it's about bending without losing shape. Together, these psychological elements form the core of resilient leadership. They help leaders manage prolonged stress without burning out, lead with empathy without exhaustion, and stay grounded during uncertainty. In a crisis, this inner strength isn't just personal — it's contagious. Teams pick up emotional cues from leaders, and when leaders show resilience, they create the environment for others to follow.

Understanding Stress and Its Impact

In crisis leadership, stress isn't just a side effect — it's a core challenge. Leaders must manage not only the external chaos of emergencies but also the internal toll that ongoing pressure takes on their bodies, minds, and relationships. Resilient leaders don't ignore stress or blindly push through it. Instead, they seek to understand how it functions, control its effects, and demonstrate healthy ways of responding for those around them.

Stress typically manifests in two distinct forms, each impacting leadership differently. Acute stress triggers the body's fight-or-flight response, enhancing focus and awareness, which can be helpful in immediate danger or when making quick decisions. However, this heightened state also narrows thinking, impairs long-term memory, and increases impulsiveness. If not managed, acute stress can cause leaders to react in ways that overlook broader strategic concerns.

Chronic stress, on the other hand, develops gradually and insidiously over time. It drains energy, reduces clarity, and diminishes emotional stability. Leaders experiencing prolonged stress may face burnout, emotional numbness, and cognitive fatigue. Their decision-making skills decline, and their ability to lead with empathy and precision begins to falter. The accumulated burden of unresolved stress can impair judgment, lower patience, and weaken the leader's capacity to inspire and connect.

The cognitive effects of stress are especially crucial during crisis situations. Elevated stress hampers the brain's executive functions, affecting judgment, shortening attention spans, and increasing reliance on routine or rigid responses. Leaders may struggle to evaluate options, process complex information, or communicate effectively under pressure. These impairments directly influence mission success, team cohesion, and public trust.

Resilient leaders address these effects through preparation, regulation, and recovery. They recognize early signs of overload—irritability, fatigue, difficulty concentrating—and take proactive steps to restore balance. They use breathing techniques, grounding exercises, and micro-recovery practices to stay centered. They emphasize getting enough sleep, staying hydrated, and maintaining physical activity, understanding that physical health is closely linked to mental clarity and emotional stability.

Equally important, resilient leaders normalize conversations about stress. They acknowledge its presence, speak openly about its impact, and model healthy coping strategies. This transparency fosters environments where others feel safe to do the same. It builds psychological safety, strengthens team cohesion, and reinforces the idea that resilience isn't about suppressing emotions; it is about managing them intentionally. In high-pressure environments, stress is unavoidable—but its effects can be controlled. Leaders who understand how stress works and manage it purposefully are better prepared to lead with clarity, compassion, and resilience. They don't just survive the storm—they guide others through it with steadiness and strength.

Cultivating Resilience

Resilience isn't a fixed trait—it's a capacity that can be strengthened through intentional practice. The psychological foundations of resilience—such as emotional regulation, cognitive framing, realistic optimism, purpose, and self-compassion—aren't exclusive to naturally steady individuals. They can be developed, reinforced, and maintained through daily habits, supportive relationships, and structured reflection. The most effective crisis leaders don't just rely on resilience—they actively seek to build it.

Daily routines establish the groundwork for emotional stability. Leaders who start their day with purpose, whether through mindfulness, journaling, physical activity, or quiet planning, create space to calm their nervous system before crises arise. These habits don't eliminate stress but help lessen its impact. One respondent shared, "He always took ten minutes to center himself before the morning briefing. It wasn't about ritual—it was about readiness." These small habits keep leaders grounded, focused, and emotionally available to others.

Peer support is equally vital. Resilient leaders understand they don't have to carry the load alone. They build trusted relationships with colleagues, mentors, and advisors who offer perspective, encouragement, and honest feedback. These connections provide emotional comfort and mental refreshment. In high-pressure moments, a quick chat with a trusted peer can restore clarity and confidence. One leader shared: "I didn't need someone to fix it—I needed someone to remind me I could." Peer support transforms isolation into solidarity and underscores that resilience is a team effort.

Reflective routines enhance resilience by turning experiences into insights. Leaders who regularly pause to evaluate their responses—through journaling, debriefs, or guided reflection—develop metacognition: the ability to think about their own thinking. They identify patterns, recognize triggers, and refine their coping strategies over time. This self-awareness improves emotional regulation and enhances decision-making under pressure. Organizations that embed reflection into leadership routines—such as end-of-day check-ins, post-crisis reviews, or monthly resilience assessments—help leaders learn from adversity and apply those lessons intentionally.

Together, these practices form a cycle of resilience: preparation, connection, reflection, and renewal. They help leaders stay emotionally agile, mentally adaptable, and purposefully engaged—even when the journey is arduous and pressure mounts. Resilience isn't just what leaders experience; it's how they navigate it. When intentionally cultivated, it becomes a source of strength. That benefits not only the leader but the entire team.

Stress Awareness in Training and Performance Reviews

If resilience is the ability to endure and recover, then stress awareness acts as a guide helping leaders navigate that landscape. Yet, in many organizations, stress remains an unseen force—felt but rarely named, acknowledged but seldom integrated into formal development or review processes. To cultivate truly resilient leadership, stress awareness must be included in both training programs and performance evaluations—not as a weakness but as a sign of strategic maturity.

Leadership training that incorporates stress awareness equips leaders with tools to recognize, interpret, and respond to stress in themselves and others. This begins with education: helping leaders understand the physiological and cognitive effects of stress, how it appears in behavior, and its influence on decision-making. Training modules can include guided reflection, case studies, and simulations that demonstrate stress responses in real time. Leaders learn to identify their own stress signals—such as irritability, tunnel vision, or fatigue—and practice techniques for management, including breathing exercises, reframing strategies, and recovery planning.

Equally important is developing emotional literacy. Leaders are encouraged to recognize their stress, discuss its effects openly, and adopt healthy coping strategies. This openness not only boosts their resilience but also fosters psychological safety within their teams. When stress awareness becomes a part of leadership conversations, it shifts the culture from silent tension to shared accountability.

Performance reviews provide another valuable opportunity to highlight stress awareness. Instead of focusing solely on results, organizations can evaluate how leaders handle pressure, stay calm, and support team well-being during critical moments. Review conversations might include questions such as: How did you respond to unexpected stressors? What recovery strategies did you use? How did you support others through uncertainty?

These prompts promote reflection, normalize emotional complexity, and encourage adaptive behaviors.

Incorporating stress awareness into evaluations also challenges outdated metrics that equate constant output with effectiveness. Leaders who pace themselves, seek support, and prioritize sustainability should be recognized— not penalized— for their approach. This shift demonstrates that resilience is not about heroic endurance but about intentional leadership under pressure.

Ultimately, integrating stress awareness into training and performance reviews transforms it from a personal challenge into a shared skill. It affirms the emotional realities of leadership and prepares individuals to lead not only with authority but also with empathy, clarity, and resilience. In doing so, organizations foster a leadership culture capable of managing crises and emerging stronger from them.

Building and Training Resilience

Resilience isn't just for those who are naturally tough—it's a skill, a discipline, and a leadership asset that can be nurtured through intentional practice, deliberate exposure, and ongoing support. Effective crisis leaders don't merely endure stress; they prepare for it, handle it, and recover with purpose. Their strength isn't measured by how much they can take in, but by how effectively they can adapt, readjust, and lead forward.

Respondents noted that resilient leaders often adopted proactive routines long before a crisis occurred. They practiced mindfulness, maintained physical health, and formed habits that supported emotional stability. These weren't just self-indulgences, they were strategic investments in clarity, endurance, and leadership ability. One leader described their morning routine as "a daily reset—so when the storm came, I wasn't starting from zero." These rituals laid a foundation of stability that helped leaders stay composed during volatility.

Building resilience starts with developing key skills. Leaders learn techniques for emotional regulation, cognitive reframing, and effective communication under pressure. They practice grounding exercises, breathing methods, and mental resets that help them stay focused when stakes are high. These tools aren't only for crises—they become part of a leader's daily toolkit, enhancing their capacity to lead with clarity and calmness in any situation.

Next is stress exposure. Using realistic simulations and escalating scenarios, leaders are placed in controlled environments that replicate the chaos of real crises. These exercises challenge their decision-making under pressure, their ability to adapt to changing conditions, and their focus amid uncertainty. This "stress inoculation" builds confidence and prepares leaders to perform when it truly matters. One respondent said, "The simulation was intense—but it showed me I could lead through it. That changed everything."

Equally essential is ongoing support. Resilience isn't built alone; it's reinforced through peer networks, coaching relationships, and structured recovery processes. After-action reviews that include emotional reflection, access to mental health resources, and mentorship programs help leaders process their experiences and learn from them. These support systems normalize vulnerability, foster learning, and prevent the gradual loss of capacity often caused by prolonged stress.

Together, these components create a cycle: preparation, performance, and renewal. Leaders learn to anticipate stress, respond effectively, and recover intentionally. Over time, resilience shifts from a mere reaction to a consistent leadership habit. It becomes integral to how leaders think, present themselves, and sustain both their own well-being and that of others amidst complexity. When organizations invest in cultivating this capacity, they don't just safeguard their leaders, they empower them to lead with endurance, empathy, and unwavering clarity.

Organizational Strategies

Resilience may start with the individual, but it relies on the system to sustain it. Leaders cannot handle a crisis alone — and they shouldn't have to. Organizations that focus on resilience foster cultures where recovery is normal, support is easily available, and well-being is seen as a strategic asset. In these settings, resilience isn't only a personal responsibility; it's a shared one.

Respondents emphasized that resilient leaders flourish in environments that emphasize pacing over burnout. These organizations don't reward exhaustion; they reward sustainability. They create policies that protect recovery time, promote open conversations about stress, and provide easy access to mental health resources without stigma. One leader recalled, "We weren't expected to power through — we were expected to pause, reflect, and come back stronger." That change in expectations made space for endurance without wear-down.

Workload pacing is a vital strategy. In high-pressure situations, the need to perform can feel endless. Organizations that value resilience understand the difference between urgent productivity and ongoing overload. They design workflows with a steady rhythm — not just intensity — allowing leaders to recover between surges and sustain their emotional capacity over time. This pacing doesn't hinder the mission; it supports the people carrying it.

Psychological safety is a fundamental element. Leaders felt confident admitting fatigue, seeking help, and showing vulnerability without fear of judgment. This transparency created ripple effects across teams, building trust, cohesion, and shared responsibility. When leaders are open about their limits, it encourages others to do the same. One respondent said, "She didn't hide her stress—she named it. That made it easier for all of us to speak up."

Supportive organizations also invested in structural safeguards. They put decompression protocols into place after major incidents, offered resilience coaching, and built peer support networks to help leaders process stress in real time. These systems weren't reactive; they were integrated into daily operations. Leaders understood recovery wasn't an afterthought — it was part of the plan.

Culture played a crucial role. When senior leaders modeled resilience — sharing openly about their recovery routines, setbacks, and coping strategies — they sent a powerful message: strength involves self-awareness. This openness helped break down outdated ideas of toughness and replaced them with a more sustainable leadership approach. Resilience was no longer about silent endurance; it became about intentional restoration.

Ultimately, resilience is more than just a personal trait; it's a collective commitment. Organizations that nurture it develop leaders who can manage crises and guide others through them with clarity, compassion, and strength. They create environments where emotional well-being is protected, recovery is prioritized, and leadership remains steady — not lost. In doing so, they ensure that resilience is not only present but widespread.

Conclusion: The Anchor in the Storm

Resilience is the leader's anchor—the quiet strength that stays steady in the storm and enables all other acts of leadership. It isn't about being unbreakable; it's about being able to recover. When faced with prolonged stress, uncertainty, and emotional strain, resilient leaders remain calm, clear-minded, and connected to their purpose. They absorb pressure without spreading panic, and they recover without avoiding their responsibilities.

These leaders don't just endure, they guide others through

perseverance. Their presence stabilizes teams, their empathy builds trust, and their discipline demonstrates sustainability. They understand that resilience isn't a solo effort; it's a shared rhythm of recovery, reflection, and renewal. One respondent described it as "the strength you don't see until everything else starts to fall apart—and then it's the only thing holding us together."

Organizations that promote resilience—through culture, training, and policy—amplify its effects. They foster environments where leaders can recharge without shame, openly discuss stress, and grow stronger through adversity. In these cultures, resilience becomes a shared strength, not just an individual trait. It is integrated into leadership styles, team interactions, and organizational responses to challenges. Resilience shifts from merely a crisis response to a foundation for continuity, compassion, and long-term success.

Ultimately, resilience is the leader's anchor—silent strength that remains steady in storms and enables all other acts of leadership. However, even the strongest leaders cannot bear the burden alone. Leadership is not a solo journey; it's a shared climb. The next chapter explores Facilitating Followership: how resilient leaders build trust, empower others, and foster shared success amid challenges.

CHAPTER 15

FACILITATING FOLLOWERSHIP

In crisis leadership, "positional authority" alone rarely motivates a team or secures their genuine commitment during a crisis. The most effective leaders instead cultivate followership—a dynamic, trust-based relationship where team members willingly align behind the leader's direction, transforming it into unity, action into shared purpose, and pressure into collective strength. This interdependent dynamic between leadership and followership, rather than opposing forces, sustains high performance by fostering mutual accountability, rapid coordination, and resilience when it matters most.

Cultivating Trust, Alignment, and Shared Momentum

Leadership is not a solo act — it's a relational effort. No matter how resilient, strategic, or visionary a leader may be, their influence ultimately depends on their ability to rally others. During a crisis, this becomes even more critical. The speed, clarity, and unity of a response rely not just on the leader's decisions but also on others' willingness to follow with trust, purpose, and shared dedication. Followership isn't passive obedience; it's active engagement. It's the process where individuals choose to align with a leader's vision, contribute their energy and expertise, and help create outcomes even under pressure. Effective leaders don't just need followership; they cultivate it. They create conditions where people feel seen, valued, and empowered to act. Respondents in this study consistently emphasized that the most trusted leaders were those who "listened before they led," "made space for others to contribute," and "earned followership through clarity and care." This chapter explores cultivating followership among team members and subordinates as a vital leadership skill—focused on building trust, effective communication, and relational intelligence. We'll see how leaders foster harmony without pressure, manage disagreement without becoming defensive, and promote cultures where people follow out of conviction rather than obligation. During a crisis, followership isn't just helpful; it's essential. It turns individual resilience into collective strength and shifts leadership from a position of authority to a partnership. These leaders didn't demand respect—they earned it. They "made people want to follow," "brought out the best in everyone," and "never had to raise their voice to be heard." Their influence came not from their title but from their presence. They led with integrity, empathy, and by example—turning compliance into commitment and task execution into shared ownership. Followership thrived in the environments they created. Team members felt "safe to speak up," "trusted to act," and "valued for their contributions." These leaders, built cultures based on psychological safety, fairness, and a shared mission. They supported their teams, managed conflict constructively, and made sure no one felt left behind. Their leadership focused on service. They "put the team first," "removed barriers," and "took care of their people before themselves." They mentored, advocated, and celebrated growth. Leadership wasn't about control; it was about empowering others to succeed. This chapter examines followership as a key strategic asset in crisis leadership. It considers how leaders build trust, encourage independence, and develop resilient teams capable of acting decisively—even when the leader is absent. In high-stakes situations, the accurate measure of leadership is not how well a leader performs, but how effectively the team functions when the leader is absent.

The Psychological Foundations of Followership

Followership is often misunderstood as passive compliance, but psychologically, it is active. Essentially, followership involves willingly aligning oneself with someone else's guidance, choosing to trust, engage, and contribute. During a crisis, this choice becomes even more critical. As uncertainty increases and stakes rise, people don't follow titles; they follow leadership signals. They seek emotional stability, trustworthiness in relationships, and psychological safety. Leaders who earn followership do so not through commands, but through connection.

Trust forms the foundation of followership. Psychologically, people are more inclined to follow leaders who show consistency, transparency, and care. Respondents in this study described trusted leaders as "predictable in their values," "honest about what they knew and didn't," and "willing to listen before deciding." This trust is not built in a single moment—it grows through repeated interactions where the leader's words and actions align. When trust exists, followers feel safe taking risks, speaking up, and dedicating their energy to shared goals.

Another key foundation is psychological safety, the belief that one can freely share ideas, concerns, and emotions without fear of punishment or embarrassment. Leaders who foster psychological safety create environments where followers can thrive. They welcome dissent, seek feedback, and address vulnerability with empathy instead of defensiveness. This openness shows that the leader values more than just compliance; they also value contribution. One respondent said, "He didn't need us to agree—he needed us to engage. That made us want to follow."

A sense of belonging also plays a crucial role. People are more likely to follow when they feel part of something meaningful. Leaders who clearly communicate a purpose, connect individual roles to the collective impact, and recognize contributions help followers see themselves in the mission. This feeling of belonging turns followership from obligation into ownership. It shifts the dynamic from "I'm doing what I'm told" to "I'm helping us succeed."

Finally, emotional connection is essential. Followers respond to leaders who show empathy, authenticity, and emotional stability. During crises, people look for clues—facial expressions, tone of voice, body language—that reveal whether the leader is calm or reactive. Leaders who keep their emotions in check and communicate clearly help followers feel grounded. Their presence acts as a calming influence, allowing others to stay focused, contribute, and move forward with confidence.

Together, these psychological foundations—trust, safety, belonging, and emotional resonance—constitute the invisible structure of followership. They influence how people interpret leadership signals, decide to engage, and maintain their commitment under pressure. In a crisis, these foundations are not optional; they are vital. Because when the path ahead is uncertain, people don't just follow strategy—they follow strength, empathy, and belief.

Trust, Safety, and Shared Purpose

Followership doesn't happen by chance; it's built through trust, psychological safety, and a shared sense of purpose. In crisis leadership, these elements form the foundation of team cohesion and performance under pressure.

Respondents described leaders who "stood up for their team," "never let resentment fester," and "made sure no one felt left behind." These leaders didn't just manage tasks; they fostered relationships. Their fairness, dependability, and authenticity created environments where people felt valued, protected, and empowered to contribute.

Trust is established through consistency. These leaders recognized effort, generously credited others, and provided feedback without blame. They created space for mistakes, understanding that learning and growth require room to develop. When people felt trusted, they took initiative. When they felt safe, they spoke up. And when they believed in the mission, they gave their best.

Psychological safety isn't a soft concept; it's a strategic advantage. In high-pressure settings, the ability to raise concerns, voice dissent, or admit uncertainty can determine success or failure. Leaders who foster safety encourage participation, listen without defensiveness, and respond respectfully—even when challenged.

Shared purpose unites everything. These leaders consistently emphasized the mission, helping team members see how their work matters and why it makes a difference. They transformed routine tasks into meaningful contributions, aligning individual efforts with collective impact.

In times of crisis, trust, safety, and shared purpose aren't optional, they are essential. They turn authority into influence, direction into unity, and teams into resilient, high-performing systems ready to face whatever lies ahead.

Cultivating Followership

Followership isn't commanded; it's earned. In high-stakes environments, people choose who to follow based on how leaders communicate, whether they feel included, and how decisions are made. The most effective crisis leaders understand that authority alone doesn't guarantee alignment. They build followership by fostering trust through clarity, connection, and collaboration. Communication is the first gateway. Leaders who communicate with transparency, empathy, and clarity create conditions for followership to thrive. They don't hide the truth or overpromise; they speak plainly, acknowledge uncertainty, and provide direction with conviction.

Respondents described trusted leaders as those who "explained the why behind the what," "kept us informed even when the news was hard," and "used their voice to calm, not command." In moments of disruption, clear communication serves as a stabilizing force. It helps followers understand complex situations and see their role within them. Inclusion deepens that connection. Leaders who invite participation show that followership isn't just about obedience; it's about contribution. They seek input, listen actively, and include diverse perspectives in decision-making. This doesn't mean reaching consensus at all costs; it means creating space for people to be heard, understood, and respected. One respondent shared, "She didn't just ask for ideas—she used them. That made us feel like we were part of the solution." Inclusion encourages ownership, and ownership turns passive compliance into active engagement. Shared decision-making is the final layer. When leaders involve others in shaping direction, especially during uncertain times, they build commitment, not just cooperation. This doesn't require relinquishing authority; it requires distributing agency. Leaders who say, "Here's the challenge—let's solve it together," invite followership rooted in mutual respect. They clarify boundaries, define roles, and empower teams to act within them. This approach strengthens alignment, accelerates execution, and builds resilience across the organization.

Together, communication, inclusion, and shared decision-making form a powerful trio for cultivating followership. They show that leadership isn't a solo effort but a shared journey. In a crisis, this becomes especially important. When people feel informed, included, and empowered, they don't just follow—they commit. They bring their whole selves to the mission and help carry the weight of uncertainty with purpose and determination.

Followership Across Organizational Layers

Followership goes beyond the front-line span of control; it exists at every organizational level. From executive teams to operational units, the willingness to align, engage, and contribute under leadership is a key factor in an organization's crisis response. However, followership varies depending on context, role, and proximity to decision-making. Understanding how it manifests across different levels helps leaders intentionally develop and maintain it systematically.

At the executive level, followership is often shown through strategic alignment and principled dissent. Senior leaders may not follow traditionally—they are usually co-leaders in their own domains—but their willingness to support a shared vision, challenge assumptions constructively, and promote unified messaging is critical. When executives demonstrate followership by listening, collaborating, and deferring when necessary, they set a tone of humility and unity. One respondent noted, "Our COO didn't need to be the loudest voice—he chose to amplify the right one. That made us all more confident in the direction."

In middle management, followership involves translating and executing. These leaders act as a bridge between strategy and implementation. Their ability to interpret executive intent, communicate it clearly to teams, and adapt it to operational realities is vital. Followership here is active and relational, involving asking clarifying questions, identifying risks, and rallying teams around changing priorities. When middle managers trust their leaders and feel trusted in return, they become key channels for alignment and morale.

At the frontline, followership is often immediate and tangible. It manifests in how individuals respond to directives, share ideas, and support each other under pressure. During a crisis, frontline followership is shaped by clarity, proximity, and emotional bonds. People follow leaders who are present, communicative, and attuned to their experiences. One team member said, "She didn't just give orders—she stood with us. That's why we followed her." Here, followership is very personal, rooted in visibility, empathy, and trust.

Even in support and administrative roles, followership remains essential. These individuals might not be in the spotlight, but their responsiveness, adaptability, and dedication to shared goals bolster the organization's resilience. When they feel informed, respected, and included, their followership acts as a stabilizing force behind the scenes.

Across all levels, followership is shaped by the leader's ability to communicate purpose, foster participation, and demonstrate integrity. It's not about hierarchy; it's about relationships. When leaders understand how followership functions at each stage, they can tailor their approach, build trust across departments, and nurture a culture where alignment is voluntary, not enforced.

Service-Oriented Leadership

Followership thrives when leaders serve. In high-stakes settings, the most effective leaders don't focus on themselves; they focus on the mission and the people executing it. Respondents consistently described these leaders as selfless, supportive, and deeply dedicated to helping others succeed.

They "put the team first," "removes barriers," and "takes care of their people before themselves." Their leadership isn't about personal power—it's about collective performance. They ensure every team member has the tools, information, and support needed to act confidently and competently, even under pressure.

These leaders don't hoard decision-making; they share it. They mentor others, delegate authority, and create space for growth. They celebrate contributions, recognize effort, and ensure credit is shared generously. Their humility isn't weakness—it's strength in service of the team.

Service-oriented leadership also involves advocacy. These leaders fight for resources, shield their teams from unnecessary distractions, and stand up for their people when it matters most. Their presence signals protection, not control. Their actions build trust, loyalty, and a sense of belonging.

By emphasizing service, they redefine leadership as a duty rather than a privilege. They foster cultures where people follow not because they must, but because they want to. In doing so, they turn teams into communities—united by purpose, strengthened through trust, and empowered to act with confidence.

Followership as a Strategic Asset

In crisis leadership, followership isn't a passive role, it's a strategic asset. Respondents emphasized that successful leaders know when to assert authority and when to empower others. This balance isn't a stylistic choice—it's a tactical necessity. Assertive authority provides clarity and structure. In chaotic moments, leaders must act quickly, set clear priorities, and establish order. Their presence serves as a stabilizing force, guiding the team through uncertainty with confidence and control. However, authority alone cannot sustain an effective response. As crises develop, adaptability and continuity rely on empowering followers. Leaders must create conditions where team members are trusted to act, given decision-making authority, and encouraged to take initiative within their roles. This decentralization enables faster pivots, more responsive actions, and greater resilience. Empowered followers are not just executors—they are active contributors. They share insights from the front lines, offer diverse perspectives, and help refine strategies in real time. Their participation enhances coordination, removes bottlenecks, and fosters a culture of shared ownership. The most effective crisis leaders recognize that leadership is a system, not a solo act. When authority and empowerment are balanced, teams become disciplined, autonomous, and capable of maintaining performance even when the leader steps back. Followership, when intentionally cultivated, acts as a force multiplier. It transforms individual leadership into collective strength—and turns direction into unity when it matters most.

Building Followership Through Understanding

Followership starts with understanding. Effective crisis leaders don't just know their team's titles—they understand their team members. They recognize individual strengths, stress responses, and readiness to take on responsibility. This deep insight allows leaders to delegate confidently, assign roles based on capabilities, and foster growth without overwhelming others. Respondents highlighted that this understanding isn't static—it's developed through continuous effort. Leaders who build followership invest time in one-on-one conversations, observe team dynamics under pressure, and simulate scenarios to see how individuals react in real time. They listen actively, give feedback constructively, and prioritize emotional resilience as much as technical skill. This intentional connection builds trust. When team members feel recognized, heard, and supported, they are encouraged to step up. They take initiative, make decisions, and contribute significantly—because they trust that their leader believes in them. Psychological safety fosters trust. Leaders who create safe environments promote honest conversations, accept differing opinions, and normalize uncertainty. In high-pressure situations, this openness provides a strategic advantage. It helps teams identify concerns early, adapt quickly, and stay coordinated even as circumstances change. Understanding also prepares leaders to guide their teams toward independence. During a crisis, leaders might not always be available for guidance. By identifying who is ready to lead, who needs support, and how to establish decision-making processes, leaders ensure continuity when the unexpected occurs. Building followership through understanding isn't about control—it's about connection. It lays the foundation for trust, sparks initiative, and is the key to developing teams that perform with confidence and cohesion under pressure.

Diagnosing Followership Health Across Teams

Effective leaders don't just assume followership; they assess it. In high-stakes environments, where alignment and engagement directly affect results, diagnosing the health of followership is as important as evaluating strategy or operations. Leaders who understand how followership functions within their teams can spot gaps in trust, cohesion, and clarity before they turn into performance issues. They see followership not as a given but as a dynamic relationship that needs attention, feedback, and care. Diagnosing followership starts with careful listening. Leaders must pay close attention to how team members respond—not just to instructions, but also to uncertainty, change, and interpersonal dynamics. Are team members asking thoughtful questions, sharing ideas, and engaging with the mission? Or are they withdrawing, deferring too much, or showing signs of disengagement? These behavioral cues help determine whether followership is active and healthy or passive and strained.

Communication patterns are another useful diagnostic tool. In teams with strong followership, dialogue flows both ways. Team members feel comfortable speaking up, challenging assumptions, and giving feedback. Leaders can gauge this by watching who participates in meetings, how openly concerns are shared, and whether dissent is welcomed or met with defensiveness. A lack of upward communication might indicate fear, fatigue, or a breakdown in trust.

Emotional tone is also crucial. Leaders need to tune into the team's energy—are people motivated, connected, and resilient, or are they just operating out of compliance and caution? One person shared a moment of clarity: "We were following orders, but we weren't following her. That's when she paused and asked what we needed to feel part of the mission again." This kind of emotional awareness helps leaders' step in early and rebuild relational harmony.

Structured feedback methods can more effectively evaluate the health of followership. Pulse surveys, one-on-one check-ins, and team retrospectives can identify patterns that might otherwise go unnoticed. Leaders can ask questions such as, "Do you feel your contributions are valued?" Do you understand the reasons behind our direction? Do you feel safe raising concerns? These prompts help leaders assess psychological safety, clarity, and engagement—all key signs of active followership.

Finally, leaders must reflect on their own behaviors. Followership health often mirrors leadership practices. Are they communicating openly? Are they encouraging participation? Are they showing vulnerability and stability? When leaders assess followership with humility and curiosity, they not only identify what's working but also learn how to lead more effectively.

During a crisis, followership is adaptable—it shifts with pressure, clarity, and connection. Leaders who regularly evaluate their state across their teams are better equipped to recalibrate, reengage, and rebuild trust when it erodes. In doing so, they ensure leadership is not just about giving direction but also about building relationships, resilience, and genuine human connection.

Training and Developing Followership

Followership isn't instinct—it's a skill. Effective crisis leaders recognize that strong followership doesn't happen by chance; it must be cultivated through deliberate effort, consistent practice, and strategic reinforcement. Respondents in this study emphasized that even the best-designed plans are only as effective as the teams executing them. Success depends on individuals who are prepared, trusted, and motivated to follow with confidence, clarity, and conviction.

Training programs that build followership focus on enhancing relational and communication skills that motivate alignment. The first essential step is trust-building. Leaders learn to encourage transparency, ethical decision-making, and values-based reasoning under pressure. Simulations challenge them to explain their choices, admit mistakes, and align their actions with mission goals. Over time, these behaviors build credibility, the foundation on which followership depends. When people trust the leader's integrity, they are more willing to follow, even amid uncertainty.

Communication and influence form the second pillar. Leaders practice delivering clear, empathetic messages in high-stakes settings. Role-playing exercises help them adjust tone, content, and delivery for different audiences, whether calming a nervous team, briefing skeptical stakeholders, or managing internal dissent. Communication becomes not just a tool for directing but a means to unify. Leaders learn that how they speak is just as important as what they say, and that influence is built through clarity and compassion.

The third focus area is shared purpose and team cohesion. Training emphasizes ownership rather than just compliance. Leaders engage in exercises that foster psychological safety, invite input, and promote alignment around a shared mission.

When people feel included and invested, they follow not because they're told to—but because they believe in the goal. This shift from obligation to belief transforms followership into a source of energy, creativity, and resilience.

These skills turn directives into coordinated action and uncertainty into shared momentum. They equip leaders to mobilize teams not just through positional authority but through relational trust, strategic clarity, and emotional connection.

Core Objectives of Followership Development

Followership isn't about obedience; it's about alignment. In crisis leadership, the goal isn't to command compliance but to foster commitment. Structured followership development programs help leaders understand why people choose to follow and how to create the right conditions for that choice, especially when pressure is high and clarity is limited. Respondents highlighted three main goals that guide effective followership development. First is understanding psychological drivers. People follow leaders who provide security, direction, and purpose. In times of uncertainty, they seek competence, fairness, and shared values. Training helps leaders recognize these drivers and respond with empathy, clarity, and conviction. When leaders understand what followers need emotionally and intellectually, they can lead more precisely and compassionately. Second, practice confidence-building behaviors. Staying calm under pressure, being transparent in decision-making, and acting ethically help build trust. Leaders learn to communicate their intentions clearly, admit their mistakes, and behave in ways that reinforce their credibility. These behaviors become habits— clear signals that inspire followership and help sustain it through tough times. Third, establishing climates of alignment is crucial. Effective leaders create environments where people willingly support the mission. They foster psychological safety, encourage input, and emphasize shared goals. When individuals feel included and valued, they contribute with energy and purpose. Followership then becomes a choice based on belief rather than obligation. Together, these objectives turn followership from a vague idea into a practical, teachable skill. They help leaders go beyond authority and build influence— creating teams that follow not because they must, but because they believe in the mission and the messenger. In a crisis, this kind of followership isn't just useful; it's transformative.

Conclusion: Leadership That Multiplies

When a leader isn't present, the ability to develop followership acts as a force multiplier. It turns individual authority into collective strength and fleeting direction into lasting momentum. Leaders who cultivate followership don't just lead—they inspire. They create environments where people choose to engage, contribute, and carry the mission forward with clarity and conviction.

Respondents emphasized that the most effective leaders build trust, empower autonomy, and foster environments where people feel safe, capable, and committed. They don't just give orders; they inspire ownership. They don't merely manage teams; they shape cultures of resilience, adaptability, and collective success. Their leadership is not transactional; it's transformational.

Followership isn't about blind obedience; it's about a meaningful, trust-based relationship. It differentiates between compliance and commitment, as well as coordination and cohesion. When leaders understand why people follow—and promote actions that build trust—they unlock their teams' full potential. They turn directives into shared purpose and pressure into unity. As one respondent cleverly stated, "Followership is the leader's multiplier—turning individual authority into collective strength and transforming direction into unity when it matters most."

But trust alone isn't enough. To retain followers, leaders need to stay open—open to feedback, challenges, and perspectives beyond their own. The next chapter explores open-mindedness: the trait of leaders who listen attentively, think flexibly, and welcome diverse voices in decision-making. We'll examine how open-mindedness improves judgment, sparks innovation, and promotes inclusive leadership that thrives amid complexity.

CHAPTER 16

OPEN-MINDEDNESS

In the unpredictable terrain of crisis leadership, open-mindedness is not a luxury—it's a necessity. Open-mindedness is a crisis leader's disciplined willingness to seek out diverse viewpoints, rigorously challenge their own assumptions, and adjust their thinking as new evidence emerges. Far from indecision or passivity, it reflects intellectual humility in action—a mindset that prioritizes truth and learning over ego and control. This approach sharpens decision quality, uncovers blind spots early, and builds trust by showing teams their input genuinely shapes the path forward.

Listening, Learning, and Leading Through Complexity

In crisis leadership, certainty can be tempting but often misleading. The pressure to act quickly, project confidence, and stay in control can cause leaders to narrow their focus, dismiss dissent, and rely on familiar habits. However, the most effective leaders resist this temptation. They remain open — not just to new information but also to fresh perspectives, voices, and opportunities. Open-mindedness is not indecision; it's disciplined openness. It's the ability to hold space for complexity without losing clarity.

Open-minded leaders listen carefully before forming opinions. They seek out different perspectives, ask thoughtful questions, and stay curious even when the stakes are high. This approach doesn't slow them down; it improves their judgment. By engaging with diverse viewpoints, they avoid blind spots, challenge assumptions, and make more inclusive, adaptable, and resilient decisions. One respondent described it this way: "She didn't need to be the smartest person in the room—she needed to hear from the smartest people in the room."

Open-mindedness also boosts followership. When leaders show they are willing to learn, revise, and respond to input, they demonstrate respect. This openness fosters psychological safety and encourages teams to speak honestly, contribute creatively, and challenge constructively. It shifts leadership from a monologue to a dialogue. During uncertain times, this dialogue becomes a lifeline — connecting people across roles, disciplines, and experiences in pursuit of shared understanding. This chapter examines open-mindedness as a vital leadership skill. We'll look at how leaders develop intellectual humility, handle disagreement without becoming defensive, and create environments where continuous learning happens — even under pressure. Because in a crisis, the ability to listen effectively isn't a luxury; it's a lifeline. Leaders who stay open are best prepared to adapt, align, and lead forward.

Respondent Perspectives: Open-Mindedness in Action

Throughout this project, respondents consistently emphasized that open-mindedness is not just a soft skill but a strategic necessity. The leaders they trust most are those who "really listen," "want to understand before deciding," and "never shut down an idea just because it is different." These leaders don't see listening as a courtesy or a checkbox; they view it as a core leadership skill. They approach decision-making with questions rather than answers and foster environments where dialogue is used for discovery rather than mere formality.

Open-minded leaders create space for dissent and embrace complexity. They don't flinch when challenged or become defensive. Instead, they engage—asking questions, clarifying, welcoming different perspectives, and showing a genuine desire to learn. Their openness is active and intentional, rooted in respect for evidence and the collective wisdom of their teams. One respondent observed, "She didn't just tolerate disagreement—she made it part of the process."

A compelling example came from an emergency manager recalling a leader during a rapidly worsening wildfire. During a tactical meeting, with pressure mounting and limited time, the leader paused and asked, "What are we missing?" That simple question gave a junior logistics officer the chance to point out a supply chain weakness no one had noticed. The leader didn't just listen; they acted. At that moment, the manager said, "It changed the trajectory of our response." It wasn't just the insight that mattered; it was the openness that made it possible.

These leaders weren't just receptive to ideas—they were willing to change because of them. They listened carefully, asked insightful follow-up questions, and reconsidered their positions when new information emerged. Their mental flexibility allowed them to adapt without losing their sense of purpose. They remained true to their principles while staying open to reason. Colleagues described them as "principled yet receptive"—confident without being stubborn, curious without being aimless.

This kind of open-mindedness didn't weaken their authority; it strengthened it. It showed that they led not out of ego but from a sense of purpose. It proved they valued truth, insight, and control over certainty. During a crisis, this attitude made all the difference. It shifted leadership from individual to collective effort, transforming teams from passive followers into active participants.

Traits That Support Open-Mindedness

Open-mindedness isn't just a personality trait—it's a disciplined blend of cognitive flexibility and emotional maturity. In crisis leadership, where ambiguity is common and certainty hard to find, these qualities become crucial. They enable leaders to stay receptive without getting stuck and to be decisive without becoming rigid. Essentially, open-mindedness isn't about agreeing with every perspective; it's about being willing to consider them with curiosity, humility, and discernment.

One of the most important mental traits is intellectual humility. Open-minded leaders understand that their knowledge is always incomplete and that their perspective is naturally limited. This humility doesn't weaken their authority—it enhances their credibility. It helps them ask better questions, consider opposing viewpoints, and revise their assumptions without shame. Respondents described open-minded leaders as those who "didn't pretend to have all the answers" and "made it safe to challenge the plan if something didn't feel right." Intellectual humility creates space for learning, which is vital when conditions change faster than anyone can anticipate.

Closely related to humility is cognitive flexibility, the ability to shift perspectives, explore multiple interpretations, and update mental models when new information becomes available. Leaders with this trait don't cling to a single story; they recognize patterns, question assumptions, and stay open to being wrong. In a crisis, this flexibility allows them to pivot quickly, incorporate new insights, and avoid rigidity that can cause blind spots or escalate problems. It's not about indecision—it's about disciplined adaptability.

On the emotional side, self-regulation is essential. Open-mindedness depends on the ability to manage discomfort, especially when faced with disagreement, ambiguity, or criticism. Leaders who control their emotional reactions are better at listening carefully, accepting difficult feedback, and resisting the urge to defend their ego. They create space between stimulus and response, giving themselves time to think before acting. This emotional stability promotes psychological safety and encourages others to speak honestly.

Another key trait is empathy. Open-minded leaders don't just listen to different perspectives—they seek to understand the experiences behind them. They recognize that people's views are shaped by context, identity, and emotion. Empathy allows leaders to listen without judgment, ask questions that deepen understanding, and respond in ways that respect the speaker's intent. This emotional intelligence doesn't weaken authority—it strengthens it by building trust and connection.

Together, these cognitive and emotional qualities form the foundation of open-minded leadership. They help leaders stay true to their values while being receptive to new information, lead clearly while embracing complexity, and make decisions that reflect not just what they know—but what they're still willing to learn. In a crisis, these qualities are not optional; they are essential. Because when the path forward is uncertain, the leader who listens best often leads most effectively.

Open-Mindedness Matters in a Crisis

Crises are characterized by uncertainty, complexity, and constantly changing situations. They occur in real time, often without precedent, demanding decisions in environments that are incomplete, unstable, and emotionally charged. During such moments, no single leader can have all the answers. Expertise is crucial — but so is openness. The ability to remain receptive to new information, emerging perspectives, and unexpected insights becomes a strategic advantage. Open-mindedness is not a luxury during a crisis — it is vital.

When leaders listen actively and without judgment, they foster psychological safety. Team members are more likely to share concerns, admit mistakes, and suggest alternative strategies when they feel their opinions are valued. This openness creates a trusting environment where information flows freely and problems are identified early. One respondent described a leader who "always had the answer before the question was asked." That approach, they said, "shut down the room." The team stopped sharing ideas, and the crisis response worsened.

The cost of closed-mindedness isn't just missed opportunities but also lower morale and diminished trust.

Open-mindedness also promotes adaptability. Leaders who remain open to new information, evolving circumstances, and changing stakeholder needs are better at adjusting plans quickly. They don't mistake decisiveness for inflexibility. Instead, they lead with clarity and adaptability, shifting direction without losing sight of their goals. This capacity to pivot is essential in dynamic environments, where yesterday's assumptions may no longer hold.

Innovation thrives in cultures that are open-minded. Creative problem-solving requires psychological space—an environment to explore, test, and challenge the status quo. When leaders support new ideas and encourage respectful dissent, they unlock their teams' full mental potential. They turn crises from setbacks into opportunities for ingenuity.

Heuristics, Biases, and Blind Spots

Even the most experienced leaders can fall into cognitive shortcuts when under stress. These mental shortcuts, known as heuristics, allow for quick decisions but often reduce accuracy and create blind spots. In a crisis, where time is limited and stakes are high, these biases can distort judgment and obstruct strategic clarity.

Availability bias leads leaders to overestimate the probability of vivid or recent events, anchoring their decisions to memory rather than facts. Anchoring bias causes them to rely too heavily on initial information, even if it's random, while confirmation bias pushes them to seek out data that supports their existing beliefs. Status quo bias makes them favor sticking to familiar paths, even if those paths are outdated, and the framing effect can change perception based on how information is presented. These biases might seem natural, but they can be misleading. Leaders may see what they expect to see instead of what is truly happening, filtering new information through their experiences or preconceptions. They can mistake speed for decisiveness or familiarity for understanding, unintentionally replacing careful analysis with instinct.

The result isn't just an analytical mistake; it's strategic blindness. One emergency response director recounted a situation where a senior leader dismissed a new evacuation model because it conflicted with the "usual protocol." The model was created using updated terrain data and weather patterns. Ignoring it led to delays and confusion. "We weren't wrong because we didn't "Care," the director said. "We were wrong because we didn't listen. This failure to listen wasn't just a communication breakdown; it was a sign of deeper cognitive rigidity. It revealed a form of trained incapacity where past experiences become liabilities rather than assets. That idea—and its counterpart, occupational psychosis, provides a compelling framework for understanding how expertise can sometimes hinder insight. The next section explores these concepts in depth, showing how habitual thinking and professional norms can limit perception and how open-minded leaders learn to overcome these tendencies through curiosity, reflection, and deliberate challenges. To understand why even experienced leaders can stumble under pressure, we examine two key concepts from social science: trained incapacity and occupational psychosis. These terms might seem abstract, but they offer valuable insights into how professional expertise can unintentionally create blind spots—especially during crises. The economist and social theorist Thorstein Veblen introduced the concept of trained incapacity in his 1923 work Absentee Ownership. He used it to explain a paradox: the skills and habits that make someone effective in one situation can become liabilities in another. Veblen argued that training shapes perception so deeply that it can limit adaptability. A person becomes so accustomed to a specific way of thinking or acting that they don't recognize when a different approach is needed. It's an oxymoron—how can being trained lead to incapacity? But it's also a profound truth: expertise can lead to rigidity. Building on this, literary theorist and philosopher Kenneth Burke introduced the term occupational psychosis to describe how professional roles influence specific patterns of thought and behavior. This "psychosis" isn't a clinical diagnosis—it's a metaphor for how deeply our jobs shape our worldview. A lawyer may default to argument and precedent; a soldier may prioritize discipline and hierarchy. These ingrained habits help us perform our roles efficiently, but they can also limit our perspective, especially when facing unfamiliar or complex challenges. In crisis leadership, these concepts have real-world impacts. Think of a firefighter trained to run toward danger. That instinct, sharpened through years of drills and experience, often saves lives during emergencies. However, during a chemical spill, the best course of action might be to evacuate and reassess. Still, the urge to act immediately can sometimes override the need to pause. Similarly, an emergency manager who strictly follows response protocols may find it difficult to improvise in a new type of crisis. Their training, once a source of consistency, can become a barrier to innovation. Even outside the urgency of an emergency, the core principle remains valid. A cybersecurity expert might excel in their specific field but overlook the human factors involved in a larger system failure. A logistics specialist could be so focused on supply chains that they ignore morale or communication problems. What they see is accurate—but incomplete. These examples highlight the paradox: the very strengths that define professional competence can create blind spots or lead to counterproductive actions. Without reflection, cross-training, and adaptive thinking, trained incapacity and occupational psychosis become genuine barriers to effective leadership. For professionals reading this book, the main point is clear: training is never completely neutral. Every habit or skill learned through experience involves assumptions, biases, and limitations. What works well in one setting might hinder adaptability or innovation in another. Leaders need to stay aware of how their expertise influences their view—and be prepared to question it when necessary.

Reinforcing Open-Mindedness

Open-mindedness may start as a personal trait, but its longevity depends on the environment where it is practiced. In high-pressure leadership situations, where the desire to appear decisive can easily overshadow the importance of staying open-minded, organizations play a crucial role in fostering this leadership quality. When open-mindedness becomes part of the culture and is strengthened through feedback, it becomes more than just a trait; it becomes a standard.

Organizational culture sets the tone. Leaders are more likely to stay open when curiosity is rewarded, dissent is welcomed, and learning takes priority over performance showmanship. Cultures that value open-mindedness don't see disagreement as disloyalty—they see it as a contribution. They encourage leaders to ask questions, admit uncertainty, and change their minds without fear of harming their reputation. One respondent noted, "In our organization, changing your mind wasn't seen as weakness—it was seen as wisdom." That cultural mindset makes all the difference.

Rituals and routines can reinforce this mindset. Regular debriefs that include reflective questions—What did we miss? Who else should we have heard from? What assumptions went untested? —show that openness is not just occasional, but an ongoing expectation. When these questions are part of operational routines, they promote intellectual humility and collective understanding. They also create space for quieter voices to be heard, surfacing insights that might otherwise be overlooked.

Feedback loops are just as important. Organizations that value open-mindedness build systems for upward feedback, peer coaching, and 360-degree reviews that assess not only what leaders decide but also how they make those decisions. These feedback approaches ask: Does this leader listen carefully? Do they actively seek out different viewpoints? Do they respond productively to challenges? When open-minded behaviors are measured, recognized, and encouraged, they become part of leadership standards—not just personal preferences.

Leading from the top strengthens the message. When senior leaders demonstrate open-mindedness—by seeking feedback, acknowledging blind spots, and giving credit when others change their views, they set a strong example. Their actions filter throughout the organization, showing that openness is a leadership strength rather than a weakness. It teaches emerging leaders that curiosity and conviction can coexist; they complement each other.

Ultimately, fostering open-mindedness requires more than just encouragement; it demands infrastructure. It calls on organizations to build cultures where listening feels safe, feedback is practical, and learning is continuous. By doing so, they don't just support open-minded leaders; they cultivate them. And during a crisis, these are the leaders who will adapt swiftly, make wiser decisions, and lead with the humility and clarity that complexity demands.

Cultivating Open-Minded Leadership

Open-mindedness isn't innate; it's something you develop. While some leaders might naturally lean toward curiosity and receptivity, maintaining openness under pressure is a skill you learn. It requires intentional practice, reflection, and dedication to growth. Effective leaders begin by examining their own biases and assumptions. They learn to recognize when their thinking is more influenced by habit than by facts, and they develop the courage to question their own conclusions.

One of the most effective ways leaders foster open-mindedness is by actively seeking dissenting opinions and cross-functional insights. They don't just surround themselves with agreement; they embrace challenges. Whether through informal conversations or structured methods like red teaming, pre-mortems, and after-action reviews, these leaders create space for alternative viewpoints to emerge. They view disagreement not as a disruption but as an opportunity for learning. In doing so, they cultivate cultures where respectful challenges are encouraged and where truth takes precedence over ego.

Tools like tabletop exercises and scenario simulations allow leaders to practice open-mindedness in a safe space. These exercises expose leaders to real-world complexity, encouraging them to adapt, listen, and adjust in real time. Red teams serve as constructive challengers—testing plans before execution and uncovering blind spots that might otherwise go unnoticed. Far from delaying decision-making, these practices enhance it. They help leaders make smarter choices by broadening the perspective through which they evaluate options.

Ultimately, open-mindedness turns uncertainty into opportunity and disagreement into insight. It broadens perspective, sharpens judgment, and welcomes wisdom from every team member. As one respondent said, "They treated every conversation as a chance to grow." That mindset—curious, principled, and receptive—is the hallmark of a leader who succeeds not by having all the answers but by listening, learning, and leading with clarity.

During crises and emergencies, inflexible thinking can be a drawback. Leaders who embrace adaptability, curiosity, and inclusive communication are better prepared to handle uncertainty and complexity. Open-mindedness isn't passive; it requires active listening, intellectual humility, and a willingness to challenge one's own assumptions. When leaders cultivate this trait, they foster environments where innovation thrives, and teams feel heard, valued, and empowered to contribute meaningfully.

However, open-mindedness alone is not enough. While it promotes diverse input and flexible thinking, leadership also requires accountability, meaning taking responsibility for decisions, fulfilling commitments, and standing by the results. The next trait, accountability, shifts the focus from mental openness to behavioral honesty. In high-stakes situations, leaders must do more than make decisions; they must accept responsibility for them. Accountability ensures that actions reflect core values, promises are kept, and trust is built through honesty and follow-through. It serves as the foundation for earning and maintaining credibility, especially when the stakes are high and the outcomes are uncertain.

Conclusion: The Discipline of Receptivity

Open-mindedness isn't just a passive trait; it's active discipline. In crisis leadership, where uncertainty is constant and clarity fleeting, being receptive becomes a strategic advantage. Leaders who foster open-mindedness don't simply tolerate diverse perspectives; they actively seek them out. They listen intentionally, reflect humbly, and adapt courageously. Their openness isn't a sign of indecision—it's a sign of strength.

Throughout this chapter, we've seen how open-mindedness fosters psychological safety, boosts adaptability, and encourages innovation. We've explored how cognitive biases and professional blind spots can skew judgment, and how leaders can address these issues through curiosity, reflection, and structured questioning. We've heard from respondents who described open-minded leaders as "principled yet receptive"— individuals who stay true to their values while remaining open to new ideas.

Most importantly, we've confirmed that open-mindedness is not innate; it is learned. Open-mindedness can be practiced, strengthened, and refined over time. Through intentional growth, leaders can expand their cognitive abilities, deepen their emotional intelligence, and foster cultures where dialogue is not just tolerated but expected. In doing so, they shift leadership from a position of control to one of connection.

But receptivity alone isn't enough. Leadership also demands accountability: the willingness to own decisions, honor commitments, and stand behind outcomes. The next chapter focuses on Accountability and Ownership: traits of leaders who align their actions with their values, accept responsibility when things go wrong, and build trust through transparency and follow-through. If open-mindedness opens the door to inclusive leadership, accountability provides the foundation that makes it credible. Together, they form a strong partnership—ensuring leaders are not only receptive to insight but also answerable for their impact.

CHAPTER 17

ACCOUNTABILITY AND OWNERSHIP

I n crisis leadership, accountability is not just a virtue—it's a requirement. When stakes are high and uncertainty looms, the most effective crisis leaders take full ownership of their decisions, actions, and outcomes—no dodging responsibility or shifting blame when things go wrong. They stand tall, give credit where due, and model integrity that earns deep trust and loyalty from their teams. This accountability is non-negotiable because blame avoidance erodes morale, stalls momentum, and turns recoverable setbacks into organizational disasters.

Standing Behind Decisions, Upholding Trust

Leadership isn't just about making decisions and taking ownership. In a crisis, where uncertainty is high and consequences are real, accountability becomes the ultimate measure of a leader's integrity. It is the mark that turns authority into credibility and action into trust. While open-mindedness encourages diverse input, accountability ensures those insights lead to responsible choices and transparent follow-up.

Accountability isn't about being perfect; it's about being present. It means being willing to stand behind decisions, admit mistakes, and stay responsible when results are unclear or unfavorable. Leaders who demonstrate this don't shift blame or hide behind procedures. They take ownership of their role, influence, and commitments. One respondent summarized it well: "She didn't just lead the plan—she owned the consequences."

Ownership is the behavioral counterpart to strategic clarity. It shows that the leader isn't just directing others; they're personally committed to the mission's success. In high-stakes environments, this approach fosters trust. Teams are more likely to follow accountable leaders—who show up when things go wrong, communicate openly, and demonstrate the responsibility they expect from others.

This chapter explores accountability as a crucial leadership skill. We will examine how it manifests in decision-making, communication, and team interactions. We'll see how leaders cultivate cultures of ownership—where responsibility is shared rather than avoided, and where trust is built through actions, not just words. In crises, accountability is more than a virtue—it's a stabilizer. It shifts leadership from simple performance to genuine partnership and ensures resilience on both personal and organizational levels.

Accountability as a Defining Mark of Leadership

Through surveys, interviews, and field reports, respondents consistently emphasized accountability as a crucial trait of the leaders they trusted most. These leaders were described as "dependable," "honorable," and "the moral core of the team." Their credibility wasn't based solely on charisma or technical skills, but on their willingness to own decisions, face consequences, and stand with their teams during challenges. One respondent remembered a leader who, during a failed deployment of emergency resources, refused to deflect blame or redirect scrutiny. "They never threw anyone under the bus," the respondent said. "They took full responsibility, even though the mistake wasn't entirely theirs. That made us want to work even harder the next time." Another shared, "If something went wrong, they faced it head-on. No excuses, no finger-pointing, just a clear plan to fix it and a commitment to learn from it." These moments weren't dramatic; they were defining. They revealed a kind of quiet strength that inspired loyalty, trust, and resilience. Notably, respondents stressed that this sense of accountability was genuine and not superficial. It wasn't about appearances or reputation management. Instead, it stemmed from the leader's character. They viewed ownership not as a burden but as a privilege—an expression of their dedication to the mission and those they serve. One team member described their supervisor as "the person who always showed up when things went sideways—not to take control, but to take responsibility." That presence, especially during times of uncertainty or failure, served as a calming influence. Another emergency coordinator shared a story about a leader who openly admitted a flawed evacuation plan during a community debrief. "He didn't sugarcoat it," she said. "He explained what went wrong, what he missed, and what we'd do differently next time. That transparency built more trust than any success ever could." In that moment, accountability became more than a leadership trait and became a cultural signal. It told the team that mistakes were not shameful but instructive, and that leadership meant standing in the light, not hiding in the shadows. These leaders demonstrated a sense of ownership that extended beyond their own actions. They fostered environments where others felt safe taking responsibility, speaking openly, and learning without fear. Their behavior set the tone for the entire organization. As one respondent mentioned, "When the leader owns it, we all feel empowered to do the same. It's contagious." In a crisis, accountability goes beyond just answering for results and involves anchoring the team in integrity. It shifts leadership from a simple role to a relationship, and from a position of authority to one of trust. The following section looks at how this principle appears in decision-making, communication, and team dynamics—and how leaders can encourage cultures of ownership that endure beyond the immediate crisis.

Accountability in Action

Accountable leaders not only own outcomes, they own the process as well. They face complexity with clarity and conviction, analyzing problems not to place blame but to understand their role in creating solutions. Their approach is proactive rather than defensive. They communicate honestly, even when the news is difficult, and remain present when things go wrong. This type of leadership doesn't hide behind hierarchy or procedures; it stands in front of them, demonstrating the integrity it expects from others.

Respondents repeatedly highlighted that accountability is more than just a trait; it is a lived experience. The leaders they trust most are those who consistently take responsibility for both successes and failures. One team member described a supervisor who, after a failed initiative, gathered the team and said, "Here's what I missed. Let's talk about what we can learn." That moment didn't just resolve the issue—it fostered deeper trust and stronger cohesion. The leader's willingness to own the mistake created space for honest reflection and collective growth.

These leaders communicated openly and honestly. They didn't hide the truth or setbacks. Instead, they spoke frankly, acknowledged their limitations, and asked for feedback. Their transparency fostered psychological safety, enabling others to speak up, share concerns, and get involved without fear of unfair blame. One respondent said, "You could tell the truth in front of her—even if it was messy. She made it safe to be honest." That safety wasn't accidental—it was built through consistent, respectful behavior.

Accountable leaders also acted on lessons learned. They didn't treat reflection as a ritual—they regarded it as a responsibility. When feedback appeared, they responded. When mistakes occurred, they adjusted. Their follow-through demonstrated that accountability wasn't just for show; it was part of their character. They saw ownership not as a burden but as a privilege, reflecting their commitment to the mission and the people they serve.

This kind of leadership doesn't enforce accountability; it encourages it. Team members aim to perform not out of fear but from pride and mutual respect. They take initiative, speak honestly, and invest in results because they know their leader will do the same. Accountability becomes contagious, spreading through the team as a shared value rather than just a management expectation.

During crises, this ethic becomes especially important. When pressure increases and clarity diminishes, teams rely on their leaders not just for guidance but for stability. Accountable leaders provide that stability—not by being flawless but by showing up consistently. They anchor the team in fairness, honesty, and follow-through. In doing so, they elevate leadership from a mere role to a relationship—one built on trust, upheld through actions, and tested in difficult times.

The Behavioral Signals of Accountability

Accountability is more than just a principle—it's a consistent way of behaving. In crisis leadership, it appears through actions that show integrity, dependability, and taking responsibility. Leaders who practice accountability don't need to state it; their actions speak for themselves. Teams notice it in how leaders show up, handle setbacks, and keep their promises. These behavioral signals build trust, especially when pressure mounts and clarity fades. One of the most apparent signs is follow-through. Accountable leaders follow through on their commitments. They meet deadlines, keep promises, and proactively communicate if circumstances change. Their dependability creates stability, especially in unpredictable environments. As one respondent noted, "You didn't have to chase her down for updates—she was already ahead of it." This consistency builds trust within the team.

Another sign of strong leadership is transparency in decision-making. Accountable leaders share not only what they decide but also why. They explain their reasoning, acknowledge trade-offs, and invite questions. This openness doesn't weaken authority; it strengthens it. It shows respect for the team's intelligence and an openness to being held to a standard of clarity. One emergency coordinator recalled a leader who began every briefing with, "Here's what we know, here's what we don't, and here's what we're doing about it." That framing helped create alignment and reduce confusion.

Responsiveness to failure also reveals a lot. Accountable leaders don't dodge blame or downplay mistakes. They confront errors directly, accept responsibility, and focus on finding solutions. Their approach isn't defensive; it's constructive. One respondent described a leader who, after a failed rollout, gathered the team and said, "This didn't go as planned. Here's what I missed, and here's how we'll fix it together." That moment not only fixed the plan but also strengthened the team's trust in the leader.

Modeling shared ownership is another essential behavior. Accountable leaders don't isolate responsibility—they share it. They empower others to take initiative, make decisions, and own results. They celebrate contributions and handle pressure, fostering a culture of mutual accountability rather than hierarchy. One team member said, "He didn't just hold us accountable, he held himself accountable to us." That reciprocity shifted the team's dynamic from compliance to commitment.

Finally, being present during tough times is a powerful signal. Accountable leaders don't disappear when things go wrong. They show up, stay engaged, and remain visible. Their presence demonstrates solidarity and steadiness. It communicates, "I'm with you—not just when it's easy, but when it's hard." That type of leadership boosts morale and reinforces the idea that the mission—and the people behind it—matter.

Together, these behavioral signals embody proper accountability. They turn abstract values into actionable behaviors and build lasting trust beyond the crisis. In the next section, we'll explore how leaders can weave accountability into team culture—creating environments where ownership is genuinely embraced rather than just expected.

Why Accountability Matters — Especially in Crisis

Accountability is not a punishment. It's a promise. It's the assurance that what we say will be reflected in our actions, that our values will be evident through our behavior, and that our leadership will be transparent to those who depend on us. In high-pressure environments, accountability is more than just a leadership virtue that unifies teams. When stakes are high and uncertainty is standard, people look for signals of stability, integrity, and shared responsibility. Accountable leaders send those signals. They build trust among colleagues, stakeholders, and the public by showing they are answerable not only for results but also for the process that produces them. Their transparency enhances credibility. Their dependability fosters resilience. And their clarity improves focus, helping teams understand their roles, boundaries, and expectations when confusion might otherwise prevail. During a crisis, accountability becomes critical. When systems fail and uncertainty increases, people seek anchors. Accountability is that anchor. It affirms: "We are still here. We are still responsible. We will not disappear when circumstances get tough." But accountability isn't just reactive; it's proactive. It involves the daily discipline of showing up, following through, and owning the outcomes—even when they aren't perfect. It's what builds trust before a crisis and sustains it afterward. Conversely, avoidant leadership erodes the foundation of coordination. It diminishes morale, fosters mistrust, and hampers decision-making, especially when clarity and unity are most needed. Leaders who dodge blame, suppress feedback, or shy away from difficult conversations send a damaging message: that responsibility is negotiable. In a crisis, this ambiguity can be as dangerous as the emergency itself. It creates a void of ownership, allowing problems to grow and teams to hesitate, unsure of who is responsible or what step to take next. The consequences of avoidant leadership are real and severe. Take the 2003 Space Shuttle Columbia disaster as an example. When reentering the atmosphere, the shuttle disintegrated, killing all seven astronauts onboard. The investigation revealed that engineers had raised concerns about foam damage to the wing early in the mission, but those concerns were ignored. The organizational culture at the time discouraged dissent and lacked clear accountability for escalating risk. Decisions were made without full transparency, and warnings were hidden beneath layers of hierarchy and hesitation. Afterwards, NASA implemented major reforms. Leaders were retrained to take responsibility for decisions, encourage different opinions, and openly explain their reasoning. Flight directors began holding organized pre-launch briefings where every concern had to be addressed, regardless of rank or perceived urgency. Accountability became a clear standard—not just an ideal. These changes not only improved safety protocols but also restored trust within the agency and with the public. NASA's recovery was not only technical; it was cultural. This case highlights a vital truth: accountability isn't optional in crisis leadership. Without it, outcomes can be catastrophic; with it, organizations can be rebuilt from within. But accountability should be more than a quick fix, it must be an ongoing practice. It requires structural, cultural, and behavioral changes. Leaders must show ownership, welcome scrutiny, and remain answerable even when the stakes are highest. Leaders who embrace accountability foster cultures of resilience. They demonstrate transparency, seek feedback, and create a safe environment for open dialogue. They don't shift blame or hide behind procedures. Instead, they step forward and say, "This was my decision. Here's what I learned. Here's what we'll do differently next time." In a multilingual, multi-stakeholder world, accountability also involves translation—not just of language, but of intent. It's about ensuring our messages are not only heard but understood, that our commitments are not only declared but also demonstrated. Accountability links leadership to legacy. Without it, we drift; with it, we persevere. To differentiate accountability from avoidant leadership, we examine their behaviors, mindsets, and results.

Building and Living a Culture of Ownership

Accountability is more than just a personal trait; it's a cultural force. In resilient organizations, it is embedded in the daily routines of leadership, decision-making, and team interactions. Leaders play a key role in cultivating this culture, not just by enforcing rules but by demonstrating ownership in ways that are clear, consistent, and inspiring. It starts with clarity. Leaders clearly define roles and decision-making boundaries, so individuals understand where their authority begins and ends. This clarity reduces confusion and encourages people to act confidently. When responsibilities are communicated clearly, accountability shifts from control to contribution. Modeling behavior matters. Leaders who hold themselves to high standards—ethically, professionally, and interpersonally—set the tone for the entire organization. Their actions become a reference point. When they admit mistakes, explain decisions transparently, and follow through on commitments, they signal that ownership is not optional—it's expected. One respondent noted, "He didn't just talk about accountability—he lived it. And that made us want to do the same."

Reflection is another crucial element. After-action reviews, when focused on learning rather than blame, foster honest dialogue. These reviews help teams recognize what worked, what didn't, and what can be improved. In one healthcare system, a hospital administrator introduced a "no-blame debrief" after each emergency department surge. Staff were encouraged to speak openly about failures and opportunities. Over time, this approach transformed the culture. Nurses, physicians, and support staff began taking responsibility, reporting issues early, and collaborating more effectively. Accountability became routine, not just a requirement.

Recognition reinforces this ethic. When leaders acknowledge responsible actions, whether it's a thoughtful decision, a candid admission, or a proactive fix—they validate the importance of ownership. This doesn't mean celebrating perfection; it means respecting integrity. In cultures of ownership, people feel recognized not only for their accomplishments but also for how they show up.

Training also plays an essential role. Accountability can be cultivated through deliberate practice. Programs that include decision-transparency exercises, structured feedback loops, and simulation-based learning help leaders develop ownership habits. At FEMA's Emergency Management Institute, simulation drills require leaders to make quick decisions and then explain their choices to peers. This process reinforces the expectation that leaders must be responsible for both their actions and their reasoning. It transforms accountability from an abstract value into a practical skill.

For accountability to be truly effective, it must be integrated into the organization's systems and culture. This involves establishing decision-making authority before crises occur, ensuring transparency through structured reviews after incidents, and aligning performance evaluations with ownership behaviors. Flat hierarchies enable real-time decisions, while psychological safety encourages honest reflection. Organizations like the U.S. Wildland Fire community institutionalize after-action reviews at all levels, making each incident a learning opportunity. Leaders are expected to document decisions, explain their reasoning, and suggest improvements. This practice shifts the culture from blame to learning and makes accountability a shared core value.

In cultures of ownership, mistakes are seen as lessons, and responsibility is a shared value. Leaders don't just manage; they empower others. Teams don't merely perform but actively participate. And accountability evolves into more than just a leadership trait—it provides the foundation for a resilient, adaptable organization.

Measuring Accountability

Assessing accountability within a team or organization involves more than just checking a list; it requires a nuanced understanding of behavior, trust, and follow-through. Accountability isn't a fixed trait; it's a dynamic practice that manifests through patterns of actions and interactions. To truly determine if it's embedded, leaders need to look beyond intentions and consider the actual experiences of their teams. One key indicator is decision transparency. Accountable leaders consistently explain their decisions and the reasons behind them. They clearly state the rationale, acknowledge trade-offs, and invite scrutiny. This openness builds credibility and shows that decisions are made in service of shared goals, not in isolation. When transparency becomes routine, it fosters alignment and helps reduce confusion, especially in high-pressure environments. Another sign is accepting responsibility. Leaders who make their own mistakes and learn from them show maturity and integrity. They don't shift blame or hide errors; they face them directly and use them as chances for growth. This attitude sets the tone for the entire team, encouraging others to be honest in their reflections and to take initiative without fearing punishment. Peer-to-subordinate trust is also an essential measure. When feedback reflects perceptions of fairness, consistency, and credibility, it shows that accountability isn't just claimed — it's genuinely felt. Trust is built when leaders follow through, communicate openly, and stay engaged during tough times. It decreases when promises are broken or responsibility is avoided. Consistent follow-through is another essential trait. Accountable leaders don't just make plans; they take action. They adapt when needed, communicate updates clearly, and ensure commitments are fulfilled. Their reliability serves as a stabilizing force, especially during a crisis, when uncertainty can easily disrupt momentum. Finally, team confidence offers a powerful perspective. When teams act decisively, take responsibility, and collaborate openly, it demonstrates that accountability is shared. People feel empowered to contribute because they trust that leadership will support them rather than blame them. As one respondent said, "We didn't just trust our leader—we trusted the culture she built." These indicators—collected through simulations, feedback tools, and real-world observation—offer a clear view of whether accountability is truly embedded. They shift assessment from theory to practice, helping organizations spot strengths, fix gaps, and reinforce behaviors that build trust.

Sustaining Accountability Over Time

Proper accountability isn't achieved through training alone; it must also be reinforced through policies, structures, and culture. Organizations that sustain accountability over time do so intentionally. They create systems that promote responsible behavior, reward integrity, and encourage reflection.

A critical initial step is to establish clear decision rights and document them in crisis plans. When roles and authorities are defined in advance, leaders can respond quickly, and teams can act confidently. Ambiguity causes hesitation; clarity fosters ownership.

Accountability should be included in job descriptions and promotional standards. When responsible behavior is recognized, rewarded, and expected at all levels, it becomes part of the organization's identity. Leaders are judged not only by results but also by how they lead, handle challenges, and maintain trust.

Regular after-action reviews focused on learning instead of blame are essential. These reviews promote honest reflection, shared insights, and continuous improvement. They show that accountability is about growth, not punishment. When teams know mistakes will be discussed constructively, they are more likely to speak up, take risks, and improve.

Multi-source feedback enhances the assessment process. Peer reviews, subordinate input, and cross-functional evaluations provide a more complete view of leadership credibility. They illustrate how accountability is perceived across the organization—not just demonstrated from the top.

Finally, organizations should reward transparency and responsible risk-taking, even when outcomes are imperfect. Leaders who admit uncertainty, explain their reasoning, and act with integrity deserve praise—not punishment. This cultural support sustains accountability as a core value, not just a rigid rule.

Maintaining accountability requires vigilance, humility, and deliberate planning. It encourages organizations to see ownership not just as a slogan but as a comprehensive system—

one strengthened through consistent behavior, evaluated through trust, and confirmed in critical moments.

Embedding Accountability in Culture

Accountability flourishes when it is not only expected from individuals but also genuinely woven into the team's culture. In high-stakes settings where decisions have significant consequences and outcomes are often uncertain, leaders must do more than demonstrate ownership—they must promote it as a shared value. When accountability becomes a core part of the organizational culture, it shifts from simple compliance to genuine commitment, and from strict enforcement to meaningful empowerment. Embedding accountability starts with clarity. Teams need to understand not only what is expected but also why it is essential. Leaders who communicate both purpose and performance foster a stronger sense of responsibility. They link tasks to the mission, roles to impact, and decisions to core values. One respondent described a leader who began every project by saying, "Here's what success looks like—and here's how we'll own it together." That framing turned deliverables into shared commitments.

Rituals and routines reinforce this ethic. Regular debriefs, after-action reviews, and feedback sessions provide opportunities for reflection and learning. When these practices become routine, not just used during crises, they demonstrate that accountability is continuous, not occasional. Leaders who ask, "What did we learn? What will we do differently?" promote ownership without shame. They shift the focus from blame to improvement. Psychological safety is critical. Accountability cannot thrive in environments of fear or defensiveness. Leaders must create conditions where people feel comfortable speaking up, admitting mistakes, and taking initiative. This involves consistent modeling—leaders who admit their mistakes, respond to feedback with curiosity, and celebrate growth as well as success. One team member said, "We didn't just have permission to be honest—we had encouragement." That support made accountability seem like a shared strength rather than a personal risk. Recognition also plays a vital role. When leaders acknowledge responsible behavior—whether it's a thoughtful decision, a candid admission, or a proactive fix, they reinforce the importance of ownership. This doesn't mean rewarding perfection; it means valuing integrity. Celebrating accountability sends a message: what matters is not just what gets done, but how it gets done. Finally, shared responsibility strengthens the culture. When accountability is spread across roles and levels, it becomes a common standard. Leaders who delegate authority, define boundaries, and empower decision-making create environments where everyone feels responsible for outcomes. One respondent said, "He didn't carry the team— he built a team that carried itself." Embedding accountability into team culture isn't a one-time effort; it's a leadership habit. It requires deliberate planning, ongoing reinforcement, and emotional intelligence. When done well, it transforms teams from reactive to resilient, from merely compliant to truly committed. In the next section, we'll explore how accountability links to ethical leadership and how leaders maintain trust when stakes are high and visibility is low. One of the most consistent findings in crisis research is that uncertainty about decision-making authority can be as harmful as the crisis itself. When leaders are unsure of who has the power to act, it can lead to paralysis or conflicting actions. Clarifying authority, embedding accountability into systems, and reinforcing it through culture are crucial steps toward effective preparedness. Organizations that implement these steps do more than develop effective crisis responses; they also foster lasting public trust. After the Challenger disaster, NASA restructured its leadership approach to acknowledge those who identified risks and took responsibility for difficult decisions. This change not only enhanced safety but also regained credibility.

ACCOUNTABLE LEADERS	UNACCOUNTABLE LEADERS
Own Successes and Failures Equally	Take Credit For Success but Shift Blame for Failures
Encourage Open Feedback and Learning	Dismiss Criticism or Suppress Feedback
Communicate Transparently	Avoid Difficult Conversations or Deflect
Create Psychological Safety Zones	Foster Fear, Mistrust, or Resentment
Act on Lessons Learned	Repeating Mistakes Without Learning

Conclusion: The Compass of Integrity

Accountability acts as a leader's compass—guiding them toward integrity, trust, and responsibility when the path ahead is uncertain. It's not about being perfect; it's about showing up. During a crisis, accountable leaders don't just give directions; they earn the trust needed to lead. Their credibility is proven not in moments of success but in how they handle setbacks. They stand firm afterward and share the consequences. And commit to rebuilding with clarity and resolve. Respondents highlighted a clear difference between accountable and avoidant leadership. Accountable leaders accept both successes and failures, communicate honestly, and foster psychological safety. They seek feedback, learn from mistakes, and create environments where responsibility is shared rather than feared. In contrast, avoidant leaders shift blame, suppress dissent, and repeat mistakes without reflection. The difference is not only behavioral but also cultural: one builds trust, the other damages it. In tough times, leadership is tested not just by the ability to manage complexity but also by the willingness to remain visible and accountable when the dust settles. This consistent presence distinguishes transactional leadership from transformational leadership. It's not just about managing events; it's about taking responsibility when it matters most. Accountability in this context extends beyond personal virtue. It forms the foundation of credible and effective crisis leadership. Leaders who consistently take ownership earn trust not by being perfect, but through transparency, humility, and follow-through. They build loyalty by demonstrating they are not above the consequences of their decisions and foster cultures where learning is prioritized—even when it stems from failure. Accountability isn't about avoiding mistakes; it's about facing them honestly and using them as opportunities to grow. By refusing to shift blame or hide difficult truths, accountable leaders act as stabilizing forces in uncertain environments. Their actions show a strong commitment—not only to the immediate situation but also to the long-term health and resilience of their teams and organizations. They exemplify ethical leadership by stepping up when things go wrong, showing that leadership is not a shield from scrutiny but a platform for principled action. As one experienced leader said, "In the end, accountability is the promise a leader makes—not just to take charge when things go right, but to stand firm, take responsibility, and lead the way forward when everything goes wrong." However, accountability is not fixed. It is a dynamic force that fosters ongoing growth. Genuine ownership encourages leaders to think, adapt, and improve. It supports a constant pursuit of better results—not for personal gain, but for team progress. Leaders who adopt this mindset turn setbacks into learning opportunities, building skills and confidence for future challenges. This commitment to growth naturally leads to the next aspect of leadership: continuous performance improvement. In the next chapter, we explore how effective leaders turn lessons into lasting skills. Through intentional reflection, structured feedback, and adaptive learning, they prepare their teams not just to recover but to come back stronger, smarter, and more resilient than before. Because in crisis leadership, the goal is not only to survive — it is to improve.

CHAPTER 18

COMMITMENT TO ONGOING PERFORMANCE IMPROVEMENT

I n the world of crisis leadership, the most effective crisis leaders are defined not by what they already know, but by their relentless commitment to continuous improvement— a mindset that rejects the illusion of ever being "fully ready" in favor of constant reflection, adaptation, and evolution. They treat every event, drill, and debrief as a chance to sharpen readiness, because in dynamic crises, static preparation erodes fast while those who evolve stay ahead of the curve.

Turning Lessons into Capability

In crisis leadership, survival isn't the final goal—growth is. The most effective leaders don't just survive disruption; they learn from it, adapt because of it, and come out stronger. Performance improvement signifies a shift that turns accountability into progress. It demonstrates a leader's dedication not only to completing the task but to doing it better—again and again. Performance isn't a one-time achievement; it's an ongoing commitment. In resilient organizations, excellence isn't measured by a single success but by the discipline to continuously evolve, adapt, and improve. Continuous performance improvement isn't just a slogan or a quarterly initiative; it's a core part of the culture. It adopts a mindset that views every outcome—whether positive or negative—as valuable data for refinement, every challenge as a chance for growth, and every team member as an active contributor to progress. In high-stakes environments where uncertainty constantly exists and expectations change rapidly, the ability to learn faster than circumstances shift provides a strategic edge. Leaders committed to continuous improvement don't wait for crises to expose weaknesses; they implement systems to identify them early. They cultivate cultures where feedback is appreciated, experimentation is encouraged, and accountability is shared. Improvement isn't reactive; it's integrated into the process. This commitment extends beyond metrics and dashboards. It requires humility, curiosity, and bravery—humility to recognize what isn't working, curiosity to explore new ideas, and bravery to pivot when legacy systems or habits resist change. It distinguishes organizations that withstand pressure from those that falter under it.

Continuous performance improvement is also a relational act. It signals to teams that their work matters, that their insights are valued, and that their growth is supported. It transforms performance from a judgment into a journey—one that is shared, iterative, and rooted in purpose.

This mark isn't about chasing perfection. It's about fostering a mindset of continuous learning, operational improvement, and strategic growth. Leaders who focus on performance enhancement view every challenge as an opportunity to diagnose. They ask not only "What happened?" but also "What can we learn?" and "How do we improve from this?" Their goal is future-oriented—not just on recovery, but on readiness.

Respondents described these leaders as "relentlessly reflective," "always scanning for ways to improve," and "never satisfied with good enough." One emergency manager recalled a leader who, after a successful response to a regional flood, convened a cross-functional review—not to celebrate, but to identify what could have been better. "He said, 'We got lucky this time. Let's make sure we don't have to rely on luck next time.'" That mindset—humble, proactive, and systems-oriented—is the essence of performance improvement.

This chapter explores how leaders turn lessons into sustained capabilities. We'll examine the tools, habits, and cultural practices that promote adaptive learning. We'll see how feedback loops, simulations, and post-incident reviews serve as engines of growth. Additionally, we'll demonstrate how leaders establish environments where continuous improvement isn't just encouraged but expected. In crisis leadership, the ability to improve isn't a bonus; it is essential.

Growth as a Shared Standard

Through interviews and field observations, respondents consistently described the most admired leaders as those who "never acted like they knew everything," "treated every challenge as a learning opportunity," and "made improvement contagious." These weren't just flattering descriptions; they reflected a more profound truth: that growth, when modeled with humility and consistency, becomes a cultural standard.

This mindset is not only admirable but also vital. In high-stakes environments where conditions change rapidly and decisions are crucial, leaders must stay adaptable, informed, and flexible. The leaders featured in this study didn't just talk about growth— they demonstrated it. They attended workshops not because they had to, but because they were curious. They pursued coaching, studied after hours, and shared ideas that benefited the whole team. One respondent recalled a leader who would return from every conference with detailed notes and a list of "three things we can try this month." That kind of intentional effort made growth tangible and actionable.

These leaders mentored selflessly. They provided feedback that boosted confidence rather than instilled fear, and they turned mistakes into lessons instead of punishments. Their humility and curiosity fostered a culture where learning was expected, encouraged, and celebrated. "You could ask questions without being judged," one team member shared. "Even if you were wrong, they'd say, 'Good—now let's figure it out together.'"

One compelling story came from a respondent who served under a leader during a complex deployment. After several operational setbacks, the team gathered for a debrief. Instead of blaming others or analyzing failures, the leader started with a simple question: "What did we learn?" That question changed the tone of the conversation. It shifted the focus from blame to growth, from defensiveness to reflection. "They made learning feel like strength," the respondent said, "not like recovery from failure."

This approach wasn't accidental; it was deliberate. These leaders recognized that growth is not a phase or a reward. It is a habit. And when leaders openly and consistently commit to that habit, they create a ripple effect. Improvement spreads. Teams begin to adopt the mindset, take initiative, and strive for excellence not out of duty, but out of shared conviction.

In environments driven by complexity and urgency, this kind of leadership isn't optional. It distinguishes stagnation from progress, survival from genuine thriving. Leaders who view growth as a discipline don't just react to change; they actively shape it. By doing so, they leave behind more than just results;

they foster a culture of learning, improvement, and evolution.

Growth as a Leadership Discipline

Growth isn't just a result of leadership; it's a core discipline. Leaders truly committed to improvement don't rely solely on instinct or charisma; they develop a set of intentional behaviors that foster a mindset of continuous growth. These behaviors aren't sporadic or performative; they are practiced, deliberate, and visible to those around them.

Such leaders analyze their decisions and incidents carefully, going beyond surface results to understand the deeper factors involved. They ask not only what happened but also why it happened and what lessons or different actions could be taken in the future. This reflective attitude demonstrates that leadership isn't about perfection; it's about making progress.

They also seek feedback from all levels of the organization, recognizing that valuable insights aren't limited to the hierarchy. They listen to superiors, peers, and subordinates equally, viewing each perspective as a potential source of clarity. By doing so, they show humility and demonstrate that growth is a shared effort, not just a top-down order.

For these leaders, change isn't a disruption to be managed — it's an opportunity to embrace. They remain receptive to new information, shifting conditions, and emerging challenges, adapting their strategies with agility rather than resistance. When plans falter, they do not retreat into defensiveness or denial. Instead, they demonstrate resilience, recalibrating with purpose and exemplifying the very adaptability they expect from their teams.

Perhaps most importantly, they make learning visible and appreciated. They share what they're reading, what they're questioning, and what they're refining. They celebrate growth—not just in results, but in effort and insight. In doing so, they inspire others to pursue their own development, creating a culture where learning isn't just permitted but valued.

These leaders are often described as resilient, forward-looking, and never complacent. Their example reminds everyone that authentic leadership requires growth—to stay relevant, sharp, and human. Growth isn't a phase; it's practice. And for those who lead with integrity, it's a promise they make not only to themselves but also to those they serve.

Pillars of Continuous Improvement

Sustainable performance improvement is never accidental. It results from a deliberate commitment to practices and principles that support learning, accountability, and adaptability at every level of an organization. While many institutions focus on efficiency through metrics and mandates, resilient ones invest in creating conditions that sustain excellence. At the core of this investment are three interconnected pillars: feedback loops, psychological safety, and adaptive leadership.

Feedback drives improvement. Without it, organizations risk existing in echo chambers—repeating patterns without reflection and reinforcing habits without scrutiny. Effective feedback loops are ongoing and multidirectional, flowing not only from leadership downward but also across teams and upward through management. When feedback is prompt, specific, and viewed as a learning tool rather than a means for blame, it acts as a catalyst for growth. Leaders who make feedback a shared responsibility foster cultures where improvement is continuous, woven into the fabric of daily work. However, feedback alone isn't enough without psychological safety to support it. Improvement depends on honesty, and honesty depends on safety.

Psychological safety is the belief that people can speak up, ask questions, or admit mistakes without fearing humiliation or retaliation. It is the unseen foundation that keeps feedback loops effective. In environments where dissent is encouraged and mistakes are seen as opportunities for learning, innovation thrives. Inclusive dialogue ensures that different perspectives are heard and valued. Without psychological safety, feedback is filtered, innovation is blocked, and progress slows. Leaders must protect this safety as fiercely as they guard budgets or timelines.

The third pillar—adaptive leadership—is what helps organizations navigate change intentionally. Adaptive leaders don't cling to fixed plans or strict hierarchies. They interpret evolving conditions, listen carefully, and change strategies in real time. They enable teams to take initiative, own their solutions, and respond to complexity clearly. Adaptive leadership isn't about having all the answers; it's about asking better questions, remaining grounded in uncertainty, and demonstrating the behaviors necessary for continuous improvement: curiosity, humility, and responsiveness.

Together, these pillars build the foundation of a resilient organization. They turn performance from a judgment into a shared, ongoing journey grounded in purpose. When feedback is embraced, safety is maintained, and leadership remains adaptable, improvement becomes not just possible but inevitable.

Why Continuous Improvement Matters in Crisis

Crisis environments are marked by volatility, complexity, and ambiguity. Threats evolve, technologies advance, and public expectations grow. What worked yesterday may be ineffective tomorrow. In this environment, continuous improvement isn't a luxury; it's essential for survival. It distinguishes reactive chaos from proactive resilience. Organizations committed to real-time learning are better equipped to adapt, recover, and lead through disruption.

Leaders who adopt continuous improvement demonstrate resilience not only in their recovery but also in their preparedness. They review decisions and outcomes, refining their approach with each cycle. This reflective practice allows them to recover faster and stronger, learning from lessons rather than just enduring setbacks. Their adaptability is intentional, not spontaneous. By applying new insights, they pivot purposefully, recalibrating strategies under pressure without losing focus or credibility.

This dedication also significantly boosts team motivation. When leadership shows growth, it spreads. Teams are encouraged to learn, contribute, and act. Improvement becomes more than a requirement; it becomes a shared value. One emergency manager shared how their team began conducting "micro-debriefs" after each shift during a lengthy disaster response. These quick, focused reflections helped identify minor adjustments that, over time, greatly improved coordination and morale. "It wasn't about fixing failure," they said. "It was about getting sharper every day."

At the organizational level, continuous improvement enhances readiness. Systems evolve alongside challenges, not after them. Protocols are revised, roles clarified, and blind spots are addressed before becoming liabilities. In a crisis, stagnation comes at a high cost. Institutions that see improvement as optional often fall behind. Those that embed it into their culture remain agile, credible, and trustworthy.

The Four Pillars of Leadership Development

To lead effectively in complex environments, leaders must develop skills across four key areas: technical expertise, strategic thinking, human performance, and policy and governance. These pillars are not separate abilities—they are interconnected capacities that influence how leaders respond, adapt, and maintain impact under pressure.

Technical skills are the core of effective crisis leadership. Mastering new tools and platforms—such as GIS mapping, AI-powered alert systems, and interagency coordination platforms—is crucial. However, simply being familiar with them is not enough. Leaders need to actively use these tools through simulations, field exercises, and joint drills that turn knowledge into confident action. One regional flood response leader used real-time GIS overlays to reroute supply convoys around washed-out roads. Their expertise with the platform didn't come from manuals; it came from practice. In moments of crisis, that expertise directly protects lives and ensures resources reach those in need.

Strategic thinking enables leaders to make quick, well-informed decisions. It is sharpened through analyzing real-world incidents, recognizing patterns, and balancing immediate needs against long-term goals. Reviewing past events helps leaders anticipate cascading effects and develop contingency plans that are both adaptable and practical. A public health director explained that studying the Ebola response helped them create a more flexible quarantine protocol during COVID-19—one that balanced containment with community trust. Their strategy wasn't improvised; it was well-informed.

Human performance skills—such as emotional intelligence, active listening, and cultural competence—are essential in high-stress environments. These are not just soft skills; they are critical survival skills. Leaders develop them through coaching, communication workshops, and conflict resolution training. Those who invest in these skills become trusted anchors for their teams. One fire chief credited their success during a multi-agency wildfire response to "knowing when to listen." By creating space for local voices, they avoided missteps and built stronger community partnerships. Their leadership was not just tactical—it was relational.

Finally, policy and governance shape the ethical and legal

foundation for responsible decision-making. Leaders must understand compliance standards, pursue certifications, and stay up to date with evolving regulations. Ethical leadership demands clarity, fairness, and public trust. A city emergency manager shared that a refresher course on ADA compliance helped them redesign shelter protocols to serve vulnerable populations better—an improvement that earned praise from both residents and oversight bodies. Their leadership was not only practical but also fair.

Together, these four pillars cultivate leaders who are skilled, insightful, and principled, ready to lead with integrity under pressure. In a crisis, technical mastery without strategic thinking is fragile. Strategic vision without emotional intelligence is isolating. And action without ethical grounding is risky. Continuous improvement ensures that these areas are not only enhanced but also integrated—forming the foundation of lasting leadership.

Embedding Growth in Organizational Culture

For continuous improvement to take hold, it must go beyond being just a leadership goal — it needs to become an organization-wide standard. Learning should be visible, supported, and shared at all levels of the organization. This involves integrating development into how organizations evaluate performance, allocate resources, and define success.

In resilient organizations, leadership development is integrated into performance reviews, succession planning, and strategic priorities rather than treated as an extracurricular activity. Leaders are expected not only to deliver results but also to demonstrate growth through reflection, skill development, and team building. Attendance at conferences, workshops, and certification programs is not just permitted — it is funded and actively encouraged. These investments show that learning is not a sideline to operational excellence but its fundamental foundation.

Reflective practice has become a routine part of work. Journaling, after-action reviews (AARs), and structured debriefs are now standard procedures, not just post-crisis rituals. These practices help teams turn experience into insights and insights into action. One emergency management agency created a "growth dashboard" where leaders tracked their development goals alongside operational metrics. The result was a culture where learning was as valued as logistics—where professional development became a public commitment rather than just a private effort.

Recognition systems also evolve to reward behaviors that promote growth rather than just outcomes. Leaders who mentor others, share lessons learned, and demonstrate curiosity are celebrated alongside those who meet performance targets. Feedback becomes a regular part of the process instead of just correcting. Cross training across different functions encourages employees to break down silos and develop a shared understanding. In this environment, learning is not just remedial — it is relational. It strengthens teams, improves systems, and sustains momentum.

Developing Continuous Improvement Commitment

To support this desirable cultural shift, organizations need to develop training programs that transform experience into insight and insight into action. These programs are active, engaging, and grounded in the realities of high-pressure environments.

After-action reviews become an essential practice, providing structured reflection after each incident. These reviews focus on learning, identifying gaps, and highlighting what went well, rather than assigning blame. Scenario-based simulations create realistic environments where leaders can test strategies, make decisions under pressure, and sharpen their instincts. These simulations help develop muscle memory for crisis response, enabling teams to rehearse complex situations before they happen.

Tools like Lean, Six Sigma, and PDCA cycles provide frameworks for identifying problems, improving processes, and sustaining progress. These tools are not just for analysts; they are designed for frontline leaders who want to make changes clear and measurable. Hospitals that trained their leaders in Lean techniques saw real improvements in patient safety and throughput—proof that structured improvement methods boost performance under pressure.

Cross-functional teams are crucial in this system. By combining different perspectives, these teams uncover systemic issues that might be hidden within isolated groups. They develop solutions together, test new approaches, and foster shared responsibility for results. This demonstrates that improvement isn't just for one department but for the entire organization.

When growth is rooted in culture and reinforced through training, continuous improvement becomes more than just a strategy; it transforms into a way of life. It shifts organizations from being reactive to resilient, from working in silos to collaborating, and from staying static to being adaptable. In environments characterized by complexity and urgency, transformation isn't optional; it's essential.

Measuring Impact

"What gets measured, gets managed." This well-known, frequently quoted saying holds particular importance in crisis situations,

where the stakes are high and the margin for error is small. Continuous improvement can't be just an abstract goal—it must be demonstrated through observable behaviors, measurable results, and repeatable processes. Without metrics, even the best intentions risk being performative. With them, growth becomes tangible. Organizations committed to resilience track how quickly lessons are put into practice after incidents—also called cycle time. The shorter the cycle, the more responsive and adaptable they are. They also observe recurrence rates, paying close attention to repeated mistakes that expose deeper systemic issues. When errors continue, it's not just a failure to act; it's a failure to learn. Effective leaders use these metrics not to assign blame but to identify blind spots and adjust systems accordingly.

Leadership behavior itself becomes a metric. Openness to feedback, adaptability in changing conditions, and responsiveness to emerging risks are no longer subjective traits—they are observable patterns. Participation rates in drills, workshops, and after-action reviews provide another perspective. When engagement is high, it indicates that learning is embedded in the culture. When it's low, it may suggest fatigue, disengagement, or a lack of psychological safety. Performance outcomes—such as faster recovery times, improved coordination, and increased public trust—are the ultimate measures of impact.

These results are not only due to technical skills learned; they reflect the cumulative influence of a *learning culture*. For example, the City of Los Angeles requires executives to complete a certain number of functional exercises each year. Agencies with high participation consistently show greater fluency and confidence in emergency operations. Their readiness is not just theoretical, but it is put into practice. Real-world examples reinforce this truth. At the Johns Hopkins Armstrong Institute, after-action reviews are conducted after every critical incident. These structured reflections have led to measurable improvements in patient outcomes, showing that disciplined learning can save lives. Toyota's Kaizen culture empowers employees at all levels to suggest improvements— even during a crisis. This decentralized approach to innovation ensures that learning is ongoing and inclusive. The U.S. Coast Guard's Lessons Learned Centers turn operational mistakes into institutional knowledge, reducing the likelihood of repeat errors and strengthening future missions. These examples make one thing clear: continuous improvement is not a luxury—it is necessary. It improves systems, builds trust, and protects lives. When done with purpose, it becomes more than a philosophy; it becomes a standard of performance.

Conclusion: Leadership as a Journey

In the world of crisis leadership, growth isn't a luxury; it's essential. The environments where these leaders operate are challenging, changing, and often unpredictable. Success isn't just about responding to a single event but about the ability to adapt through every challenge, improve judgment, develop skills, and build cultures of excellence along the way.

The most effective leaders are not judged by their titles or tenure but by their dedication to continuous growth. They don't see development as just a phase or a performance metric; they see it as a discipline. Their resilience isn't reactive; it's proactive. They seek feedback, embrace change, and show adaptability in ways that inspire others to do the same. By doing so, they transform their teams from passive responders into active learners, capable of handling complexity with confidence and clarity. One respondent summarized this mindset clearly: "A single response does not measure a leader's true legacy, but by an unwavering commitment to grow stronger with every test, turning each challenge into a steppingstone for future excellence." Leadership is not a destination; it is a journey. And that journey is defined not by perfection but by progress. This mindset lays the foundation for the Continuous Preparedness Loop that follows. It is a cycle of learning, adapting, and refining that turns improvement from a one-time effort into an ongoing culture of readiness. In the next chapter, we will examine how this loop operates across operational, strategic, and relational levels—and how leaders can embed it into their organizations' core to ensure that preparedness is never static but always advancing.

CHAPTER 19

THE CONTINUOUS PREPAREDNESS LOOP

Effective crisis leaders understand that readiness is not a checklist—it's a cycle. Preparedness is not a linear checklist or one-time event that leaders can check off and declare "done." Instead, the most effective leaders embrace a continuous preparedness loop—a cyclical process of plan, prepare, practice, perform, review, and refine that keeps readiness dynamic and resilient. This mindset matters because a linear approach breeds complacency and brittleness, leaving gaps that crises exploit, while the loop turns every experience into sharper vigilance, faster adaptation, and compounding strength over time.

The Continuous Preparedness Loop

Preparedness isn't a checklist; it's a cycle. In high-stakes environments, readiness can't be reduced to static plans or one-time training. It must be dynamic, iterative, and deeply embedded in the leadership culture. The Continuous Preparedness Loop captures this reality: a living system of learning, adapting, and refining that ensures organizations stay agile in the face of evolving threats.

This loop isn't just a theoretical idea—it's a practical system based on the rhythms of real-world crisis response. It starts with reflection: leaders and teams analyze what happened, what they learned, and what needs to change. Then, these insights lead to adjustments—new protocols, updated roles, and revised training. These changes are tested through drills, simulations, and live operations, generating new data and lessons. The cycle repeats, each time enhancing readiness and resilience.

Leaders who embrace the loop understand that readiness is an ongoing process. They reject the idea of a final state and instead promote a mindset of continuous preparedness. They realize that yesterday's solutions might not fix tomorrow's challenges, and that the best way to honor past successes is to build on them. Thus, the loop becomes more than just a process—it becomes a way of thinking. It transforms improvement from reactive to a steady rhythm.

In the pages ahead, we will explore how the Continuous Preparedness Loop functions across operational, strategic, and relational areas. We'll examine how leaders can activate the loop within their teams, assess its impact, and sustain its momentum over time. Because in a world where crises are inevitable, the most resilient organizations aren't the ones with the best plans, they're the ones with the best habits.

Leadership Beyond the Checklist Mindset

Throughout this project, respondents consistently described the most effective crisis leaders as "proactive," "steady," and "never complacent." These leaders didn't rely on binders gathering dust or plans shelved for audits. They were practitioners of preparedness—leaders who viewed readiness as a dynamic practice rather than a static document.

One respondent shared, "They believed preparedness was everyone's job." Another recalled, "They led by example—always assessing, planning, and testing so we'd never be caught off guard." These leaders didn't wait for emergencies to activate their teams. They fostered a steady rhythm of readiness through a cycle of assessment, planning, preparation, testing, and reassessment. Their approach was systematic but flexible—practical yet not perfunctory.

What set these leaders apart was their ability to keep a steady sense of urgency without causing panic. They knew that vigilance didn't mean anxiety. Their teams stayed alert, not alarmed—because the leaders fostered a culture where being prepared was normal, not exaggerated. One emergency coordinator described a supervisor who started every Monday with a five-minute review of recent drills, upcoming risks, and readiness gaps. "It wasn't dramatic," they said. "It was just part of how we worked."

These leaders didn't just run exercises—they learned from them. They emphasized structured reflection after every drill or incident, documenting what worked, identifying what didn't, and applying those lessons to future plans. Their motto was clear: "Good enough is never good enough." One respondent recalled a regional director who, after a successful multi-agency simulation, still held a post-exercise review to ask, "Where did we get lucky?" That question shifted the focus—not as a celebration of success, but as a way to find blind spots.

Another respondent described a hospital administrator who integrated the preparedness loop into daily operations. After a surge event, the administrator led a cross-functional debrief within 24 hours, gathering insights from clinical staff, logistics, and patient services. Those insights were then turned into revised protocols and retraining modules within the week. "It wasn't just about fixing what broke," the respondent said. "It was about strengthening what held."

These examples reveal a deeper truth: effective leaders don't see preparedness as a checkbox to complete; they see it as a continuous cycle to maintain. They recognize that readiness isn't a final goal but a consistent practice. By always demonstrating that discipline, they foster organizations that are not only prepared for the next crisis but also equipped to learn from it.

Closing the Loop: From Reflection to Action

The most effective leaders don't just recognize lessons; they ensure those lessons lead to change. They complete the cycle between experience and improvement. This includes updating emergency plans, revising protocols, adopting new technologies, and offering targeted training. It's not only about understanding what went wrong, but also about taking action to fix it.

One respondent described a leader who, after a chaotic multi-agency response, personally led a series of post-incident reviews. They didn't just listen; they acted. Within weeks, communication protocols were updated, roles clarified, and new drills organized. "They didn't let the lessons sit in a binder," the respondent said. "They turned them into progress."

The Purpose of After-Action Reviews: Looking Ahead, Not Back

After-Action Reviews (AARs) and Post-Incident Reviews (PIRs) are often misunderstood. They are not about assigning blame, praising individuals, or making anyone feel bad — or good — about their performance. They are not about the past, even though they happen after an event. Their main goal is to improve future performance.

An AAR is a leadership tool used for learning. It focuses on identifying areas for improvement, refining systems, and strengthening teams. The best leaders make it clear from the start: "This is not about fault — it's about future readiness." When communicated this way, AARs create a safe space for honest reflection and constructive dialogue.

This disciplined mindset—where preparedness is viewed as a shared, ongoing responsibility—naturally leads to the functioning of the Continuous Preparedness Loop. Leaders who embrace this mindset don't just promote readiness; they act on it. They activate the loop by integrating it into daily routines, tracking progress with clear behaviors and results, and maintaining its momentum through regular reflection and cross-team collaboration. What begins as a leadership commitment becomes an organizational habit—a practice that ensures teams aren't just prepared for the next crisis but are constantly evolving to anticipate it. In the next section, we explore how this loop functions in practice: how it starts, how progress is measured, and how it becomes a powerful driver of resilience across teams and systems.

Facilitating Meaningful Reviews

In resilient organizations, after-action reviews (AARs) and post-incident reviews (PIRs) are not merely administrative routines; they are leadership practices. When conducted with purpose and integrity, these reviews become sources of insight, accountability, and operational improvement. They turn experience into learning and learning into readiness.

A high-quality review begins well before the actual meeting. Skilled facilitators prepare by gathering relevant data, identifying key participants, and clarifying the session's goals. This preparation ensures that the review isn't just a vague discussion but a focused inquiry. Participants arrive knowing why they are there, what will be discussed, and how their input will influence future decisions. Equally important is the tone. Reviews should be viewed as opportunities to learn, not to assign blame. Leaders set this tone by demonstrating curiosity, humility, and creating psychological safety. When participants feel comfortable speaking openly, especially about mistakes or missed signals—the review becomes a space for growth rather than defensiveness. One emergency manager shared how their team begins each AAR with a simple question: "What surprised us?" That question encourages honest reflection without blaming anyone.

The reconstruction phase involves reviewing the event in order, often using guiding questions or visual tools. In one wildfire response AAR, facilitators used visual storyboards to map decisions, delays, and resource movements. This approach revealed that the main bottleneck was not a planning error, as initially thought, but a series of unexpected road closures. That insight led to an updated logistics protocol and faster deployment in future incidents. The review didn't just explain what happened; it clarified why it happened.

Analyzing reconstruction flows involves identifying strengths, locating gaps, and investigating root causes. Good reviews avoid oversimplification by digging deeper than surface issues to uncover systemic problems, communication breakdowns, or decision-making blind spots. The goal isn't to assign blame but to foster understanding.

Action planning connects insight to action. Recommendations should be specific, assigned to individuals, and include clear deadlines. Vague goals—like "we should communicate better"— are replaced with precise actions: "By next quarter, revise the incident notification protocol and train all shift leads on its use." Ownership is assigned, deadlines are set, and accountability is built into the process.

That final step—follow-up—is where many reviews fall short. Without tracking progress and sharing results, even the most insightful review risks becoming superficial. Leaders who treat reviews as living documents revisit them regularly, update stakeholders on progress, and use them to guide future exercises and planning cycles. In doing so, they show that learning is not episodic—it is an ongoing process.

Organizations that approach reviews this way cultivate cultures of resilience and trust. They demonstrate that reflection is not a luxury—it is a leadership discipline. And in environments driven by complexity and urgency, that discipline becomes a strategic advantage.

Tools and Techniques for Meaningful Review

The effectiveness of a review depends not only on the mindset of its participants but also on the tools and techniques that guide the process. Modern organizations have moved beyond informal debriefs and adopted structured methods that help uncover insights, identify root causes, and turn lessons into measurable improvements. These tools don't replace leadership; they enhance it. They provide support for reflection, clarity for analysis, and accountability for action.

One of the most common techniques is Root Cause Analysis, which helps teams go beyond surface symptoms to identify deeper systemic issues that lead to failure. Methods like the "Five Whys" ask participants to pose iterative questions—"Why did this happen?" and "Why did that happen?"—until the root cause is uncovered. Fishbone diagrams, also called Ishikawa diagrams, provide a visual way to map contributing factors in categories such as personnel, equipment, environment, and process. These tools are especially useful in complex systems where multiple variables interact and where blame is often wrongly placed on the most obvious error rather than on the underlying conditions.

Storyboarding is a powerful technique, especially in fast-paced situations. By creating visual timelines of events, decisions, and dependencies, teams can reconstruct incidents more accurately. This method helps participants see how one decision influenced another, where delays occurred, and how information was transmitted—or not. In a wildfire response review, facilitators used storyboards to outline the sequence of resource deployment. What initially seemed like a planning failure was actually a logistics bottleneck caused by unexpected road closures. That insight led to a revised plan and faster mobilization in the next incident.

To promote honesty, many organizations now use anonymous feedback tools in their review processes. Digital platforms enable team members to share observations, concerns, and suggestions without fear of retaliation. This is especially vital in hierarchical or high-pressure environments where junior staff might be reluctant to speak openly. When used carefully, anonymous input can reveal blind spots, challenge assumptions, and foster inclusive learning.

Performance dashboards help link lessons learned to measurable results. These dashboards track key indicators—such as response time, coordination efficiency, and error recurrence—allowing leaders to determine if review insights are actually leading to improvements. When combined with action plans and delegated responsibilities, dashboards go beyond just data; they serve as tools for accountability.

The U.S. Army pioneered the modern formal AAR model by conducting reviews after every mission, regardless of the outcome. These sessions are mandatory and a vital part of the operational routine. This approach has enhanced coordination, adaptability, and decision-making across the force. It has also been adopted in other fields, such as emergency services, aviation, and wildfire management. In each case, the core principle remains unchanged: reflection is not a luxury, it's a necessity.

These tools and techniques do not guarantee insight, but they set the stage for it. When combined with skilled facilitation and a culture of psychological safety, they turn reviews from mere checkboxes into opportunities for strategic learning. They ensure that the Continuous Preparedness Loop becomes a tangible practice, not just a concept.

Learning Lessons from Past Battles

Long before modern review processes became formalized, military and naval leaders understood an essential truth: the best way to prepare for the next battle is to analyze the last one. Throughout history and across civilizations, commanders have conducted post-engagement reviews—not as bureaucratic chores but as strategic imperatives. Victory was rarely due solely to luck; it often resulted from learning, adapting, and maintaining discipline through examining failures.

In ancient Greece, Athenian generals routinely debriefed after campaigns, recording tactical decisions and battlefield outcomes in public forums. Thucydides' History of the Peloponnesian War isn't just a chronicle—it's an early example of operational analysis, illustrating the interactions of leadership, terrain, morale, and timing. Similarly, Roman legions conducted structured reviews after battles, with centurions reporting on unit cohesion, discipline, and performance. These reflections influenced future campaigns and contributed to the development of Roman military doctrine.

Centuries later, naval powers such as Britain and France formalized battle reporting as an integral part of officer training. Admirals were expected to submit detailed reports on engagements, including what went wrong, lessons learned, and ways to improve future operations. The British Royal Navy earned a reputation for its comprehensive post-action reviews, which helped refine tactics during the Napoleonic Wars and beyond.

During the American Civil War, commanders on both sides kept journals and prepared reports after battles that military academies later analyzed. These documents became essential texts for understanding leadership under fire, the impact of terrain on combat, and the effects of miscommunication. By World War I, the scale of the war demanded more formal review methods. By World War II, after-action reports had become a standard part of operational procedures across Allied forces.

What unites these examples is a shared dedication to reflection as a tool for preparedness. Whether through oral debriefs, written reports, or tactical simulations, military leaders have long recognized that experience alone isn't enough—analyzed experience is what fosters competence.

From Tradition to System: The Road to AAR

This tradition of reflective practice laid the groundwork for the U.S. Army's development of the After-Action Review (AAR) process. Although informal debriefs had always been part of army culture, the Vietnam War underscored the need for a more structured, repeatable way to capture lessons learned. In the 1980s, the Army formalized the AAR as a key component of training and operational feedback, transforming centuries of tradition into a scalable, teachable system.

In the next section, we'll explore how the AAR process evolved, how it transformed leadership development, and how its principles can be applied beyond the battlefield—to crisis response, organizational resilience, and high-stakes decision-making across sectors.

Because the question is no longer 'did we win?' but 'what did we learn, and how will we lead better next time?'

The U.S. Army and the Origins of the AAR

The After-Action Review (AAR) is one of the most lasting and influential tools in continuous preparedness efforts, and the U.S. Army pioneered its modern form. Developed after the Vietnam War and formalized in the 1980s, the AAR emerged from the need to improve operational learning, reduce repeated mistakes, and foster a culture of reflection within military units. It was designed not as a punitive exercise but as a structured approach to turning experience into insight and insight into action.

At its core, the Army's AAR process is straightforward. After every mission, training exercise, or operational engagement—regardless of the outcome—units come together to review what was supposed to happen, what occurred, why it happened, and how to improve next time. This method encourages honest discussion, shared accountability, and a focus on growth rather than blame. The goal is to learn, not to judge.

What makes the Army's approach unique is its consistency and discipline. AARs are not just for major failures or high-profile missions; they are a vital part of everyday operations. Whether the event was a live-fire exercise or a humanitarian deployment, the review should be structured to facilitate learning. This regular practice emphasizes that every experience is an opportunity to learn and that collective knowledge is essential.

The methods used in Army AARs have evolved over time. Facilitators often use visual tools such as maps, timelines, and decision charts to reconstruct events. They ask guiding questions to encourage reflection and employ root cause analysis tools to dig deeper than surface symptoms. Importantly, rank is ignored during the review. Junior soldiers are encouraged to speak openly, and senior leaders are expected to listen. This flattening of hierarchy fosters psychological safety and helps ensure that insights are not filtered by status.

The impact of this approach has been significant. Units that regularly conduct AARs show greater adaptability, improved coordination, and faster decision-making under pressure. Lessons learned from one engagement are quickly applied to future situations. Over time, this creates a feedback loop that enhances operational readiness and reinforces institutional memory.

The Army's AAR model has proven so effective that it has been adopted widely outside the military. Emergency services, aviation authorities, wildfire management teams, and public health agencies have all modified the framework to suit their operations. For instance, wildfire incident management teams now hold structured debriefs after major deployments, using visual storyboards and cross-functional input to improve logistics and communication protocols. In aviation, AARs are used to review flight operations, maintenance procedures, and crew coordination, thereby increasing safety and reliability across the industry.

Even in civilian crisis response, the core principles of AAR—clarity, honesty, and a commitment to improvement—have proven invaluable. FEMA, for example, incorporated AARs into its post-disaster evaluations, which helped identify gaps in logistics and coordination after events like Hurricane Katrina. These insights guided reforms that improved performance in subsequent responses such as Hurricane Harvey.

In the end, the U.S. Army's legacy with the AAR is more than just a procedure—it's a mindset. It embodies the belief that excellence comes from reflection, not perfection. It sees readiness as an ongoing, active process rather than a static state. And it recognizes that leadership involves more than just making decisions; it's about learning from those decisions.

A Personal Reflection: Learning from the Field

During my doctoral program's field research at Fort Leavenworth, I analyzed AAR sessions from simulated battle exercises. What stood out most was the discipline and honesty integrated into the process. Leaders didn't just review tactics; they also evaluated logistics, communication, morale, and decision-making under pressure.

In multiple sessions, Battalion Command Groups reviewed their failures and breakdowns with the Controller and the Threat Commander participating. It was an interactive post-battle classroom where lessons were learned in every session. The discussions provided an in-depth look at sustainment planning for the next battle, whether real or simulated. The main point was clear: strategy without command leadership, support logistics, and real-time human performance during high-stress situations is just a dream. These reviews weren't just procedural and technical; they were not merely box-checking exercises. Instead, they focused on exploring human performance by the command group leaders. Commanders considered aspects of situational awareness, communication, tone, trust, and decision-making. During the review sessions, it was clear that those who embraced honesty and openness learned more quickly. Those who reacted defensively learned less and ultimately slowed the Battalion Command Group's progress.

The AAR became a reflection—not just of performance, but of human performance, leadership, and character. And always, the focus was on the future. The best AARs didn't dwell on what went wrong—they asked questions, "How do we do better next time?" That shift—from backward-looking critique to forward-looking improvement—is what makes the Continuous Preparedness Loop so powerful. I have one memorable case study that I hope illustrates this point.

Case Study: Tanks, Fuel, and the Myth of the Magic Fairies

As I mentioned, during that research project at the CATTS Center at Fort Leavenworth, among other tasks, I was responsible for analyzing hours of video footage from after-action reviews (AARs) following simulated battle exercises. Most sessions followed familiar patterns—debriefing maneuvers, identifying friction points, and discussing what they would do differently next time. However, one session stood out not just for its instructional value but also for its unexpected humor and a lasting lesson on the role of post-event review sessions for a young doctoral student.

The battle scenario involved a mechanized unit tasked with leading a column of tanks through contested terrain at the Fulda Gap on the West German/East German border. The mission failed. The tanks stalled halfway, unable to achieve their goal of blocking the Eastern Bloc armor's advance. During the after-action review, one officer looked visibly frustrated. He had ordered the NATO tanks forward to block the gap, but the simulation controller overruled the move. The officer claimed the simulation was therefore flawed. "This wouldn't happen in the real world," he argued. "There must've been a glitch."

The Controller, a seasoned battle simulation facilitator with the calm demeanor of someone who had seen this movie before, waited patiently. Then, with a slight smile, he replied, "Sir, your tanks couldn't move forward because they had no fuel."

The officer blinked. "That's not possible. We had everything in place."

The controller didn't flinch. "Sir," he said, "tanks don't get refueled by magic fairies."

There was a brief silence. Then, the room erupted into laughter, not harsh but cathartic. The tension eased, bringing clarity. The officer hadn't issued fuel-delivery or refueling orders to the subordinate responsible (nothing happens without orders being issued, even during a multi-day battle simulation). The simulation, accurate to its design, followed the logic of the plan—or, more accurately, the lack of one. Poor communication led to poor coordination. Failure in followership led to a loss of command and control. Cascading "small" failures inevitably caused mission failure.

What could have been an easy, defensive, self-justifying (and blame-shifting, scapegoating) exchange in this case — as it occasionally did in some AAR sessions I observed at CATTS — instead, it became a turning point, a moment of critical reflection, and an opening for adaptability.

That moment turned into a masterclass in sustainment planning and served as a reminder of the true purpose of reviews. They weren't about blaming others but about identifying root causes, questioning assumptions, and building shared understanding. The phrase "magic fairies" became an ongoing joke in later sessions of that Battalion Command Group, functioning as a quick reminder that even the best strategy can fail without practical foresight. Several useful "takeaways" emerged, including paying attention to details, avoiding assumptions, and following procedural checklists. Mundane chores and tasks might be just as mission critical as high-level strategic planning. More importantly, from my perspective, it permanently changed how I see the purpose of AARs. They aren't about revisiting past mistakes; they're about preparing for what's next. The goal isn't to dwell on failure but to gain insights that help improve the next plan, not just analyze the last one. This attitude—humble, curious, and future-focused—is what turns a review from a simple formality into a leadership tool.

After many hours of reviewing and coding AAR videos, I carefully analyzed them. The command officers, primarily and to their credit, viewed the review as a learning opportunity to prepare for the "next battle" (whether real-world or simulated). It was common to see them acknowledge oversights and commit to using these lessons to guide the group in handling situations, not just in that review but also to improve performance in future operations. The review discussions consistently shifted from hints of blame to efforts to understand how to improve next time. Verbally, it was never about dwelling on "what went wrong," but rather about maintaining a focus on "what do we need to do differently next time based on what we learned."

During the Marks of a Leader project, which has taken place over the decades since its inception at Fort Leavenworth, respondents have shared examples and discussed with me the importance of a continuous improvement mindset for effective leaders. This mindset, they suggested, is not focused on fault-finding or blame assignment but always on how the team and the leader can improve during "the next time" based on what happened and what we have learned." The initial research really helped me see these ideas in a helpful framework, which I now include in my training workshops and teaching contexts. I have told the story about Tanks, Fuel, and the Myth of the Magic Fairies to many classrooms of students, seminars and workshops, and even in major keynote presentations. It helps convey this aspect of leadership.

Institutionalizing the Loop

Organizations that excel at preparedness don't see after-action reviews as optional or occasional; they consider them essential. For these groups, the review cycle isn't just a supplementary step; it's deeply integrated into their culture. The Continuous Preparedness Loop becomes a fundamental part of how they think, plan, and lead.

This begins with a clear rule: reviews must happen after every significant event, exercise, or near miss. Whether the result was success, failure, or something in between, the review remains crucial. It's not just for crises that go wrong; it's regular practice to learn from everything that occurs. This consistency sends a strong message: learning isn't reactive; it's part of the routine.

But mandating post-incident reviews is only the initial step. High-performing organizations assign clear ownership for the recommendations resulting from those reviews. Action items are not allowed to drift aimlessly in a sea of good intentions. Instead, they are assigned to specific individuals or teams, with precise deadlines and follow-up procedures. This ensures that insights don't just stay in a report; they become real change.

Tracking implementation is equally vital. Leaders review unresolved issues, monitor progress, and ask tough questions about what has been accomplished and what still needs to be done. This creates a feedback loop that enhances accountability and prevents the repetition of the same lessons at a higher cost. One emergency management agency created a "lessons ledger," a living document that records the status of every recommendation from past reviews. It became a tool not just for compliance but also for continuity—ensuring institutional memory remains intact despite staff changes or the passage of time.

Sharing lessons across teams and departments is vital for organizations that create a feedback loop. Insights are shared openly rather than kept secret. Cross-functional meetings, internal knowledge hubs, and collaborative reviews ensure that one team's experience benefits everyone. For example, in the U.S. wildfire community, the National Wildfire Coordinating Group ensures that lessons learned from major incidents are incorporated into national training curricula within 90 days. This quick transfer of insights into training helps prevent future problems and speeds up learning across different areas. Perhaps most importantly, these organizations promote transparency and learning—not just success. Leaders who admit mistakes, share lessons, and show curiosity are valued, not punished. This cultural message is crucial. It shows teams that growth matters more than perfection and that the goal isn't to avoid failure at all costs, but to learn from it whenever possible. The Federal Emergency Management Agency (FEMA) provides a clear example. After facing heavy criticism for its response to Hurricane Katrina, FEMA conducted a thorough review of its logistics systems. The agency didn't just admit fault; it took decisive action. It restructured supply chains, improved tracking systems, and invested in pre-positioned resources. When Hurricane Harvey struck more than a decade later, those improvements proved effective. Resource deployment was faster, coordination was more efficient, and public confidence increased significantly. The cycle was not only closed but also became standard practice. In these organizations, the Continuous Preparedness Loop is not a one-time event. It is a way of operating, a shared discipline, and a cultural norm. It ensures that learning is ongoing rather than sporadic. This approach turns preparedness from a plan on a shelf into a dynamic system—one that adapts as quickly as the threats it aims to address.

Conclusion

Readiness by Design Every crisis leaves two legacies: the visible damage that demands immediate attention and the invisible lessons that shape future resilience. The difference between merely surviving and truly growing is how leaders choose to close the loop. The Continuous Preparedness Loop isn't just a framework; it's a leadership philosophy. It turns experience into insight, insight into action, and action into ongoing readiness. Leaders who adopt this cycle don't wait for the next crisis to test their systems. They test them proactively. They reflect with discipline, revise intentionally, and rehearse purposefully. Their teams become confident, capable, and cohesive — not by accident, but deliberately. Preparedness isn't a one-time achievement; it's an ongoing process. These leaders understand that readiness isn't created in the moment of crisis — it's built during the moments in between. Above all, they recognize a deeper truth: an After-Action Review isn't about the past; it's about the future. It's not about judgment; it's about learning. It's not about what happened; it's about what comes next. This mindset shifts the culture from reactive to proactive, from procedural to purposeful. It ensures that every challenge becomes a steppingstone, not a stumbling block. As we move forward, the next chapter explores how continuous readiness is forged through targeted leadership training and development. Resilient systems demand resilient leaders—because resilience is learned, not innate—and we'll cover best practices to build trust under pressure, master complexity, and sustain the preparedness cycle with clarity and conviction.

CHAPTER 20

LEADERSHIP TRAINING AND DEVELOPMENT

The Marks of a Leader project has yielded meaningful and actionable insights into the qualities that define effective leadership in the complex fields of crisis management, emergency response, disaster coordination, and continuity operations. Most notably, the findings reinforce a compelling and often underappreciated truth: exceptional leadership in high-consequence environments is driven not by technical knowledge or credentials, but by human performance capacities.

The 15 Marks of an Effective Leader detailed in this project's results go beyond just a list of desired traits—they form an evidence-based, comprehensive framework that reflects the real-world challenges of leadership under pressure. These marks provide both a theoretical foundation and a practical guide for selecting, training, assessing, and developing leaders to manage the urgent and often unpredictable problems of crises.

Rethinking Leadership: From Credentials to Capability

A notable finding is that demographic attributes and traditional qualifications—such as age, gender, academic degrees, and certifications—rarely appear among respondents as indicators of effective crisis leadership. Instead, they emphasized qualities like adaptability, decisiveness, communication, composure, emotional intelligence, and collaboration. This insight challenges the common assumption that leadership potential is tied to seniority or formal authority. It confirms that leadership excellence relies on behavioral skills and mindset, not pedigree or rank.

Crucially, these findings dispel the myth that effective crisis leaders are "born." The 15 marks are learnable, teachable, and measurable. They are not limited to naturally gifted individuals but are competencies that can be developed through intentional professional growth, experiential learning, and structured training programs.

Human-Centered Competencies

It is important to note that the real drivers of effective leadership in high-stakes situations are human performance knowledge, mindsets, strategic thinking, cognitive processes, and traits. Obviously, technical skills and having a plan(s) are essential, but they are not enough on their own to enable leadership success in these contexts. What truly distinguishes effective leaders is their behavior in the moment: how they think, respond, communicate, and adapt when conditions change and pressure mounts. These behaviors stem from a core set of human-centered skills that consistently appeared in the Marks of Leader research—not as abstract ideals but as tangible behaviors observed by those on the front lines.

These competencies are not fixed traits. They are teachable, trainable, and improvable. They can be developed through deliberate practice, thoughtful coaching, and immersive experience. When intentionally cultivated, they become the main drivers of leadership, especially during a crisis.

Decisiveness, for example, isn't just about making quick choices. It's about making timely, well-informed decisions even amid uncertainty. Leaders develop this skill through simulations, pressure drills, and coaching in risk assessment. One emergency manager described a mentor who would pause mid-scenario and ask, "What do you know, and what do you need to decide?" That approach helped teams differentiate between signal and noise and act decisively, even when information was incomplete.

Communication is another vital element. During disruptions, leaders must communicate clearly, empathetically, and credibly. This skill is improved through role-playing, media training, and emotional intelligence workshops. A public health director recalled how media coaching helped them shift from technical jargon to straightforward reassurance during a community outbreak—building trust not just with facts but with tone.

Adaptability is the ability to change strategies and priorities quickly. It develops through dynamic scenario drills and cross-team projects that encourage leaders to adjust instantly. One fire chief shared how a simulation involving multiple agencies revealed a gap in resource coordination. Instead of sticking to the original plan, the team adapted by reassigning roles and reallocating resources in real time. The exercise not only tested adaptability but also strengthened it. Situational awareness—the ability to accurately perceive and interpret unfolding events—improves through red-teaming, wargaming, and pattern recognition training. Leaders learn to spot anomalies, anticipate second-order effects, and modify their responses accordingly. In one case, a logistics officer credited their success in rerouting supplies during a flood to pattern drills that trained them to recognize early signs of infrastructure failure.

Resilience is the ability to sustain energy and remain calm during extended stress. It is developed through stress exposure exercises, mindfulness practices, and guided reflection. Leaders who focus on cultivating this skill become stabilizing influences for their teams. One respondent mentioned a supervisor who, during a multi-day emergency activation, took time for quick check-ins, breathing exercises, and humor. "They didn't just keep going," the respondent said. "They helped us keep going." Accountability—taking responsibility for decisions and results—is strengthened through after-action reviews, ethical decision-making workshops, and mentoring. Leaders who demonstrate accountability foster cultures where learning outweighs perfection. They don't deflect—they reflect. One team member recalled a leader who started every review with, "Here's what I missed. Let's build from that." Improving followership often overlooks the importance of empowering others and promoting decentralized decision-making. It develops through rotating leadership roles and teamwork-based problem-solving activities. Leaders who understand followership know when to step back, delegate, and allow others to lead. This fosters agility, trust, and shared responsibility. Open-mindedness—the willingness to embrace new perspectives and constructive challenges—improves through red-teaming, structured debates, and cognitive bias coaching. Leaders who adopt this trait don't just tolerate dissent—they foster it. They understand that challenge sharpens thinking and that diverse viewpoints are a strategic advantage. These qualities are more than just theoretical; they are the core traits most valued by those involved in the Marks of Leader research. What stood out wasn't their past accomplishments but how they managed pressure, connected with others, and helped teams persevere, adapt, and succeed together. Ultimately, it wasn't about titles or credentials; it was about presence, practice, and the human ability to lead with integrity when it matters most.

From Insight to Action: Building the Future of Leadership

If the Continuous Preparedness Loop is the engine of resilience, then leadership development is its fuel. To meet the demands of today's volatile, high-stakes environments, organizations must rethink how they cultivate and evaluate leaders. The traditional model—focused on technical knowledge, positional authority, and tenure—is no longer sufficient. What's needed is a shift toward human-centered competencies: the true drivers of performance under pressure.

This shift begins with training programs that match the complexity of the challenges leaders face. Instead of static lectures or abstract case studies, development should be immersive, hands-on, and repeated. Simulations, coaching, and after-action reviews offer structured opportunities for leaders to practice decision-making, communication, adaptability, and emotional intelligence in unpredictable, fast-changing situations. These are not soft skills—they are essential skills for survival. They should be approached with the same seriousness as tactical and strategic training.

One emergency services agency transformed its leadership academy by incorporating live scenario drills, peer coaching, and guided reflection sessions. Participants weren't just shown how to lead; they were encouraged to lead, experience failure, reflect on it, and try again. The result was a group of leaders who didn't just memorize protocols, they understood how to apply them under pressure, in real-time, with real consequences.

Leadership development must be ongoing. It can't be limited to onboarding or promotions. It should be adaptable, evolving with new threats, technologies, and priorities. This means fostering a culture that sees learning as a lifelong journey, not just a one-time event. Leaders should be encouraged to seek feedback, get coaching, and reflect throughout their careers.

Evaluation systems must grow alongside leadership development. Judging leaders only by tenure, rank, or resume misses the core point. What truly matters is demonstrated skill under pressure, the ability to think clearly, act decisively, and lead collaboratively when it counts most. Including peer feedback, 360-degree reviews, and live simulations should become standard in promotion processes and talent pipelines. These methods offer a fuller view of a leader's impact, showing not just what they know but how they perform and lead in real situations.

One public health department implemented a performance review system that incorporated peer assessments, scenario-based evaluations, and participation in post-incident debriefs as part of its leadership standards. Promotions were no longer solely based on years of service; rather, they were earned through evidence of readiness, responsiveness, and relational leadership. The change not only improved team cohesion but also increased trust across the organization.

Building the future of leadership involves turning insight into action. It means creating systems that reward growth, not just achievement. It entails preparing leaders not only for routine tasks but for critical moments that test judgment, reveal character, and influence outcomes. It also requires understanding that the leaders we need tomorrow must be cultivated today through intentional practice, honest feedback, and a culture that treats leadership as a responsibility, not just a title.

CATTS Center: A Model Worth Examining

As I have mentioned many times in this book, during my doctoral research program at the University of Kansas, I had the privilege of collecting and analyzing data at the Command and Tactical Training Simulation (CATTS) Center at Fort Leavenworth. As I have already mentioned, CATTS is part of the U.S. Army's

Mission Command Training Program and plays a key role in boosting operational readiness through immersive battle command and staff training.

At point I want to call attention to yet another key part of the CATTS success model. The entire training orientation is one that emphasizes *real-time decision-making under pressure,* replicating the chaos and complexity of actual crisis situations. Its scenario-based simulations, command post drills, and unpredictable enemy teams create a highly intense training environment. The center also offers structured lessons in systems integration and the military decision-making process, supported by feedback mechanisms and performance analytics.

In my career I have encountered many formal and static training programs, methods, and designs. Some of the are based on linear learning models and assume that skills mastery is a threshold (achieved and one) event. This widespread utilization of insufficient approaches has and continues to frustrate me. That so many rely on these very low order approaches to training and expect to achieve preparedness and readiness at the same time there are better proven models and learning/teaching options more likely to be effective that are not being used or dismissed as *"too expensive, too costly, require too much effort, or we don't have to time for that commitment."*

I have long suggested a formal leadership decision-making

training approach to clients, students, and conference attendees that is an alternative to such underachieving approaches. These include the models that I observed working so very well at CATTS; especially those that focus or at least include *real-time decision-making under pressure training methods.*

I acknowledge that a full-scale simulation center (replicating CATTS) is likely beyond the fiscal resources of most (if not many) small and medium-sized organizations and perhaps even a few large ones. Still, a mindful approach to human factors decision-making training using the base approach is replicable in various ways. For example, one memorable insight for me at CATTA was by observing the use of a real time **Threat Commander**—an officer trained in Soviet doctrine who functioned as an opponent along with the environmental and contextual challenges that the simulation controlled orchestrated to challenge the Battalion Command Group —to stress-teste the US Army (NATO) commanders in those simulated battles. The Threat Commander's role was, for me, like a masterclass in red-teaming and highlighted the importance of adversarial thinking in leadership development. Red teaming, from tabletop to full-scale exercises, combined with focused debriefing reviews can be a highly effective approach to testing plans, procedures, and people.

A Personal Reflection

My graduate students often tell me I tend to be a storyteller in class (which they say is a positive comment, not a complaint), as they say this helps make the content more meaningful, with personal anecdotes acting as anchors they will remember long after class or during research. So, I ask for your forgiveness for this brief narrative diversion, which is intended to make a point. I wanted to share that during my time at the CATTS Center at Fort Leavenworth, I was often drawn to the Fulda Gap Battle Scenarios not only because they were a key Cold War flashpoint but also because they felt personal to me. My father, a US Army soldier, served near Fulda (during the Korean War – Cold War era), stationed along the border where U.S. forces observed East German and Soviet troop movements—while their counterparts across the "gap" observed them as well. He was part of the silent vigilance of that time—watching, waiting, and preparing for a conflict that, thankfully, never happened.

Years later, long after working on a research project at CATTS and the follow-up Marks of a Leader project, I teamed up with a colleague, a crisis-communication professor at Ilmenau University of Technology in what was once East Germany. His father served on the opposing side in that Cold War-era conflict. Over dinner, we discussed Germany's reunification and the course of history. I further learned that his father served at

Fulda during the same years as my father—except he wore a different uniform, stood behind a different wire, and looked at the same horizon from the other side of the gap. Two men, conscripted into the armies of former enemies stationed across the border from each other in a divided Germany, who would unknowingly become fathers of sons. Those sons would grow up to become collaborative academic colleagues and research partners studying crisis decision-making and communication, sitting in a restaurant enjoying Thuringer Bratwurst and drinking Altenburger Brauerei - Bock Bier (which my colleague insisted was the best sausage and beer in a unified Germany, and further claimed that foods and beers from other regions of Germany were mere attempts at copies of these local delicacies). At that dinner conversation, I had a "small world" moment, discovering the unexpected interconnectedness of events in the universe. Perhaps the fictional Forrest Gump was right when he said, "I don't know if we each have a destiny or if we're all just floating around accidental-like on a breeze, but I, I think maybe it's both. Maybe both are happening at the same time." That realization stopped me in my tracks, but it also motivated me to stay curious and open to things I may not fully understand. At least, my colleague and I weren't just analyzing crisis simulations or refining academic leadership doctrines. We were proof that something larger is at play: that history bends, divisions can heal, and authentic crisis leadership—at its best—is about discovering connection, not seeking control. The Fulda Gap, once a symbol of potential confrontation and conflict in the mid-20th century, had now become a metaphor for progress and reconciliation. What had been a line of separation was now a shared point of reference.

That eye-opening experience also deepened my appreciation for the human side of crisis leadership (and history). It reminded me that behind every strategic plan are people, families, children (some yet to be born), memories, and legacies. It also reinforced a truth I carry into every leadership conversation: the most powerful changes in life are not always tactical, strategic, or technological. Sometimes, they are relational. Sometimes, they are personal. These are aspects I now aim to emphasize more in my research and teaching.

Preparing Leaders, Not Just Appointing Them

Ultimately, this research affirms a simple yet powerful truth: effective crisis leaders are made, not born. They grow through intentional practice, guided reflection, and structured development opportunities. The future of emergency, disaster, and continuity management depends not on the leadership competences we are born with, but rather it depends on those which we develop. Effective leaders are equipped not just with knowledge of plans and technical expertise, to effectively respond to crises but rather how to guide other humans through them with clarity, courage, and skill.

As we move from cultivating leadership skills to evaluating them, it's clear that creating effective crisis leaders is only part of the solution. The other part involves our ability to assess those skills in real-world situations accurately. The next chapter examines how organizations can build strong, behavior-based evaluation systems that go beyond traditional metrics to measure what truly matters: how leaders perform under pressure, adapt to complexity, and motivate others in the most challenging circumstances. By aligning assessment with the 15 Marks of Effective Leadership, we can ensure leadership development is purposeful, accountable, measurable, and mission focused.

As we transition to the next chapter, we'll explore best practices for leadership training and development—covering how to design programs, choose methods, and create environments where human-centered skills are not only taught but also practiced, because the future of readiness relies not just on plans and protocols but also on people prepared to lead.

CHAPTER 21

LEADERSHIP ASSESSMENT AND EVALUATION

The Marks of a Leader project revealed a striking truth: traditional qualifications—technical expertise, credentials, and degrees—were rarely cited by respondents as indicators of effective crisis leadership. Instead, human performance traits such as adaptability, emotional intelligence, decisiveness, and communication emerged as the defining characteristics of leaders who succeed under pressure. The findings presented in this work challenge long-held beliefs about what makes a leader effective, particularly in crisis situations. For many years, leadership assessments have focused heavily on technical expertise, official credentials, and hierarchical status. However, in moments of disruption, these indicators often fall short. What truly matters is not what leaders know, but how they act when the stakes are high and the way forward is uncertain.

Leadership in a crisis is a behavioral art. It shows in how people make judgments under pressure, handle stress during long periods of uncertainty, connect with others across different roles and emotions, and respond flexibly to rapidly changing situations. These are vital traits—they are essential skills. In short, soft skills are no longer considered soft; they are the tough currency of effective leadership.

This shift redefines the core purpose of leadership assessment. It moves us beyond static checklists and performance reviews focused on past achievements. Instead, it asks: How does a leader show up today? How do they handle ambiguity, build trust, and make decisions that balance urgency with wisdom? These questions can't be answered by résumés or titles alone. They require observation, reflection, and systems designed to see leadership in action.

In this chapter, we explore how organizations can develop evaluation models that reflect this reality. We examine tools and techniques that emphasize human-centered skills—such as emotional intelligence, adaptability, and situational awareness—and consider how to measure leadership not just in theory but in practice, because in environments marked by volatility and complexity, the leaders who succeed are not those with the most knowledge but those who grow the most.

Evaluating What Matters Most

The 15 Marks of a Leader provide more than just a conceptual model—they function as a practical guide for identifying, developing, and selecting leaders capable of excelling in complex environments. These marks shift the focus from fixed qualifications to adaptable skills. They emphasize not only what leaders know but also how they act—how they learn, adapt, communicate, and lead under pressure. In doing so, they challenge traditional evaluation methods and promote a more human-centered, meaningful approach to leadership assessment.

Organizations that concentrate on these competencies aren't just preparing for the next promotion cycle—they're preparing for the next crisis. They recognize that the leaders who will guide them through disruption aren't always those with the longest résumés or the highest rank. Instead, they're the ones who can stay calm in uncertain situations, make sound decisions with incomplete information, and foster trust across fractured teams. These qualities cannot be judged solely by tenure or academic success. They need to be observed, measured, and actively cultivated.

This calls for a fundamental reevaluation of how leadership is assessed. Traditional metrics such as years of service, formal education, and hierarchical rank provide limited insight into a leader's capacity to succeed in unpredictable environments. Instead, organizations should adopt multidimensional strategies that evaluate behavioral performance under stress. These strategies must be integrated at every stage of the leadership lifecycle—from initial selection and onboarding to ongoing training, promotion, and post-incident review. For example, an emergency management agency revised its hiring process to include live simulations and behavioral interviews that assessed candidates' ability to prioritize, communicate, and adapt in real time. Rather than asking hypothetical questions, they placed candidates in dynamic scenarios and observed their responses. The result was a clearer understanding of leadership readiness—focused on action rather than assumptions. Similarly, a healthcare system incorporated 360-degree feedback and peer evaluations into its leadership development program. Team members evaluated not only technical skills but also emotional intelligence, accountability, and collaboration. These insights were then used to customize coaching and training plans, ensuring development was tailored and performance focused.

Post-incident reviews also offer valuable opportunities for evaluation. By analyzing how leaders behaved during actual crises—how they communicated, made decisions, and supported their teams—organizations can identify strengths, uncover weaknesses, and enhance leadership skills. One fire department began including leadership reflections in its after-action reviews, asking supervisors to share lessons learned, how they adapted, and what they would do differently next time.

These reflections became part of the evaluation record, emphasizing that growth is just as vital as execution. Ultimately, determining what matters most involves viewing leadership as an ongoing, practical effort rather than a fixed credential. It means understanding that the most effective leaders are defined not by their past accomplishments but by how they continue to grow. It also requires establishing systems that reward not only success but also the ability to lead with clarity, courage, and resilience, especially when it matters most.

Building a Behaviorally Anchored Evaluation System

Practical leadership assessment in crisis environments should go beyond a checklist; it needs to be comprehensive, experiential, and rooted in the realities leaders face when stakes are high. The most significant evaluations do not just measure what leaders know; they demonstrate how leaders act. They highlight the nuances of decision-making under pressure, the quality of personal engagement, and the ability to adapt quickly. To do this effectively, organizations must develop behaviorally anchored systems that reflect the complexity of leadership in practice.

Simulation-based evaluation is a highly effective method in this approach. Tabletop exercises and full-scale drills now do more than test technical protocols—they aim to reveal emotional regulation, team dynamics, and strategic agility. In a training exercise for emergency services, a simulated mass casualty incident required leaders to coordinate across jurisdictions, handle media inquiries, and make triage decisions swiftly. Observers watched not only what decisions were made but also how they were made—who listened, who delegated, who froze, and who adapted. The exercise served as a reflection, uncovering strengths and blind spots that wouldn't have been visible in a classroom.

Behavioral observation is essential in these settings. Skilled facilitators and trained evaluators observe leaders in action, noting how they communicate, collaborate, and manage stress. Their feedback is detailed, practical, and based on observable behaviors. One organization created a rubric to track leadership qualities, including empathy, clarity, decisiveness, and composure. During a wildfire simulation exercise, a team leader who calmly redirected resources while recognizing the emotional impact on responders received high scores—even in logistics management—because they also demonstrated human-centered leadership.

Coaching and mentorship are essential complements to these assessments. Performance coaches help leaders reflect on their behaviors, identify areas for growth, and internalize key skills. These conversations aren't about fixing flaws; they aim to increase awareness and build capacity. A hospital system paired emerging leaders with experienced mentors who had navigated previous crises. The result was a culture of shared wisdom, where learning was continuous and personally meaningful.

Validated assessment tools add extra rigor. Psychometric instruments given before and after training can track progress in emotional intelligence, resilience, and decision-making. These tools provide data that complement observational feedback, giving a fuller picture of a leader's growth. One agency used resilience scales to evaluate how leaders handled extended stress during a multi-week deployment. The results helped tailor future training to improve endurance and recovery strategies.

360-degree feedback completes the system. Input from peers, subordinates, and supervisors gives a complete view of leadership impact. It shows how leaders are seen—not only by those above them, but also by those they serve and support. This feedback is vital during crises, when relational trust and psychological safety often determine whether teams stay together or fall apart.

Post-incident reviews provide a final, often-overlooked opportunity to assess behavior. Structured debriefs should go beyond simply reviewing procedures to include analysis of leadership actions. How did leaders communicate? How did they handle conflict? How did they support their teams? One fire department added a behavioral reflection section to its AAR template, encouraging leaders to evaluate their own performance and seek feedback from their crews. The outcome was a deeper, more honest learning experience.

By applying these principles in training and assessment, organizations foster a culture that values human-centered leadership. They enhance resilience not only through systems and protocols but also through people—leaders who are self-aware, adaptable, and able to guide others through uncertainty. Real-world case studies reinforce this truth. During the Christchurch earthquake in 2011, compassionate communication and flexibility helped build public trust and operational unity. In the 1982 Tylenol crisis, ethical decision-making and transparency protected both reputation and public safety. Captain Chesley "Sully" Sullenberger's calm, decisive leadership during US Airways Flight 1549 demonstrated the importance of situational awareness and emotional control under extreme pressure.

Conversely, the Fukushima disaster in 2011 showed how communication failures and a lack of emotional intelligence can increase confusion and fear. Hurricane Katrina revealed weaknesses in collaboration and accountability, undermining response efforts and damaging public trust. During the COVID-19 pandemic, leaders who demonstrated empathy, transparency, and adaptability achieved better public health outcomes — not because they had all the answers, but because they led with compassion.

These examples emphasize a consistent theme: technical expertise alone isn't enough. Their actions don't just define successful leaders in a crisis, but by how they execute them. Human-centered leadership behaviors—built on clarity, compassion, and courage—are the accurate indicators of readiness.

From Assessment to Impact

Training in the *Marks of a Leader* focal areas does more than improve individual skills; it changes the very fabric of leadership within an organization. Leaders who develop these traits gain the ability to assess situations clearly, make sound decisions under pressure, and inspire trust in others. But the impact goes beyond the individual. These qualities—emotional intelligence, stress management, adaptability—spread outward, strengthening team cohesion, building trust, and fostering organizational resilience from within. When leaders stay calm in chaos, their teams mirror that calmness. When they communicate with empathy, they create psychological safety. When they adapt quickly, they show agility that others emulate. These behaviors are contagious. They set the tone, shape the culture, and influence how others respond—not just during crises, but also in daily teamwork and problem-solving. This is why leadership evaluation must go beyond a checklist; it should act as a mirror. When done well, it reflects not only what a leader has achieved but also how they lead, develop, and influence those around them. It reveals who they are right now, who they are becoming, and how far their growth can carry their teams. It captures leadership as a journey, not just a static profile.

These insights can be transformative if we act with them in mind as we move forward. They can influence succession planning, guide coaching strategies, and shape organizational priorities. When evaluation systems are behaviorally anchored and human-centered, they help organizations see not only who is ready to lead but also who is prepared to grow. They shift the focus from pedigree to potential, from position to presence.

One public safety agency started including behavioral reflections in its promotion process, asking candidates to describe how they had grown through adversity, supported their teams, and adapted to changing conditions. The outcome was a leadership group chosen not only for what they had accomplished but also for how they had led—and how they are likely to lead in the future.

Ultimately, the purpose of assessment is not to rank leaders; it is to develop them. It aims to cultivate a culture where growth is visible, valued, and encouraged, where leadership is seen as a practice rather than just a title. Additionally, the impact of that practice is measured not only by outcomes but also by the strength, cohesion, and resilience of the teams it influences.

Leadership Assessment and Evaluation

Practical leadership assessment is a continuous, intentional process rather than a one-time event. It depends on behavioral observation, experiential learning, and strategic reflection. The Marks of a Leader framework offers a human-centered approach to evaluate leadership not just by accomplishments but also by how those accomplishments are achieved. This method shifts the focus from static credentials to dynamic skills, emphasizing how leaders think, respond, and connect under pressure. The core of this model includes four interconnected pillars: approach, method, pacing, and purpose. The approach sets the philosophical foundation of the assessment system. In traditional models, evaluation often emphasizes authority, tenure, or technical skills. In contrast, the Marks of a Leader approach emphasizes observable behaviors—such as empathy, adaptability, decisiveness, and accountability—as the true signs of leadership potential. This requires evaluators to adopt a mindset of curiosity rather than judgment, viewing assessment as a tool for growth rather than gatekeeping. Leaders are not just measured; they are understood.

Method refers to the tools and techniques used to observe leadership in action. Behaviorally anchored rubrics, simulation-based evaluations, 360-degree feedback, and post-incident reviews all contribute. These methods aim to reveal how leaders perform in real-world situations, not just how they appear in idealized settings. For example, a tabletop exercise might assess a leader's ability to manage conflicting priorities, while a live simulation could demonstrate how they regulate emotions and communicate under stress. The goal is to create environments that simulate complexity, allowing leadership to emerge naturally.

Pacing relates to the rhythm and frequency of evaluations. Leadership development is continuous, not episodic. Evaluations should be integrated throughout the leadership journey, from selection and onboarding to promotion and post-crisis reflection. This pacing helps track growth over time and ensures feedback is timely and actionable. One organization held quarterly leadership reflections linked to operational reviews, enabling leaders to evaluate their behaviors in context and set goals for the next cycle. This rhythm reinforced the idea that leadership is practice, not just a performance.

Purpose underpins the entire system. The main aim of leadership assessment isn't to rank or reward—but to build readiness. It seeks to identify who can lead through uncertainty, grow during adversity, and build trust when it truly counts. These insights shape succession planning, guide coaching strategies, and influence organizational culture. When purpose is clear, evaluation becomes a strategic asset — not just a procedural formality.

Together, these pillars form a leadership assessment system that is strict, relational, and resilient. Based on the Marks of a Leader, they ensure organizations don't just identify talent but also develop it. They help build teams led by individuals who are not only skilled but also deeply connected—to their mission, their team, and their own growth. In a world where crises happen frequently, that kind of leadership isn't optional; it's essential.

Looking Ahead

This chapter advocates a significant shift in how we understand and assess leadership, especially during crises. It challenges the long-standing reliance on traditional credentials, tenure, and formal authority, instead highlighting the importance of human-centered performance under pressure. Using the 15 Marks of a Leader framework, the chapter shows that effective leadership is defined not by what leaders know but by how they act when it matters most. Traits like adaptability, emotional intelligence, decisiveness, and clear communication stand out as the key differences—observable, teachable, and measurable skills that shape outcomes in volatile environments. To capture these qualities, the chapter promotes multidimensional evaluation strategies that reflect the complexity of real-world leadership. Simulations, behavioral observation, coaching, 360-degree feedback, and post-incident reviews are presented not as optional but as essential tools for assessing eadership in action. Through case studies from aviation, public health, emergency response, and corporate ethics, we learn that technical expertise alone isn't enough. What separates success from failure is a leader's ability to connect, adapt, and act decisively under pressure. But assessment is only part of the equation. As we continue to improve leadership development, the next challenge is ensuring sustainability. How can we make sure these insights aren't just fleeting but truly embedded? How do we create systems that not only identify great leaders but also foster their growth—over time, across roles, and through every stage of organizational life?

Chapter 22 shifts our focus to these questions. The emphasis shifts from individual assessment to the broader ecosystems that influence leadership development. Developing effective crisis leaders requires more than just training modules and performance reviews; it demands an organizational culture that values growth, supports ongoing learning, and aligns structures with the behavioral standards outlined in the Marks of a Leader framework. In the next chapter, we will explore how organizations can cultivate environments that promote excellent leadership, sustain growth over time, and integrate leadership into strategic planning, talent development, and daily operations when leadership becomes a shared cultural priority. Not just a personal trait or departmental effort, the entire organization becomes more resilient, adaptable, and prepared for any challenges ahead.

CHAPTER 22

Implications for Organizational Culture and Policy

The findings from the Marks of a Leader project do more than redefine individual leadership—they challenge organizations to rethink the very systems and cultures that shape leadership behavior. At the heart of this transformation is a simple but profound insight: effective crisis leadership is not rooted in hierarchy or credentials, but in human performance. This realization carries far-reaching implications for how organizations cultivate, support, and sustain leadership excellence.

The previous chapter made a compelling case for rethinking leadership evaluation, shifting from static credentials to dynamic, behavior-based assessments. But identifying and measuring leadership traits is only part of the challenge. The real difficulty lies in integrating those insights into the organization's core. Leadership development can't be limited to isolated programs or individual coaching sessions; it must be embedded—woven into culture, policy, and daily practice. This chapter explores how organizations can use the Marks of a

Leader framework across three interconnected areas: culture, systems and structures, and succession planning. Each area has a specific purpose, but together they build a strong foundation for a resilient leadership environment—one that prepares individuals and teams to excel amid complexity rather than merely surviving it.

First, we examine organizational culture, which comprises shared values, norms, and behaviors that shape how leadership is understood and practiced. Cultures that highlight human-centered qualities—such as empathy, adaptability, and accountability—foster environments where these traits thrive. When leaders are recognized not only for their results but also for their leadership style, it clearly communicates character matters. Organizations that focus on transparency, emotional intelligence, and collaborative problem-solving build trust, psychological safety, and lasting cohesion.

Next, we focus on systems and structures, the formal mechanisms used to recruit, evaluate, and develop leaders. These systems should align with behavioral skills, not just technical qualifications. Recruitment should assess how candidates perform under pressure. Evaluation methods should include simulations, peer feedback, and post-incident reviews. Development programs need to be experiential, iterative, and based on real-world challenges. When systems reflect the realities of crisis leadership, they develop leaders who are prepared for it.

Finally, we evaluate succession planning and bench strength—the strategic development of future leaders. Organizations should create pipelines that identify, and support talent based on performance rather than pedigree. This involves looking beyond titles and years of service to see how individuals demonstrate leadership in real situations. It also calls for investing in mentorship, rotational leadership programs, and feedback processes for development. Additionally, it requires recognizing leadership potential early, supporting it consistently, and actively promoting it.

Together, these areas form a comprehensive approach to leadership resilience. They ensure that the principles outlined in the Marks of a Leader are not only learned but also actively practiced. They foster environments where leadership is a shared responsibility, growth is ongoing, and readiness becomes part of the culture—rather than just a procedure. In the pages ahead, we'll explore how organizations can activate these areas, align them with strategic priorities, and build systems that support leadership excellence across generations and disruptions.

This chapter explores how organizations can move from gaining insights to implementing them—by applying human-centered leadership principles across systems that influence culture, policy, and long-term resilience. The Marks of a Leader framework demonstrates that effective crisis leadership is defined not by pedigree or position but by behavior: how leaders adapt, communicate, decide, and connect under pressure. To embed these insights into organizational practices, we must analyze three interconnected areas that together shape leadership development and sustainability: culture, systems and structures, and succession planning.

First, we focus on culture—the invisible framework that influences how leadership is perceived, rewarded, and reinforced. Culture isn't created through slogans or manuals; it is shaped by what organizations celebrate, accept, and imitate. When human-centered qualities like empathy, accountability, and adaptability are consistently recognized and demonstrated, they become core to the organization's identity. Leaders who model these traits signal what is important, and teams begin to reflect those values. Cultures that prioritize psychological safety, continuous learning, and relational trust create a strong foundation for leadership to flourish—not only during crises but also in everyday decisions.

Next, we examine systems and structures—formal mechanisms for recruiting, evaluating, and developing leadership. These systems should align with behavioral competencies rather than solely with technical skills or hierarchy. Recruitment should emphasize how candidates lead in uncertain situations. Evaluation methods need to include simulations, peer feedback, and post-incident reviews that showcase leadership in action. Development programs should be experiential, iterative, and based on real-world challenges. When systems mirror the realities of crisis leadership, they foster the growth of genuinely prepared leaders.

Finally, we review succession planning and bench strength—the strategic development of future leaders. Organizations need talent pipelines that focus on performance, not just pedigree. This means looking beyond titles and tenure to assess how individuals lead. It also involves investing in mentorship programs, rotational leadership opportunities, and feedback processes that promote growth. Moreover, it requires identifying leadership potential early, supporting it consistently, and promoting it purposefully.

Together, these domains create the foundation for a resilient leadership culture—one that trains individuals and teams to succeed amid complexity, not just survive it. When culture, systems, and succession planning align with the behavioral standards outlined in the Marks of a Leader, leadership transcends a role—becoming a shared, ongoing practice. In the pages ahead, we'll explore how organizations can activate these domains, embed them into strategic planning, and foster environments where leadership excellence is not only cultivated but continually elevated.

Shaping Culture Around Human-Centered Leadership

Organizational culture is the invisible framework that influences which behaviors are encouraged, accepted, or discouraged. Mission statements or policy manuals do not define it; instead, it is shaped by what leaders demonstrate, what teams celebrate, and what systems support. To align with the Marks of a Leader framework, culture must shift from being solely transactional and compliance-focused to one that actively nurtures human-centered qualities: empathy, adaptability, decisiveness, resilience, and emotional intelligence.

This shift begins with psychological safety. In high-pressure settings, people must feel comfortable speaking up, challenging assumptions, and sharing feedback without fear of retaliation. When leaders invite dissent, listen with curiosity, and respond with humility, they create conditions where learning happens continuously and trust becomes lasting. One emergency response agency incorporated "challenge sessions" into its planning cycle, encouraging junior staff to question assumptions and suggest alternatives. The result wasn't chaos—it was clarity.

Behavioral recognition is just as important. Organizations should reward not only results but also the behaviors that lead to them. When emotional intelligence, collaboration, and ethical decision-making are recognized alongside technical achievements, they become central to leadership identity— recognition rituals, whether formal awards or informal acknowledgments, emphasize what truly matters. A healthcare system began emphasizing "quiet leaders" who demonstrated calm, compassionate leadership during patient surges. The message was clear: humanity is not a soft sk ll — it's a strategic asset.

Reflective practice should be woven into daily operations. After critical incidents, teams need to debrief not only on what happened but also on how they lead. What decisions were made? What emotions surfaced? What lessons were learned? These reflections foster collective wisdcm and promote behavioral growth. One fire department introduced a "leadership lens" to its after-action reviews, encouraging supervisors to evaluate their communication, adaptability, and team support during the incident.

Finally, well-being and recovery must be recognized as essential elements of leadership sustainability. Leade s who suffer from burnout cannot lead effectively. Organizations should prioritize mental health, stress resilience, and recovery strategies—not as perks but as operational necessities. When leaders are supported in their own well-being, they are better equipped to help others. One public health agency developed "resilience pods"—peer-led spaces for reflection and decompression after extended crisis deployments.

Culture change begins with what leaders demonstrate and reward. When senior leaders showcase and promote the 15 Marks of a Leader, they make it clear that these traits are essential, not optional. When systems and structures support these signals, culture becomes not just aspirational but also actionable.

Aligning Systems and Structures

While culture sets the tone, systems and structures determine whether leadership behaviors are consistently supported, measured, and maintained. To embed the Marks of a Leader into the core of an organization, leadership development must be reflected in how leaders are recruited, assessed, promoted, and supported. This requires a fundamental recalibration of key organizational mechanisms.

Recruitment and selection should go beyond traditional hiring practices that mainly focus on credentials, tenure, and technical skills. Crisis leadership demands behavioral skills, especially under pressure. Job descriptions need to clearly highlight traits like adaptability, emotional intelligence, and ethical decision-making. Behavioral interviews should include scenario-based questions to assess how candidates handle ambiguity, stress, and interpersonal conflicts. Simulation exercises—such as real-time decision-making drills—can showcase how candidates lead when the stakes are high and circumstances are constantly changing.

Promotion and advancement should be based on both past performance and potential for future leadership. Organizations must gather 360-degree feedback from peers, subordinates, and cross-functional partners to evaluate relational and behavioral skills. Leadership portfolios can document competencies aligned with the 15 Marks, including examples from drills, incidents, and team feedback. Promotion standards should reflect organizational values, not just operational metrics, ensuring those promoted to leadership roles embody the culture they are meant to foster.

Training and development should extend beyond procedural instructions to immersive, behavior-based learning. Scenario-based training must replicate the complexity, urgency, and emotional intensity of real crises. Modules on resilience and emotional regulation help leaders manage stress and maintain energy over time. Peer learning and coaching, especially across different functions, promote shared growth and innovation.

One organization created "leadership labs" where emerging leaders practiced decision-making in simulated crisis environments, followed by guided reflection and coaching.

Feedback and accountability systems are essential for reinforcing desired behaviors and supporting ongoing improvement. After-action reviews should evaluate leadership actions, team interactions, and communication effectiveness—not just procedural compliance. Upward feedback channels must be safe and accessible, allowing team members to share honest feedback on leadership performance. Performance dashboards should track behavioral metrics alongside operational results, ensuring assessments are balanced and aligned with the organization's leadership philosophy.

When these systems align with the Marks of a Leader, leadership development becomes a continuous and integrated process. The traits most vital for crisis leadership are not only encouraged but also expected, assessed, and rewarded.

Succession Planning and Leadership Bench Depth

In high-stakes environments, leadership continuity isn't just a luxury; it's a necessity. The Marks of a Leader project emphasizes that effective crisis leadership isn't innate but developed. This presents both a challenge and an opportunity: how can organizations intentionally build leadership capacity at all levels? Succession planning should shift from a reactive, title-based approach to a proactive, behavior-focused strategy. It must concentrate on identifying individuals showing leadership potential through their actions, mindset, and interpersonal skills—even before they assume formal leadership roles. Early identification is crucial. Organizations need to observe how individuals handle pressure, collaborate across teams, and demonstrate qualities like empathy, decisiveness, and adaptability in everyday situations. Layered development paths offer ongoing leadership opportunities, increasing responsibilities, exposure to complex challenges, and avenues for reflection and feedback. Rotational assignments across different functions and crisis scenarios enhance agility and broaden perspectives. Leader shadowing, especially during high-pressure events, allows promising individuals to observe experienced leaders in action, helping them internalize behaviors and decision-making patterns. Successor selection should prioritize behavioral readiness over tenure or technical skills. Behavioral readiness assessments can evaluate emotional intelligence, teamwork, and decision-making under pressure. Scenario testing—using simulations and role-playing—demonstrates how candidates lead in complex, high-stakes situations. Values alignment interviews verify that successors not only perform effectively but also embody the organization's leadership culture and principles. Succession planning should be transparent, inclusive, and adaptable, encouraging participation and feedback from across the organization. When future leaders are selected based on proven human performance traits, organizations develop a leadership pipeline that is not only skilled but also culturally aligned and prepared for crises.

Conclusion

This chapter has explored how the Marks of a Leader framework can be embedded into the core of organizational life—through culture, systems, and succession planning. We have learned that developing effective crisis leadership isn't just about luck, charisma, or authority. Instead, it comes from intentionally aligning values, behaviors, and institutional support. When organizations focus on human performance qualities—such as emotional intelligence, adaptability, decisiveness, and resilience—they create ecosystems where leadership isn't only cultivated but also maintained, reinforced, and expanded.

Leadership development, in this context, must be systemic. It can't be limited to HR departments or confined to executive retreats. It should be reflected in how leaders are selected, trained, evaluated, and supported throughout their careers. From immersive simulations that test judgment under pressure to behavioral feedback loops that foster self-awareness and growth, and inclusive policies and transparent succession planning—every part of the organization needs to reinforce the traits that define effective leadership amid complexity. When these elements are aligned, leadership becomes a shared responsibility, a cultural norm, and a strategic asset—not just a role or title.

This chapter also highlights that leadership excellence isn't a static goal; it's an ongoing practice. It requires intentional development, is demonstrated through everyday actions, and must be sustained by organizational commitment. Organizations embedding the Marks of a Leader into their culture and systems aren't just preparing for the next crisis; they are building the capacity to lead through any challenge that arises.

Looking ahead, the question is not only how we develop leaders today but also how we prepare for the leadership demands of tomorrow. The next chapter combines two vital perspectives: a detailed look at the aspects of human performance uncovered in this research and a forward-looking prediction of the challenges shaping crisis leadership in the coming decades. From climate change to cyber threats, from geopolitical instability to the erosion of public trust, the future will require leaders who are not only technically capable but also behaviorally adaptable, ethically grounded, and emotionally resilient.

Chapter 23 will explore what these emerging demands mean for leadership development, readiness, and evaluation. It will offer a plan for how organizations can adjust their metrics, mindsets, and strategies to nurture leaders prepared not just for the next crisis but for the next era of complexity, because the future of leadership won't depend solely on credentials but on character, clarity, and connection. In a world full of volatility, these qualities will be the actual currency of trust, influence, and resilience.

CHAPTER 23

THE 15 MARKS OF A LEADER: STRATEGIC REFLECTION

The Marks of a Leader framework is more than a list—it is a lens. It offers a way to see leadership not as a title or a technical function, but as a dynamic human performance discipline. These 15 characteristics emerged from rigorous research, field experience, and practitioner insight. They represent the behavioral DNA of effective crisis leadership.

Why These Marks Matter

This chapter provides a strategic reflection on the value, implications, and applications of the 15 Marks of a Leader. It discusses how understanding these behavioral traits can transform leadership development, influence assessment, and shape organizational culture. It also offers practical takeaways—knowledge, skills, and abilities (KSAs)—that should be prioritized in preparing leaders for high-stakes environments across various sectors.

The Marks are not just aspirational slogans or abstract ideals. They are behavioral skills that manifest in moments of pressure, ambiguity, and consequence. Each Mark highlights a specific way leaders respond when the stakes are high, and the path forward is unclear. Whether it's decisiveness despite incomplete information, adaptability in changing conditions, or ethical accountability when values are challenged, these traits define how leadership is demonstrated—not just how it is perceived.

What makes these Marks especially powerful is their universality. They span across sectors, roles, and types of crises. In emergency management, healthcare, military operations, education, and corporate continuity, the same human-centered qualities consistently distinguish successful leaders from those who struggle. A hospital administrator managing a pandemic surge, a logistics officer overseeing disaster relief, a school principal responding to a threat on campus, and a CEO handling a reputational crisis may work in very different settings—but the behavioral demands they face are remarkably similar. In every case, leading with clarity, empathy, and resilience is the key.

One respondent, a regional emergency manager, described her most trusted leader as "the person who could walk into a chaotic room, listen before speaking, and make a decision that felt both firm and fair." Another, a healthcare director, recalled a colleague who "never lost composure, even when the ICU was overwhelmed. He didn't just manage the crisis—he managed our morale." These stories reinforce what the data indicates: technical expertise may open the door, but behavioral fluency keeps it from collapsing.

The Marks also represent a shift in how leadership is understood and developed. They move the focus from what leaders know to how they act. They challenge organizations to go beyond credential-based hiring and instead prioritize performance-based growth. The question is no longer, "Does this person have the right qualifications?" but "Can this person guide others through uncertainty, fear, and complexity?" This change redefines leadership as a practical experience—one that must be observed, supported, and improved over time.

By grounding leadership development in these behavioral traits, organizations can foster cultures that value growth over pedigree and readiness over résumé. They can identify emerging leaders based on presence, not titles. And they can ensure that those entrusted with guiding others through disruption are not only technically capable but also behaviorally prepared.

Translating the Marks into KSAs

Each Mark of a Leader signifies more than just a trait; it embodies a blend of knowledge, skills, and abilities (KSAs) that can be taught, practiced, and assessed. This translation is essential. It helps organizations move from simply endorsing ideas to executing them effectively. It transforms values into competencies, and competencies into curriculum. For example, the Mark of Decisiveness might relate to KSAs like risk assessment, quick decision-making, and confidence in uncertain situations. Adaptability could involve strategic flexibility, emotional regulation, and the ability to adjust quickly under pressure. Resilience may include stress management, recovery strategies, and maintaining energy during prolonged disruptions. Each trait becomes a development goal, something leaders can aim for, reflect on, and improve.

In tactical terms, this translation offers sector-specific guidance:

- ➤ Emergency Management: KSAs should include quick prioritization, interagency coordination, and public-facing communication under stress.
- ➤ Healthcare Leadership: Focus on emotional regulation, ethical clarity, and collaborative triage decision-making.
- ➤ Military and Defense: Emphasize situational awareness, mission alignment, and adaptive command presence.
- ➤ Corporate Continuity and Risk: KSAs around reputational agility, stakeholder trust-building, and transparent crisis messaging.
- ➤ Education and Campus Safety: Skills in trauma-informed leadership, community reassurance, and cross-functional coordination.

By connecting the Marks to KSAs, organizations can develop targeted, engaging training programs. They can create assessment systems that mirror real-world crisis leadership, using simulations, behavioral interviews, and peer feedback to evaluate leaders' performance—not just their knowledge. They can also implement coaching methods to help leaders develop these skills and establish feedback processes to encourage ongoing growth.

This approach also supports scalability. It allows organizations to include the Marks of a Leader in job descriptions, promotion criteria, and succession planning. It ensures leadership development is continuous, not sporadic. Additionally, it provides a shared language for what effective leadership looks like—across teams, roles, and challenging situations.

A university respondent shared this comment with me: "We started using the Marks as part of our onboarding rubric, not just for senior administration leaders, but for department chairs and student services directors. It changed the tone of our hiring conversations. We weren't just asking about experience as we had been doing; we were now asking about presence, situational awareness, building followership, adaptability, communication, prioritization, and relational trust."

In the upcoming chapters, we will continue exploring how these KSAs can be integrated into organizational life—covering everything from training programs to performance dashboards. Since leadership is defined by behavior and supported by structure, the result will be not just better leaders but a stronger, more resilient organization.

Here's how each Mark breaks down into core KSAs:

THE 15 MARKS OF A LEADER

MARK OF A LEADER	KNOWLEDGE	SKILLS	ABILITIES
Coordination Facilitator	Team dyframics, operational planning	Synchronizing efforts, managing interdependen-	Aligning people and processes under pressure
Decisive	Decision frameworks, risk analysis	Making timely choices, managing ambiguity	Acting confidently with limited information
Critical Thinker	Analytical models, cognitive bias awareness	Evaluating options, identifying patterns	Applying structured reasoning in dynamic
Prioritizes	Time/resource management, urgency	Ranking tasks, allocating attention	Distinguisning critical from peripheral under str-
Experienced	Lessons learned, domain-specific knowle-	Mentoring intultive judgment	Drawing from past to guide present decisions
Goal-Oriented	Strategic alignment, mission clarity	Maintaining focus, outcome tracking	Driving toward results despite disruption
Communicator	Audience analysis, messaging strategies	Clear speaking/writing active listening	Conveying essential into across diverse pla-
Situationally Aware	Environmental scan- ning, human factors	Reading cues, adjusting tone	Maintaining real-time awareness of evolving dy-
Adaptability	Change management, confingency planning	Shifting strategies, improvising	Remaining flexible and composed amidur-
Personal Resilience	Stress physiology, recovery strategies	Emotional regulation, stamina building	Sustaining performance under prolonged pressure
Facilitates Followership	Motivation theory, team cohesion	Inspiring trust, fostering unity	Building shared pur- pose and psychologica-
Open-Minded	Cognitive diversity, feedback culture	Listening, suspending judgment	Welcoming new ideas and adjusting perspectives
Accountable	Ethical frameworks, transparency standards	Owning outcomes, modeling integrity	Taking responsibility and promoting ethical con-
Ongoing Performance Improvement	Reflective practice, learning science	Self-evaluation, feedback integration	Continuously refining behavior and decision- making

Competency Checklists to Lived Culture

The knowledge, skills, and abilities (KSAs) derived from the Marks of a Leader form the foundation of a behaviorally anchored leadership model—one that moves beyond abstract ideals to measurable, trainable, and observable actions. These KSAs turn intangible qualities into practical steps. They help organizations define what effective leadership looks like, not just in theory but also in high-pressure, real-world situations. They provide a roadmap for developing leaders who can navigate ambiguity, build trust, and make sound decisions under pressure. This framework challenges traditional leadership development in three main ways, each requiring a shift in how we assess, train, and support leaders.

Credentials to Competencies

Traditional leadership models have long emphasized tenure, rank, and academic qualifications as signs of readiness. However, in a crisis, these indicators often fall short. The Marks of a Leader framework shifts the focus to behavior—specifically, how leaders respond under pressure. Are they able to stay calm amid chaos? Can they communicate effectively and with empathy? Are they capable of making quick decisions with limited information? One respondent, a senior logistics coordinator in a disaster response agency, shared: "The leader I trusted most didn't have the longest résumé. But when the phones were ringing, the trucks were stalled, and the press was circling, he kept us focused. He didn't panic, he prioritized." Another, a school superintendent, recalled a principal who "stepped into a lockdown situation and immediately began calming students, coordinating with law enforcement, and reassuring parents. That wasn't in the handbook. That was leadership." These stories reveal a key truth: leadership readiness isn't about what's on a resume, but about how leaders behave when the stakes are high.

Static Training to Dynamic Practice

Leadership cannot be learned solely through lectures or slide decks. It must be experienced, tested, and refined. Immersive simulations, stress inoculation exercises, and real-time feedback loops are essential; they are critical. These experiences enable leaders to practice for real situations, fail safely, and develop the behavioral muscle memory needed in high-pressure environments. During a workshop at the University of South Alabama Center for Disaster Healthcare Preparedness, an administrator shared that her entire healthcare system had redesigned its leadership development program to include quarterly crisis simulations, each followed by structured debriefs and coaching. Scenarios ranged from mass casualty incidents to cyberattacks on patient records. Leaders were assessed not only on their decisions but also on their communication, emotional management, and support for their teams. The result was not only improved preparedness but also a cultural shift toward continuous learning and behavioral accountability. At a disaster recovery conference workshop, one participant from a regional fire department wrote in his evaluation, "We stopped asking who had the most certifications and started asking who could lead a crew through a burning building. Our simulations don't just test tactics; they test trust."

Generic Feedback to Behavioral Precision

Vague praise like "strong communicator" or "good under pressure" is no longer sufficient. Evaluation systems need to be designed to measure specific, observable behaviors aligned with the Marks. This includes structured behavioral observations during drills and real incidents, 360-degree feedback that emphasizes interpersonal impact, and performance dashboards that track growth over time.

A financial technology company reached out to tell me they have implemented a behavioral assessment rubric directly linked to scores, enabling evaluators to assess leaders using categories based on The Marks of a Leader and other traits they identified as aligned and suitable for their context, such as ethical clarity, technological skill, forecasting ability, and collaborative intelligence. They also said that feedback is no longer just anecdotal but now based on collected and measured evidence. Similarly, a respondent in a university senior leadership evaluation shared that, "We started using behavioral snapshots in our evaluations. Instead of evaluating a college dean simply by saying 'She's a natural leader,' we now provide specific examples, most of which are based on the Marks of a Leader characteristics you discussed. For instance, we now write: 'She de-escalated a conflict between departments during a budget crisis with transparency and empathy.' That has changed everything. These tools offer leaders practical insights and give organizations a clear view of who is ready to lead—and who is still developing.

By integrating these principles into leadership development, organizations cultivate a culture where human performance is not only recognized but also nurtured, evaluated, and rewarded. They shift from merely assessing potential to actively accelerating it. They foster environments where leadership is not a title to achieve, but a practice to embody.

This captures the essence of lived culture. It's not about what's written in policies, but what's shown during moments of pressure. When the Marks of a Leader become part of everyday language, training, and evaluation, leadership shifts from just being theoretical. It becomes real, teachable, and transformative.

The Enduring Value of the Marks of a Leader

The Marks of a Leader framework is more than just a research project—it's a curated collection of real experience, practical insight, and fundamental human truths. It shows what seasoned leaders have proven repeatedly: that titles, charm, or credentials do not define leadership under pressure. It is characterized by behavior—how a leader thinks in uncertain situations, responds to adversity, and connects amid complexity.

This project shows that the most important leadership qualities are not the easiest to teach or measure, but the ones most vital to develop. Emotional regulation, adaptabiity, ethical clarity, and collaborative intelligence are not luxuries in crisis leadership; they are essentials. They distinguish between reacting and responding, confusion and clarity, and survival and resilience. These qualities do not happen by chance; they must be intentionally cultivated, consistently reinforced, and carefully evaluated.

The 15 Marks offer more than just a framework—they establish a shared language for leadership development. One that spans sectors, ranks, and roles. They provide a blueprint for training, a foundation for evaluation, and a guide for shaping culture. They motivate organizations to go beyond transactional leadership models and adopt a more human-centered, performance-driven approach. They help us shift from asking, "Who's in charge?" to asking, "Who's ready to lead?"

Respondents from different fields echoed ths change. A military officer said, "The best leaders I've served under weren't the loudest—they were the ones who stayed grounded when everything else was spinning." A hospital administrator shared,

"During the pandemic, our most effective leaders weren't the ones with the most degrees. They were the ones who could listen, adapt, and make decisions that felt human." These reflections reinforce the main point: leadership isn't about pedigree—it's about presence.

But perhaps most importantly, the Marks present a vision for the future, a future where leadership is not limited to a select few but is developed in many. A future where readiness is not just about technical skills but also about behavior. A future where leaders are chosen not for what they've memorized, but for how they perform when it matters most. This vision is not just aspirational; it is practical. It calls for systems that identify, support, and elevate leaders based on their behavior rather than just their knowledge.

The implications are clear. To build resilient organizations, cohesive teams, and capable leaders, we must invest in the human side of leadership. We need to treat "soft skills" as vital strategic assets. We should create training that mirrors real-world situations, give feedback that promotes growth, and foster cultures that value courage, clarity, and connection.

Leadership is not a static trait; it is continuous practice. The Marks of a Leader serve as guides for that practice. They are the qualities we need to teach, the behaviors we must measure, and the values we are dedicated to upholding.

Ultimately, leadership in crisis is not about being in charge, it's about being ready. Readiness is not defined by authority or position, but by mindset and intention. It begins long before the crisis hits, in the quiet choices leaders make about how they show up, what they stand for, and how they treat others. Authentic leadership is revealed not in command, but in care; not in control, but in clarity. It's the difference between reacting and responding, between managing tasks and stewarding people through uncertainty.

Preparation for crisis leadership starts with choosing to lead differently—with purpose, integrity, and compassion. It means cultivating emotional intelligence, practicing ethical decision-making, and building trust before it's tested. Leaders who embrace this approach don't just prepare for disruption—they shape the conditions for resilience. They understand that leadership is not a role to perform, but a responsibility to embody. And when the moment comes, they are not simply ready to act, they are prepared to serve.

CHAPTER 24

THE HUMAN SIDE OF CRISIS LEADERSHIP

L eadership in crisis is not defined by titles, credentials, or organizational charts—it is revealed in moments of pressure, ambiguity, and human complexity. After years of research, fieldwork, and reflection, the Marks of a Leader project has made one truth unmistakably clear: the most effective crisis leaders excel in human performance. They are not merely experts in procedure; they are anchors in chaos—calm, adaptive, emotionally intelligent, and ethically grounded.

This chapter provides both a summary and a forward-looking strategy. It consolidates the project's main findings and anticipates the evolving demands of leadership in an increasingly unpredictable world. It serves as a call to action for organizations, educators, and leadership developers to rethink how they prepare leaders—not only for today's crises but also for future disruptions.

The term "soft skills" has long been used to describe human-centered traits that define effective leadership—empathy, communication, adaptability, resilience, and ethical judgment. However, these skills are anything but soft. They are difficult to teach, even harder to measure, and essential when the stakes are high. In fact, they are the key abilities that determine whether a leader can guide others through uncertainty, rebuild trust, and make sound decisions under pressure.

As global threats become more complex—such as climate change, cyber warfare, pandemics, misinformation, and geopolitical instability—traditional leadership models are falling short. The future will require leaders who can think systemically, act with emotional clarity, and collaborate across boundaries. It will also demand a new kind of preparedness—one rooted not only in technical knowledge but also in behavioral flexibility and human connection.

This chapter explores what the future may look like. It examines the limits of traditional leadership development, highlights the importance of human performance in crisis management, and offers a blueprint for cultivating the next generation of leaders. These insights are practical; they come from real-world experience, are backed by evidence, and reflect the perspectives of those who have led through challenging situations.

Leadership in the coming decades won't be judged by how well someone follows a plan — it will be judged by how effectively they lead when the plan falls apart. That kind of leadership begins with understanding the human side of crisis.

The Persistent Undervaluing of Soft Skills

Despite overwhelming evidence that human-centered skills are essential for effective crisis leadership, soft skills are still often undervalued in many leadership development programs. This contradiction arises from a systemic bias toward what is easy to measure, standardize, and credential. Degrees, certifications, and technical skills provide concrete proof of qualifications. They conveniently fit into spreadsheets, promotion criteria, and institutional checklists. However, empathy, composure, adaptability, and emotional intelligence are more difficult to quantify, teach, and justify in budget meetings.

In structured environments like healthcare, the military, and emergency services, emphasizing procedural compliance and technical skills is understandable. These systems depend on accuracy and consistency. Yet, during a crisis, it is rarely the checklist that brings peace; it is the leader's presence, communication, and ability to connect. The irony is that the qualities most critical in high-stakes moments are often regarded as less important in training and assessment.

Cultural myths worsen this problem. Leadership is still too often linked to authority, rank, or charisma. Pop culture promotes the "hero expert" archetype—leaders who rely on knowledge and decisiveness, not humility or emotional intelligence. Some of the most effective crisis leaders are not those with the loudest voices or the highest titles, but those who listen, adapt, and lead with clear, grounded judgment.

Undervaluing soft skills is also a problem in training design. Many leadership programs tend to stick with what's easiest to deliver: lectures, policy reviews, and procedural walkthroughs. Teaching emotional regulation, active listening, or ethical reasoning requires vulnerability, expert guidance, and immersive practice. It takes time, nuance, and effort. Therefore, these skills are often overlooked—not because they aren't important, but because they're inconvenient.

Ignoring soft skills can cause serious issues. During crises, relying only on technical skills without emotional intelligence can lead to loss of trust, low morale, and poor teamwork. Leaders lacking adaptability or communication skills might worsen confusion instead of resolving it. Without psychological safety, teams can fall apart even if their operational plans are strong.

To prepare leaders for crisis realities, we must stop treating soft skills as optional. They are not the garnish on the leadership plate; they are the foundation. As the world becomes more complex, their importance will only grow.

Forecasting the Future of Crisis Leadership

The leadership challenges of the coming decades will differ from those of the past. Crises are increasing in frequency, interconnectedness, and unpredictability. Climate disruptions, cyber threats, global pandemics, geopolitical instability, and misinformation campaigns are not isolated incidents — they are cascading system failures that demand a new kind of leadership. Future crisis leaders must operate across disciplines, jurisdictions, and cultures. They will face dilemmas that balance speed with ethics, data with intuition, and control with collaboration. Success in these environments will depend less on technical skills and more on behavioral adaptability.

Key traits for future crisis leadership include:

- ➢ Systems Thinking: Grasping how decisions influence interconnected areas.
- ➢ Emotional Regulation: Maintaining clarity and composure under prolonged stress.
- ➢ Ethical Foresight: Making principled decisions in morally ambiguous situations.
- ➢ Collaborative Intelligence: Leading across boundaries with trust and shared authority.
- ➢ Adaptive Communication: Crafting messages that resonate across diverse audiences under pressure.

Technology will play a bigger role—but it won't replace the human element. AI, predictive analytics, and real-time data will improve decision-making, but they cannot replace trust, empathy, or moral judgment. Leaders will need to know when to rely on the algorithm—and when to override it. The future of leadership depends on how well we train leaders to handle pressure, not just on their planning skills. It will require immersive training, continuous feedback, and a culture that values growth over perfection. Additionally, it involves shifting soft skills from the margins to the core of leadership development.

If the future of crisis leadership relies on human-centered traits, then how we train, coach, and support leaders must also focus on these qualities. Traits like emotional regulation, adaptability, systems thinking, ethical clarity, and collaborative intelligence aren't innate gifts reserved for a few. They are skills that can be learned, refined, and strengthened through deliberate practice and organizational commitment to development.

Immersive Practice: Rehearsing for Reality

Traditional leadership workshops and lectures, while useful for teaching concepts and frameworks, are not enough to prepare leaders for operating under pressure. The challenges of crisis leadership, quick decision-making, emotional regulation, and teamwork cannot be learned passively. They must be experienced, tested, and improved in environments that reflect the complexity and intensity of real-world crises. To develop leaders truly ready for crises, immersive, scenario-based training environments should become standard. These simulations are not theatrical exercises or abstract role-playing; they serve as high-fidelity rehearsals for actual situations. They simulate the emotional intensity, time pressure, and uncertainty of real emergencies, pushing leaders to make decisions with incomplete information, manage team dynamics under stress, and communicate effectively when every word counts.

One core method is stress inoculation training, which boosts resilience by gradually exposing leaders to increasingly challenging situations in controlled environments. These exercises help individuals recognize their physiological and mental reactions to pressure, develop coping mechanisms, and increase their tolerance for ambiguity and discomfort. Over time, leaders not only learn to withstand stress but also to operate effectively within it. For example, a public safety agency integrated stress inoculation into its command training by simulating media scrutiny, resource shortages, and ethical dilemmas to build psychological resilience.

Real-time crisis simulations take this further by immersing leaders in unfolding chaos. These scenarios challenge participants to adapt quickly, prioritize conflicting demands, and lead amidst disruption. They reveal not only technical skills but also behavioral depth—how leaders respond when plans fall apart, teams fracture, and decisions have real consequences. One healthcare system used live simulations to test pandemic surge protocols, observing how leaders balanced clinical urgency with staff morale and public communication. The insights gained shaped both policy and professional growth.

Cross-functional drills are equally important. Crises often involve multiple departments, and effective leadership requires coordination across disciplines, jurisdictions, and cultures. These exercises bring together various stakeholders— emergency managers, communicators, clinicians, logisticians— and challenge them to manage conflicting priorities, resource constraints, and differing viewpoints. The goal is not only operational alignment but also the development of relationship skills. Leaders learn to listen, negotiate, and collaborate under pressure. One city government conducted a multi-agency flood response drill that identified communication gaps between departments and led to the creation of a unified command protocol.

These immersive experiences develop the "muscle memory" leaders need to stay calm, decisive, and connected when it matters most. They turn leadership from a theoretical idea into a practical skill. And they ensure that when a real crisis occurs, leaders are not improvising; they are activating abilities they have already practiced.

There is a clear need to examine how these "new paradigm" training methods can be integrated into leadership development systems, aligned with behavioral evaluation frameworks, and scaled across organizations. This topic is highly relevant to me because it aligns with my work in training, teaching, assessment, and curriculum development. In crisis leadership, readiness is not just a mindset; it is a skill that must be developed.

Designing Scalable Simulation Programs

While immersive, scenario-based training is essential for developing crisis-ready leaders, designing and implementing these simulations must also be scalable. Not every organization has access to a dedicated training facility, a team of facilitators, or the budget for extensive exercises. However, every organization—regardless of size or sector—can and should create opportunities for leaders to practice real-life scenarios. The key is customizing simulation programs to match the organization's operational environment, resource levels, and leadership development stage.

For large, complex organizations like government agencies, healthcare systems, or multinational corporations, simulation programs can be layered and multi-modal. These entities typically have the infrastructure to support full-scale drills, cross-functional exercises, and real-time crisis simulations. They can incorporate behavioral observers, use advanced scenario scripting, and include technology such as virtual reality or AI-driven "injects" to enhance realism. For example, a national emergency management agency might run a multi-day simulation involving cyberattacks, misinformation campaigns, and cascading infrastructure failures, testing not only tactical responses but also strategic coordination and leadership under extended pressure.

Mid-sized organizations—such as regional nonprofits, school districts, or municipal governments—can use modular simulation models. These programs break down complex scenarios into smaller, manageable parts that can be delivered gradually. A targeted role-play on media response might follow a tabletop exercise, followed by a debrief on ethical decision-making. These organizations can also collaborate with local emergency services, universities, or peer institutions to co-host simulations and share facilitation resources. For example, a regional hospital might partner with public health and law enforcement to simulate a mass casualty event, rotating leadership roles among departments to develop cross-functional skills.

Small organizations and resource-limited teams—such as startups, rural clinics, or volunteer-led groups—can still conduct high-impact simulations using affordable, creative methods. Scenario cards, facilitated discussions, and time-limited decision drills can be done during staff meetings or retreats. Even a 30-minute "what would you do?" exercise can reveal assumptions, test instincts, and create a common language around leadership behaviors. A small nonprofit might simulate a donor data breach, prompting leaders to handle reputational risks, stakeholder communication, and internal coordination within a single afternoon.

Sector-specific customization is essential. In healthcare, simulations must focus on clinical urgency, patient safety, and emotional labor. In education, scenarios might include student safety, parent communication, and media scrutiny. In corporate environments, simulations could address supply chain disruptions, executive decisions, or brand reputation. The behavioral demands—adaptability, clarity, empathy, decisiveness—stay consistent, but the context and outcomes differ. Effective simulation design respects both.

To ensure scalability, organizations should consider three design principles:

- ➢ Right-size the realism: Match the simulation's complexity to the team's maturity. Start simple, then gradually add ambiguity, time pressure, and emotional intensity as leaders develop.
- ➢ Built-in reflection: No matter the scale, the true power of simulation is found in the debrief. Structured reflection turns experience into insight and insight into growth.
- ➢ Make it repeatable: Simulations should not be one-off events. Establish a cadence—quarterly, biannually, or tied to leadership transitions—so that practice becomes part of the culture.

Ultimately, scalable simulation programs aren't about copying a single model; they focus on applying principles of immersive, behavior-driven training tailored to each organization's needs. When implemented effectively, they democratize leadership development, making powerful learning accessible to everyone. And they ensure that when the next crisis arises, leaders at all levels are not just aware—they are prepared.

Closing Reflection and Call to Action

The Marks of a Leader project began with a deceptively simple question: What truly defines effective leadership during a crisis? What followed was more than just research results; it was an insight. Across various sectors, disciplines, and personal experiences, one truth became clear: leadership under pressure isn't about credentials, titles, or technical skills. It's about human performance—how leaders think, act, decide, and connect when the stakes are high, and the path forward isn't obvious.

Throughout this book, I have examined the 15 behavioral traits that distinguish effective leaders during times of disruption. These traits—covering emotional intelligence, ethical clarity, adaptability, decisiveness, and collaborative strength—are not just abstract ideals. They are observable, teachable, and essential. They determine whether a leader can guide others through fear, uncertainty, and complexity. However, these qualities are often overlooked in traditional leadership development, which tends to emphasize pedigree over presence and position over practice.

This work challenges that notion. It shows that the most crucial leadership traits are not innate talent; they are skills that can be developed. They can be cultivated through immersive training, refined with feedback, and sustained through culture. They are what distinguish reaction from response, confusion from clarity, survival from resilience. Looking ahead, the need to develop these traits has never been more urgent. The crises approaching will be more complex, interconnected, and unforgiving. They will test not only our systems but also our humanity. In this environment, leadership must change—not gradually but fundamentally. Organizations should invest in experiential learning, expert coaching, and behaviorally anchored assessment systems. They need to foster cultures that value emotional intelligence, ethical decision-making, and relational trust. Leadership should be viewed not just as a title to earn but as a practice to embody.

This is more than just a change in curriculum; it is a transformation in consciousness. It recognizes that the leaders who will shape the future are those capable of leading with clarity amidst chaos, with empathy through uncertainty, and with courage in complexity. They will be the ones who understand that leadership is not about control; it's about connection. It's not about perfection but about presence.

The call to action is clear. We must develop systems that cultivate these traits, measure them, and reward them. We need to prepare leaders not just to withstand crises but to lead through them—with integrity, resilience, and humanity. We must do this intentionally, urgently, and collaboratively. Because the future will not wait for us to catch up; it will demand leaders who are prepared.

And readiness begins with the decision to lead differently.

The Marks of a Leader framework is more than just a model—it's a movement. It establishes a common language for leadership that crosses sectors, ranks, and roles. It guides organizations in selecting, training, evaluating, and promoting leaders based on their behavior rather than just their knowledge. It inspires us to view leadership as a human-centered discipline rooted in clarity, character, and connection.

This book ends with a challenge and a promise. The challenge is to move away from outdated ideas that link leadership only with authority or achievement. The promise is that a new kind of leadership is achievable—one that is more inclusive, adaptable, and resilient. This type of leadership emphasizes the human side as the key strength for navigating the unknown. Let this be the moment we choose to lead differently. Let this be the moment we shape the future of leadership—together.

Epilogue
A JOURNEY COMPLETED,
A LEGACY IN MOTION

When I started this project, I was convinced that leadership, especially during crises, could be the difference between recovery and failure, trust and chaos, lives saved and lives lost. That belief has only grown stronger through my research and work on this book. What began as a question: What truly defines effective leadership under pressure? Has developed into a framework, a common language, and, I hope, a valuable addition to the field.

Although I have a background in social sciences, especially persuasion and communication, this book was never meant only for scholars. It's for practitioners who need to make quick, error-free decisions. It's for those in classrooms, command centers, boardrooms, hospitals, and city halls. These are people who understand that, in a crisis, leadership goes beyond titles. It's a test of character, clarity, and skill.

In the preface, I set out three goals for this book:

- ➢ To help readers identify the traits and mindsets that set effective crisis leaders apart—those who earn trust, inspire action, and stay composed when others falter.
- ➢ To help them avoid common leadership mistakes, including blind spots, breakdowns, and habits that undermine mission success and team confidence.

➢ And to help them develop a leadership model grounded in human factors—one that defines the essential knowledge, skills, and attitudes (KSAs) for resilience, readiness, and ethical responsibility.

I believe this project has accomplished those goals and more. At the start of this book, I outlined three clear objectives, each emphasizing that titles or credentials do not define leadership during a crisis; instead, it is behavior under pressure that does. Now, as we finish this journey, it's essential to reflect on how those objectives were achieved—and why they matter in a world that demands more from its leaders than ever before.

➢ **Identifying the Traits of Effective Crisis Leaders**

Throughout these chapters, we have identified and examined the behavioral traits that distinguish high-performing leaders in times of disruption. From decisiveness and emotional intelligence to prioritization and critical thinking, the Marks of a Leader framework offers a clear, research-based profile of effective crisis leadership in action. These traits are not just abstract ideals, they are observable, teachable, and repeatable behaviors that build trust, motivate action, and help maintain composure when others falter.

By grounding these traits in real-world examples, practitioner insights, and human factor analysis, this book has helped readers move beyond vague notions of leadership and toward a concrete understanding of what excellence looks like under pressure.

➢ Avoiding Common Leadership Mistakes

Leadership failure in a crisis is rarely due to a lack of effort—blind spots, breakdowns, and unchecked behavioral habits are often to blame. This book identifies those patterns: indecisiveness, rigidity, poor listening, emotional detachment, and misaligned priorities. More importantly, it offers strategies to recognize and correct them.

By highlighting both failures and successes across sectors—from healthcare and education to public safety and corporate response—this work prepares readers to anticipate pitfalls and make deliberate choices that safeguard mission success and boost team confidence. This project shows that leadership mistakes are not unavoidable; they are preventable if we understand what to look for and how to respond.

➢ Developing a Human-Factor-Based Leadership Model

At its core, this book presents a leadership model rooted in human factors. This framework outlines the essential knowledge, skills, and attitudes (KSAs) needed for resilience, readiness, and ethical responsibility. The Marks of a Leader are not just traits; they are fundamental elements for training, assessment, and development.

This model is practical and designed for real-world use. It helps select leaders, shape curriculum, guide coaching, and inform organizational culture. It provides a common language for leadership development—one that connects sectors, roles, and experience levels. It also recognizes that during a crisis, what matters most is not just what leaders know, but how they behave.

Why This Matters

In a world increasingly shaped by volatility, complexity, and disruption, effective crisis leadership is no longer just a theory; it's a necessity. Institutions bend or break depending on how their leaders respond. Communities either recover or fall apart based on how trust is built and maintained. Organizations either thrive or falter based on how well they prepare their people to lead when the margin for error vanishes.

This book was written for this moment. It provides a framework that is measurable, actionable, and adaptable. It translates research into practice and offers a path forward—not just for understanding leadership, but for developing it.

Marks of Effective Leadership

The effort to understand leadership continues, but the foundation is here. Using the 15 Marks of a Leader, we identified the key behaviors during high-pressure situations. We turned these behaviors into practical KSAs and showed how they can be taught, practiced, and evaluated. We also provided a plan for incorporating them into leadership development, organizational culture, and crisis preparedness.

Beyond that, I believe this work can help change the conversation about effective leadership. I hope it challenges the outdated notion that success depends on charisma, credentials, or a command-and-control style. Research shows that the leaders who make the most significant difference are often those who stay calm in chaos, listen before speaking, and act with integrity when no one is watching. These are not just ideals; they are observable behaviors, and anyone willing to put in the effort can achieve them.

Over the past twenty-five years, I have watched the risk landscape change. I have studied leadership successes and failures during pandemics, terrorist attacks, school shootings, natural disasters, and institutional collapses. I've seen how public trust can vanish in an instant and be rebuilt through steady, human-centered leadership. I believe that the quality of leadership during emergencies directly affects not only operational results but also emotional, political, and cultural outcomes.

This book isn't just a reflection on what I've learned; it's a guide to prepare for the world we live in, where crises are not rare interruptions but constant realities. A world where leadership is crucial and preparation is essential. A world where people follow not just titles but leaders who bring order to chaos, calm fears, and offer hope during uncertain times.

A Leadership Framework for a Chaotic World

Although this book represents the culmination of a long and personal research journey, it is not the end of the work. The Marks of a Leader is a living framework—designed to grow, adapt, and evolve as we face different challenges. It is not a static model or a finished doctrine. Instead, t is a dynamic tool for reflection, development, and action. And it now belongs to all of us.

It is part of the trainers who will include it in leadership programs, helping individuals develop the behavioral skills that matter most under pressure.

It belongs to the executives who will use it to shape organizational culture, moving beyond slogans and toward measurable, mission-aligned leadership behaviors. It belongs to the educators who will teach it to the next generation of leaders, equipping them not just with knowledge but with the character and clarity to lead in uncertain situations. And it belongs to the leaders themselves—those who will strive to embody these traits in the field, in the moment, and in the face of adversity. "The Marks of a Leader" offers more than insight—it provides infrastructure. It delivers a measurable, assessable, and trainable set of human performance traits that can make leaders more effective when it matters most. These traits are not abstract ideals; they are observable behaviors that can be cultivated, reinforced, and evaluated. They create a common language for leadership development and a practical roadmap for readiness. In a world increasingly characterized by volatility, complexity, and disruption, the need for resilient, adaptable, and ethically grounded leaders has never been more urgent. Traditional models—based on hierarchy, credentials, or charisma—are no longer enough. We need leaders who can think clearly, act decisively, listen deeply, and prioritize wisely. We need leaders who can earn trust, inspire action, and guide others through chaos with calmness and compassion.

This framework was built for that world. It is rooted in research, shaped by real-world experience, and refined through dialogue with those who lead in the most demanding environments. It is designed not just to describe leadership but to develop it.

So, while this book may end, the effort to better understand leadership continues. The Marks of a Leader is not just the conclusion of a project but a call to action—a call to build cultures of readiness. It's a call to prepare leaders not for perfect conditions but for the realities we face. It's a call to lead with intention, integrity, and impact.

Because the next crisis will not wait, and when it arrives, it will judge us not by our titles or intentions but by our readiness to lead.

This is your invitation. If you find this work valuable, I encourage you to share it. Please pass it along, challenge it, or expand on it. Use it to spark conversations, influence decisions, and boost preparedness. The next crisis won't wait for us to get ready. It will arrive unannounced and unforgiving. When it does, it will test leaders not by their good intentions or credentials, but by their ability to lead.

Call to Action: Leading into the Future

The world we live in is becoming more unpredictable. Crises occur suddenly, escalate rapidly, and expose weaknesses in our institutions, communities, and beliefs. In this environment, leadership is more than just a title; it's a challenge. The leaders who will shape the future are those who create clarity, not just wait for it.

The Marks of a Leader introduces a new approach to crisis leadership. It emphasizes a behavior-based strategy, rooted in human factors, and designed for practical application. It's not just a concept to admire but a framework to put into action. It's meant for use in classrooms, boardrooms, training centers, and on the ground. It should be challenged, refined, and expanded by those who lead under pressure.

Use the Marks to choose leaders who can gain trust when it counts most.

Use them to train teams that can stay effective amid chaos.

Use these elements to develop cultures that focus on readiness, resilience, and ethical responsibility.

Prepare for the next crisis—not with fear, but with focus.

Because the next crisis won't wait, and when it happens, it won't judge us by our intentions or credentials. It will judge us by our ability to lead.

Let this framework serve as your guide and compass. Allow it to steer your growth, decisions, and influence. And let it expand— through your insights, feedback, and leadership.

Leadership isn't a fixed trait; it's an ongoing practice. The Marks of a Leader serve as milestones in that journey. They are the qualities we need to teach, the behaviors we must assess, and the values we must uphold. Because, in the end, history doesn't just remember leaders during times of peace and prosperity. It often defines them—permanently—by how they respond when everything starts to fall apart.

Let us be the ones who are prepared or assist others in becoming prepared.

That work begins now. The future is watching.

Lead effectively.

Appendix A

MODEL TRAINING CURRICULUM

This curriculum is part of the CrisisMasters© Series, developed by Emperiria, a consulting and professional development group dedicated to strengthening leadership and operational readiness in high-stakes environments.

Why Emperiria?

The name Emperiria (ἐμπειρία), rooted in classical Greek, means "knowledge gained through lived experience." It's related to the word "empirical," which refers to knowledge that has been demonstrated to be valid and reliable.

It reflects the idea that actual leadership ability isn't just based on theory but is developed through action, reflection, and tested judgment. In crisis leadership, this concept is essential: the most effective leaders are those who have practiced, adapted, and succeeded under pressure.

Emperiria specializes in translating this philosophy into practical, evidence-based training programs. Our approach is grounded in real-world insights, behavioral science, and operational excellence. We don't just teach leadership—we help organizations develop it from within.

The Marks of a Leader™ Training Curriculum

This curriculum is designed to develop and evaluate the 15 core behavioral traits outlined in the Marks of a Leader framework that you have here in this book. It is organized to support current and future leaders in roles related to continuity, crisis, disaster, and emergency management across various sectors. It targets the characteristics and methods that have been discussed in this book.

Program Overview

- Target Audience: Leaders and emerging leaders in high-consequence environments
- Delivery Format: In-person, virtual, hybrid, and field-based options
- Duration: Typically, 8–10 weeks, with flexibility for condensed or extended formats (which vary the number of weeks) for the entire program but smaller sets of modules can be offered in shorter durations.
- Structure: Five progressive phases, culminating in a capstone simulation
- Implementation Support

This curriculum is not intended for casual copying or attempted replication. It is a comprehensive, behaviorally grounded program that requires expert guidance, tailored design, and careful evaluation. As the creator of this model and founder of Emperiria, I am available to support your organization in:

- Conducting leadership assessments and readiness diagnostics.
- Customizing curriculum delivery to fit your operational context.
- Facilitating immersive training and simulation exercises.
- Providing coaching, feedback, and post-training evaluation.
- Advising on integration into talent pipelines and succession planning.

If your organization is serious about building resilient, high-performing leaders for complex environments, I invite you to connect directly. Let's design a program that fits your mission, elevates your people, and prepares your teams to lead when it matters most.

Contact Information

- Dr. Robert C. Chandler, Ph.D.
- Email - bob@emperiria.com
- Business Cell: +1 (731) 741-1812

Appendix B

LEADERSHIP SELF-ASSESSMENT INSTRUMENT

Instructions

This tool is intended for personal professional development purposes only and does not constitute clinical or legal advice. For each of the 15 leadership marks, rate yourself using the following scale based on your typical behavior and mindset in crisis, emergency, or high-pressure situations:

Rating Description

5   Strongly Agree – This describes me consistently

4   Agree – This generally describes me

3   Neutral – This sometimes describes me

2   Disagree – This rarely describes me

1   Strongly Disagree – This does not describe me

Assessment Table

#	Leadership Mark	Description	Rating (1–5)
1.	Coordination Facilitator- I can organize and align people and processes during dynamic or chaotic situations.		☐
2.	Decisive - I make timely, confident decisions—even with limited or ambiguous information.		☐
3.	Critical Thinker - I analyze situations logically and make informed judgments under pressure.		☐
4.	Prioritizes - I quickly distinguish between what is urgent and what is most important.		☐
5.	Experienced - I draw effectively from past professional experience to guide actions.		☐
6.	Goal-Oriented - I stay focused on key objectives despite uncertainty or disruption.		☐
7.	Communicator – I clearly and consistently convey critical information to all stakeholders.		☐
8.	Situationally Aware – I accurately assess changing conditions and the human dynamics involved.		☐
9.	Adaptability – I respond constructively and f exibly to changing conditions.		☐
10.	Personal Resilience - I manage stress well and maintain calm, composed leadership.		☐
11.	Facilitates Followership - I inspire trust and create cohesion and unity in teams.		☐
12.	Open-Minded - I welcome diverse perspectives and avoid rigid thinking.		☐

13. Accountable - I take responsibility for decisions, outcomes, and behavior. ☐

14. Ongoing Improvement - I regularly reflect and act on lessons learned to improve performance. ☐

15. Preparedness Loop - I actively engage in planning, practice, evaluation, and readiness. ☐

Optional Reflection Questions

1. Top Strengths: Which 2–3 marks did you rate highest, and how have they served you well in critical situations?

2. Growth Areas: Which marks received the lowest ratings? What specific situations challenged you in those areas?

3. Development Plan: What actions or learning steps could help you improve in your lowest-rated areas over the next 6–12 months?

4. Support System: Who in your professional network can help you grow in one or more of these leadership areas?

About the Author

D r. Chandler is the founder and principal of Emperiria, which provides assessment, training, organization, and team development, and management coaching solutions. He has advised, mentored, and taught both graduate students and professional practitioners in vital areas of human performance. He is a respected researcher, trainer, and subject matter expert. With over 40 years of academic and professional experience, he offers evidence-based strategies for crisis prevention, mitigation, response, and recovery. His expertise encompasses communication, decision-making, teamwork, situational awareness, crisis management, ethics, and personal resilience. He is passionate about applying research-based best practices in practice and frequently speaks about the importance of training and preparation to improve performance.

Dr. Chandler is a frequently invited keynote speaker at professional conferences and symposiums worldwide, and a popular presenter for national webinars, workshops, and off-site seminars. He is a globally recognized expert in crisis leadership, organizational resilience, communication, human performance, and high-stakes decision-making. Known for his engaging, insightful, and practical style, he regularly speaks at national conferences, professional development events, and executive leadership programs. His workshops and training sessions consistently earn top evaluations from participants, who praise their relevance, clarity, and real-world application. Dr. Chandler's work bridges academic research and practical application, drawing on decades of field experience, scholarly expertise, and a deep understanding of human performance under pressure.

In recognition of his contributions to leadership education and preparedness training, Dr. Chandler has received numerous awards for excellence in teaching, scholarship, and service. His reputation as a trusted advisor and energetic educator continues to make him a highly sought-after figure in both public- and private-sector leadership circles.

Dr. Chandler is also widely recognized for his innovative insights and his ability to translate complex research into practical, easy-to-understand, and applicable findings. He is known for popular practical templates such as the "Chandler" 3-3-30 Rule, 60 & 6 Principle, DA4 Emergency Notification Message Structure, Marks of a Leader, Chandler Message Map Model, New Paradigm for Crisis Leadership, More Effective Crisis Decision-Making, Crisis Master Competency Certificate, and The Chandler Crisis Lifecycle Model.

Dr. Chandler is a both a researcher and scholar. He has authored, co-authored, or edited numerous respected professional and academic articles and industry-specific "white papers." He has previously published 11 books, either as an author, editor, or co-author. Recognized as an applied researcher, he is highly regarded as a subject matter expert and consultant on best practices and thought leadership. His specialization includes organizational and business communication, with a focus on crisis communication within organizations—covering communication during emergencies, crises, and disasters. He also has expertise in health and risk communication for pandemics and public health crises, effective risk communication, behavioral and psychometric assessment, incident notification, crisis leadership, teamwork, multicultural and intercultural diversity, organizational integrity, public relations, human performance in critical situations, and program evaluation. Additionally, he excels in designing training curricula, instructional delivery, assessment, training and development, and analyzing the effects of mediated communication on cognitive and emotional outcomes.

Robert (Bob) C. Chandler, Ph.D.

Business Cell: +1 (731) 741-1812

Email: bob@emperiria.com

Website: www.emperiria.com

Author's Note on AI Collaboration

In writing The Marks of a Leader, I relied heavily on my own experiences, research (including feedback from respondents), and reflections on crisis leadership. The personal stories, insights, reflections, and principles in this book stem from my scholarship, professional practice, and personal journey. After completing a master's thesis, a doctoral dissertation, numerous academic papers and journal articles, professional white papers, and contributing to more than a dozen other books and publications—all before the rise of AI—I was encouraged to modernize my approach by incorporating AI technology into the editing and review of my manuscript.

To expand my comfort zone and ensure clarity, consistency, and polish, I used AI—specifically Claude, Microsoft Copilot, ChatGPT, and Grammarly—as collaborative ecitorial helpers in various roles and for different purposes. (As editors, AI tools can be just as strict with strikethroughs, deletions, and reminders to "write less like a rambling academic" as any human editor I've worked with over the decades.) These tools helped improve grammar, streamline structure, and enhance readability, all while preserving my conclusions, tone, and intent. They did prompt me to learn how to insert (press Alt and WIN+) an "em dash" when I wanted to imply "a pause" in my text phrasing. At no point did AI generate content independently or replace my analysis or creative decisions. Instead, these tools served as editorial partners, much like trusted human colleagues and editors I've worked with before, hopefully helping boost the clarity and craftsmanship of my writing.

I have come to believe that the thoughtful use of emerging technologies can empower authors rather than diminish them. By merging human insight with digital precision, we can create work that is both authentically genuine and more widely accessible to general population readers.

As a lifelong debater (interscholastic and intercollegiate) and former debate coach and professor of argumentation, I welcome questions and even challenging counterpoints; that's how we enhance knowledge and understanding. I can't blame AI for any of the conceptual claims in this book—but if (and my assumption is that it is) there's a bit more clarity here than in some of my earlier works, then my AI editors deserve credit.

Ultimately, the ideas, interpretations, and conclusions here are mine, shaped by my values, stories, and vision of effective crisis leadership. AI helped me express them more clearly. So, if you disagree with anything, you only have me to blame or debate.

Acknowledgments

The Marks of a Leader research project—and this book—would not have been possible without the generous support, collaboration, and encouragement of many individuals and organizations. What began as a question about leadership under pressure turned into a multi-decade journey of research, reflection, and discovery. I am sincerely thankful to everyone who has accompanied me on this journey.

I sincerely thank Dr. Mike Hazen for supervising my master's thesis at Wake Forest University and Dr. Cal Downs for supervising my doctoral dissertation at the University of Kansas, respectively. Elements from the research of those projects inform some of the ideas in this book.

I am especially grateful to Dr. Cal Downs and Dr. Ken Johnson for inviting me to collaborate at the CATTS Center in Fort Leavenworth during my doctoral studies at KU. The insights I gained from that valuable experience significantly shaped the core conceptual framework and methodological design of this project and, in turn, undergird this book.

I want to acknowledge Dr. Vince Hazleton. I thank him for his support of my research on the Marks of a Leader during my time as a faculty member at Illinois State University. His support and encouragement helped me refine the questions that guided this project during those critical years of exploratory research.

I also want to sincerely thank Pepperdine University for supporting the bulk of the field research for this project through the Blanche E. Seaver Professor of Communication Endowment. I am especially grateful to the late Dr. W. David Baird—Seaver College Dean Emeritus and Howard A. White Professor Emeritus of History—whose generous support and faith in the project allowed me to collect and analyze the original survey data, which was foundational in this project.

To my colleague and research partner, Dr. JD Wallace: thank you for your collaboration in designing the foundational original survey instrument, collecting, and analyzing the preliminary data, and interpreting the initial findings. Your insight and partnership were invaluable. I also extend my appreciation to the professional associations and organizations that graciously allowed us to invite their members and conference attendees to participate in the study.

To all the generations of graduate and undergraduate students who, in one way or another, participated in this research project, thank you. Your questions, critiques, and curiosity helped improve the framework and challenged its assumptions. I am especially grateful to my master's students, who listened to countless lectures, engaged in sense-making discussions (and more than a few lively debates), and assisted me in interpreting respondents' feedback. Your thoughtful participation in discussions, the papers you wrote to support or challenge the framework, and the honest critiques you shared strengthened this book.

To the professionals I spoke with, interviewed, asked you to complete a survey instrument, and discussed these concepts with —individually, in small groups, and those who shared their stories at conferences and public speaking events—thank you for your candor, wisdom, and willingness to reflect on leadership during difficult circumstances. Your voices are woven throughout this work to the best of my notes and recollections. Finally, to my academic and professional colleagues who encouraged me to pursue this line of inquiry and recognized its importance, thank you for believing in the role of behavioral factors in effective leadership and for challenging me to keep going. Many of you have encouraged me over the years to write this book. I apologize for not writing it sooner.

And most importantly, I want to acknowledge Anita—my senior year in college debate partner and ultimately my brilliant, patient, exceptional mom for our three children, business owner-manager, and long-suffering wife—who taught me that arguing with someone in debate competitions is the most fitting preparation for marriage I can imagine. Thank you for enduring the chaos of manuscript deadlines, my coffee-fueled ramblings about leadership marks, and the mysterious disappearance of our weekends. Your grace under pressure (and your pointed reminders about the laundry) kept me grounded. Now that this book is finally finished, I swear solemnly to tackle the chore list... starting right after a celebratory nap.

With deepest gratitude to all who walked this path with me— your wisdom, support, and shared commitment made this book possible.

Robert C. Chandler, Ph.D.
January 1, 2026 – Nashville, Tennessee

www.ingramcontent.com/pod-product-compliance
Lightning Source LLC
Chambersburg PA
CBHW061546120626
46550CB00004B/1387